THE OLYMPIA & YORK STORY

TOWERS OF DEBT

THE RISE AND FALL OF THE REICHMANNS

PETER FOSTER

KEY PORTER BOOKS

Canadian Cataloguing in Publication Data

Foster, Peter, 1947–
   Towers of debt

Rev. ed.
Previously published under title: The master builders.
Includes index.
ISBN 1-55013-445-0 hardcover
ISBN 1-55013-498-1 paperback

1. Reichmann family. 2. Olympia & York Developments — History. 3. Consolidation and merger of corporations — Canada — History. 4. Real estate developers — Canada — History. I. Title.

HD316.F68 1993   338.8'6'0971   C92-095374-3

Key Porter Books Limited
70 The Esplanade
Toronto, Ontario
Canada M5E 1R2

Distributed in the United States of America by:
Publishers Group West
4065 Hollis
Emeryville, CA 94608

The publisher gratefully acknowledges the assistance of the Canada Council and the Ontario Arts Council.

Typesetting: Computer Composition of Canada Inc.

Printed and bound in Canada

93 94 95 96 97 98 6 5 4 3 2

CONTENTS

Preface / v

Acknowledgements / vii

  1. Empty Pockets / 1

  2. The Road to Morocco / 11

  3. Gold on the Table / 19

  4. The Flagship / 30

  5. The "Deal of the Century" / 41

  6. Grand Designs / 51

  7. Bell Cows and Brass Knuckles / 61

  8. Bumping into the Bronfmans / 75

  9. Image and Reality in a Changing Empire / 84

10. Drawing a Bead on Gulf / 99

11. Paul and Bill Do the Bump / 110

12. The Reichmanns are Coming! / 123

13. Saturday Night Specials and White Knights / 136

14. "A Battle over Money" / 150

15. Unhappy Union / 164

16. Losing It / 180

17. Canary Wharf: Cheaper by the Dozen / 192

18. Strange Bedfellows / 211

19. Bad Press / 227

20. Shadowy Figures / 240

21. Complex Choreography / 253

22. The Crunch / 265

23. Seeking Protection / 277

24. Credit Where Credit Is Due / 295

Chronology / 303

Index / 308

Preface

THIS BOOK IS SUBSTANTIALLY DIFFERENT FROM THE FIRST book that I wrote on the Reichmanns, *The Master Builders* (1986), although it inevitably covers much of the same ground. As well as completely revising and condensing the subject matter of that book, I have added a new introduction and an additional seven chapters that deal with subsequent events, including the crash of the Reichmann empire and its aftermath.

The Reichmanns refused to cooperate personally with my first book, although they allowed me interviews with a number of their senior executives. In 1990, I approached them again in connection with a magazine article I was writing. This time, Paul Reichmann agreed to see me. In addition to long interviews with Paul Reichmann in Toronto and London in 1990, I interviewed his elder brother Albert, and Albert's son Philip. I also had another round of interviews with senior O&Y executives, including Lionel Dodd, Michael Dennis, George Iacobescu, and Richard Griffiths. The article was delayed by more than a year, during which I carried out considerable further research, and eventually appeared in *Canadian Business* in October 1991. Titled "Deep Pockets?" it attempted to analyze the condition of the Reichmann empire, and questioned the continuing rosy views of the Reichmanns' financial position.

I had been discussing an update of *The Master Builders* with Anna Porter for more than a year when the Reichmann crisis exploded early in 1992. I set out to revise and update the earlier book in the light of subsequent events. In this, I was greatly helped by the fact that I had covered a number of key related topics in magazine articles.

In the wake of *The Master Builders*, I had returned to the Hiram Walker affair and its aftermath in a story for *Saturday Night* magazine, "Cheerio, Hiram Walker!" which appeared in April 1989. I have to express thanks to Walkerville union leader Ron Dickson for allowing me to see his fascinating unpublished memoir, "Takeover: A Personal Journal," which provided me with further insight into the Reichmanns' battle for Hiram Walker.

Again, *Saturday Night* commissioned me in 1990 to write about Robert Campeau and Paul Reichmann. The result, "Strange Bedfellows," appeared in March 1991. The chapter that appears under that name in this book has been revised and updated in the light of subsequent events and additional information.

I feel I should also mention here Elaine Dewar's article, "The Mysterious Reichmanns," which appeared in *Toronto Life* in November 1987. Dewar's article was wildly ambitious and fatally flawed, a fact for which its author has paid a heavy personal price. Nevertheless, the subsequent court case provided some fascinating details of the Reichmanns' background. It also forced me to think further about the Reichmanns' relationship with the media.

Acknowledgements

I FEEL IT APPROPRIATE TO NAME ONCE MORE THE PEOPLE WHO assisted me with *The Master Builders*: Carol Alkerton, Brian Bannon, Dunnery Best, Gail-Ann Bost, Theresa Butcher, Pat Brasch, Harry Carlyle, William Clark, Howard Cohen, Betty Corson, Estelle Nopolsky-Davis, Jamie Deacie, Ron Dickson, Jim Doak, Kathy Duffield, Trevor Eyton, Bob Fenner, Dan Frank, Norm Fraser, Doug Gibson, Ira Gluskin, Jim Hamilton, Dick Haskayne, Gerry Henderson, Bob Heule, Sir Derrick Holden-Brown, Bill Hopper, Peter Hunter, William Kilbourne, Bernd Koken, Gerry Maier, Sheilagh McEvenue, Paul McGoldrick, Bob McGrath, Stephen McLaughlin, Bill Menzell, Dan Mernit, Al Milne, Ed Minskoff, Bill Nankivell, John Norris, Bob Patterson, David Philpotts, Alf Powis, Sheryll Reid, Bill Richards, Keith Roberts, Robert Robinson, Peter Rosewell, Gary Ross, Andy Sarlos, Thorn Savage, Harry Schachter, Tim Sheeres, Bill Shields, Jim Soden, Ron Soskolne, Frank Ternan, Bob Vallance, and Joe Wright.

Among those who helped give me further insight, or other forms of assistance, after *The Master Builders*, but before the Reichmanns' severe problems developed, I must thank Bob Barnes (and his better half, Mags), David Beattie, Conrad Black, David Brown, John Clemes, Michael Dennis, Lionel Dodd, Bud Downing, Bill Fatt, Jim Ferguson, John Fraser, Norm Fraser, Nick Fry, Ian Gearing, Gerry Gianni, John Giffen, James Grant, Richard Griffiths, Stanley Hartt, Cliff Hatch, Sr., Cliff Hatch, Jr., Pat Howe, George Iacobescu, Mike Jackaman, Randy Litchfield, Jacquie McNish, John Mead, Barbara Moon, Pom Pomeroy, Tony Pratt, Miguel Rakiewicz, Doug Sawchuk, Bob Tebbs,

Norma Tuninga, John Usborne, Jim Webber, Dick Wertheim, Ian Wilson-Smith, and Doug Young.

With the new book, as with the original one, I received assistance from a large number of people on the grounds of anonymity. Anonymity became particularly important in the wake of the crash. I take this opportunity to thank them. I stress, naturally, that my conclusions, as in the original work, are my own.

Anna Porter is always a joy to deal with. Had it not been for her, I might have started writing this new book much too soon! Also at Key Porter, Phyllis Bruce was, as ever, the voice of sweet reason and sensible compromise. I have also to thank Jonathan Webb with whom, apart from anything else, I went on a brief but fruitful voyage of technological discovery, ably aided by Softprobe's Miriam Brown. Barbara Czarnecki saved me from myself. Meg Taylor did a wonderful job of editing.

1

Empty Pockets

PAUL REICHMANN HAS ALWAYS BEEN EASIER TO DESCRIBE than to fathom. He has, except when he smiles, the air of an undertaker. Polite and courtly, shy and sensitive, he always appears quite without vanity or personal pride. He dresses somberly, and invariably, in dark suit and tie, white shirt and black shoes. He always wears a yarmulke or homburg, a sign that he is a servant of his God. His speech, which still bears a strong mid-European accent, also tends toward mid-European sentence structures, verbal labyrinths reflecting the complexity of his thinking. Employees have been known to take tape recorders into meetings with him and, like cryptographers, later bend with strained ears and knitted brows over their master's voice. Even then, there have often been communications problems. As one consultant who worked for Paul Reichmann for many years put it: "Even when I've worked out what he's said, I still can't necessarily understand what he's saying." Insiders reckoned he ran Olympia & York more like a medieval monarchy than a company, telling nobody more than they needed to know, and with a positive "pride in disorganization."

Despite his supposed otherworldliness, one key element in creating an almost superhuman public image was Paul Reichmann's skill in dealing with the press. Although billed as reclusive, Paul Reichmann has been involved in countless interviews, although most have been given on a "background" basis, that is, not for attribution. Somehow, he made each journalist feel he or she was privy to something truly exclusive. He always seemed remarkably frank, and somehow vulnerable, almost overeager to be fully understood. But Paul Reichmann always had an agenda when dealing with the media: to boost the notion of the Reichmanns as men with "deep pockets." That was a key part of the Reichmann myth.

For their part, the media showed a remarkable willingness to take the Reichmanns' word for their financial status. Periodically, in the lists of the financially mighty, the Reichmanns appeared among the world's richest families. In September 1991, when *Fortune* produced its annual list of the world's wealthiest people, there were the Reichmanns at number four, sitting snugly between King Fahd of Saudi Arabia and the Mars family of candy fame.

But where could these figures possibly originate? And how could they be corroborated? It might be possible to put a value on the Reichmanns' assets, but to reach a true figure of net worth, knowledge of overall debt was necessary, and only O&Y's very largest bankers had a glimpse at that. Nevertheless, it was comforting for bankers and other lenders to see a figure of U.S.$12.8 billion beside the family name, even if they suspected, or even knew, that it could not possibly be accurate.

One thing was definite: if there had been a list of world borrowers, among private companies, the Reichmanns would undoubtedly have been number one. The simple fact was that Paul Reichmann was, outside governments, perhaps the greatest borrower the world had ever seen. In early 1992, the negative consequences of that status finally caught up with the empire.

The murmur had been building throughout the previous year. How could the Reichmanns *not* be in trouble? The Toronto-based brothers — Paul, his elder brother Albert, and his younger brother Ralph — were the world's largest private real estate developers, and real estate worldwide was in the dumps. Through their main company, Olympia & York Developments Limited, the Reichmanns controlled more than forty North American buildings with some 43 million square feet of rentable space. Holding fourteen Manhattan skyscrapers, they were the Big Apple's biggest landlords. But the Big Apple's rental juices had been drying up just as the brothers desperately needed the money for their most ambitious project, the £1.5 billion first phase of London's Canary Wharf.

The Reichmanns had progressed through ever grander and more ambitious projects, involving larger and more sophisticated buildings and more elaborate and attractive public spaces. But Canary Wharf was ambitious in another sense: the Reichmanns were attempting to produce a gravitational shift in Britain's capital, creating the heart of a "third business district" in a previously derelict part of London's Docklands, 2½ miles east of the Bank of England.

In the spring of 1992, with the first phase of Canary Wharf close to completion, Londoners could, from a distance of thirty miles, gape at, or grumble about, the development's huge, glistening, steel-clad, pyramid-topped principal tower. Up close, they could marvel at the exceptional quality of the other buildings, at the architectural detail and the no-expenses-spared "street furniture," at the magnificently manicured gardens, at the revolutionary (for Britain) combination of commercial and retail space. But perceptions are important in selling developments, and the Docklands suffered not only from a low-rent image, but also from chronic transportation difficulties.

The main public access to Canary Wharf was the Docklands Light Railway. The inefficiency of the "Toytown Railway," as it had been derisively dubbed, had driven the Reichmanns and O&Y's managers to distraction, and further damaged the project's credibility. Transport was being addressed by new systems, including a proposed extension of the Jubilee subway line. But the Reichmanns had promised to kick in £400 million toward the costs, and the first payment was due at the end of March 1992. Moreover, even if the subway extension went ahead on schedule, it would still not be completed until 1996.

The British are renowned traditionalists, and there had been widely voiced doubts from the beginning about whether major companies and institutions would give up their traditional haunts. So far, they were unwilling. Canary Wharf's problems had been exacerbated because authorities in the City and West End of

London — concerned about losing tenants to the new project — had relaxed their own development regulations, thus spawning a surge of new commercial construction. This additional space, plus the prolonged recession, had led to a real estate crash. Despite increasingly expensive inducements, O&Y's leasing thrust had been stalled for almost eighteen months, with less than 60 percent of the project accounted for. No major British financial institution had taken significant space. Neither had any Canadian institution. Meanwhile, the project's enormous costs were being funded primarily by North American debt, serviced from North American cash flows, which were rapidly drying up.

In New York, downtown vacancy rates were almost 20 percent, while rents had slumped 30 percent below the levels of 1987. The most dramatic example of O&Y's tenant problems was the collapse of Drexel Burnham Lambert, the very symbol of Wall Street's excesses in the 1980s, whose star employee had been junk-bond king Michael Milken. Faced with a multiplicity of charges by the Securities and Exchange Commission, Drexel had plea-bargained its way to a stunning U.S.$650 million settlement, which had helped drive it into default. Drexel had filed for protection in February 1990 and soon after vacated its offices at the Reichmann-owned Manhattan building at 60 Broad Street, leaving a ghostly outline of its name on the wall outside, a stack of empty floors, and a hole in the Reichmanns' income.

Although O&Y claimed that average vacancy rates in its downtown Manhattan buildings, including the World Financial Center, were running below the industry average, at around 15 percent, that was still much higher than earlier Reichmann forecasts. Rental renewals were also at lower-than-forecast rates. All this meant both lower cash flows and lower asset values, squeezed finances and nervous bankers.

The company had been having similar problems in Toronto. A giant new development, BCE Place, was sucking tenants out of the Reichmanns' flagship development, First Canadian Place, against a background of overbuilding and rent declines that mirrored the New York and London markets.

O&Y's investment portfolio had also been struggling. Its market value had slumped more than Can$1 billion in 1990, to just over Can$5 billion, and continued to fall through 1991 to less than Can$4 billion, as key holdings like oil company Gulf Canada and newsprint giant Abitibi-Price had suffered flagging resource markets and a multitude of other problems. The rumbles grew louder: what was keeping them afloat?

In June 1991, stories had flashed around the world that O&Y had defaulted on a loan to Citibank. An O&Y spokesman had described the rumor as "malicious and groundless." A representative of Citibank had dubbed it "patently ridiculous." Although the rumor may have been malicious, it was certainly neither groundless nor ridiculous, at least not patently so. For nothing had ever been patent about the finances of the Reichmann empire.

Bankers had for years told themselves and the media that the Reichmanns were "men of their word." There was a compelling reason for this: the Reichmanns had never shown their books to the majority of those who had loaned them billions of dollars. Much of the empire's financial structure and rationale existed not on paper, but in the head of Paul Reichmann, the man dubbed O&Y's "strategic mastermind."

Although it was a matter of loyalty within the family to speak of the three brothers as equal partners, Ralph had little involvement. Albert was regarded as a good developer, and had taken the lead in O&Y's business and philanthropic sorties in Eastern Europe and the Soviet Union, but his chief role had always been that of sounding board and confidant for Paul. It was Paul who had become the wizard of real estate finance, turning future streams of rental income into cash for expansion. It was Paul who hatched the strategy of diversification into natural resources. It was Paul who had fallen in love with Canary Wharf. If the empire was in trouble, it was Paul who was now on the spot.

In the late 1980s and early 1990s, O&Y and a number of its many subsidiaries had raised cash by issuing short-term promissory notes or bonds, commonly known as "commercial paper." For borrowers, commercial paper is cheaper than a bank loan. For short-term investors wanting to invest at least $100,000, commercial paper offers higher rates than alternatives like treasury bills. As far as traditional conservative corporate finance theory is concerned, funding real estate with commercial paper is a no-no; you never borrow short to invest long. But nobody questioned the Reichmanns. Paul Reichmann was widely acknowledged as a financial genius; if he was borrowing short to invest long, then classic financial theory had to be wrong.

Only the most credit-worthy corporations had access to the commercial paper market. Investors in commercial paper bought at least partly on the basis of the issuer's reputation. O&Y had enormous mystique, despite the continuing doubts over Canary Wharf. Moreover, the fact that there was always O&Y commercial paper available made O&Y a permanent part of the market, further increasing investors' sense of security. Investment dealers had no problem with O&Y needing as much money as they could raise, since their income depended on commissions of one-eighth of 1 percent on the amount of paper sold. For them, it was the more the merrier.

Of course, investors bought commercial paper on a more scientific basis than their subjective assessment of O&Y's name. Commercial paper issuers' credit-worthiness was rated by independent bond rating agencies, which received their income both from the companies they rated and from subscriptions to their rating reports. Toronto-based Dominion Bond Rating Service, DBRS, was one of two Canadian bond rating agencies. The other was the Canadian Bond Rating Service. In recent years, as the commercial paper market had grown, Canadian investors had increasingly come to rely on the ratings of DBRS and CBRS. DBRS, for its part, may also have been lulled by the Reichmann mystique, that their word was as good as their bond.

DBRS's head, Walter Schroeder, had met with Paul Reichmann on a number of occasions and asked to see the overall figures of O&Y. Reichmann had told him there was no need: the paper — and bonds — DBRS was being asked to rate were all backed by security, in the form of a building or basket of investments, that was isolated from the underlying risk of O&Y; it did not matter what happened to the parent company; paper holders and bondholders would always be secured. Without these assurances, DBRS would not have rated O&Y's commercial paper and building-backed bonds. Without the DBRS rating, the commercial paper and bonds would have been very difficult to sell.

Early in 1992, some disturbing signs began to appear in the commercial paper market. Dealers noticed that O&Y's commercial paper managers were willing both to be more flexible in maturities, and to pay higher rates, than other issuers. Instead of thirty, sixty, and ninety days, they were prepared to take money for periods from two weeks to six months. Also, their rates were "gapping," that is, they were offering higher rates of interest than other companies with similar ratings. This led some other commercial paper issuers with the same rating as O&Y to issue paper and then use the proceeds to buy O&Y paper for a matching period, thus earning the "spread" between the rate they paid and the higher rate offered by O&Y. Some dealers, smelling trouble, stopped marketing O&Y paper.

Issuers of commercial paper usually give comfort to their investors by establishing bank lines of credit to support the redemption of paper in the event there are problems rolling it over. But to obtain such lines of credit, a company has to pay a fee. O&Y did not like paying fees. Instead, it backed its commercial paper issues with specific pieces of collateral.

One Reichmann program was backed by the Exchange Tower in Toronto, the building in which the Reichmanns had their headquarters and which also housed the Toronto Stock Exchange. If anything went wrong, then those who took Exchange Tower paper could ultimately seize the building. But of course those who bought the Exchange Tower paper never imagined for a second they would have to seize the building. If they had, they never would have bought the paper. Nevertheless, having such a tangible and visible piece of security made commercial paper holders comfortable.

In 1990 and 1991, DBRS had produced brief overviews of the

O&Y empire, which noted the hurdles facing Canary Wharf. In 1990, DBRS had said it believed there was "substantial net worth (equity) above and beyond outstanding debt." In the 1991 report, the agency declared it believed there was "reasonable" net worth. In November 1991, DBRS, aware of further deterioration in property markets and the Reichmanns' share portfolio, returned to O&Y for a further review. On February 13, it issued another report which made no comments about overall net worth and lowered the rating on one of O&Y's commercial paper issues, O&Y Commercial Paper II — which was backed by publicly traded shares from the Reichmanns' portfolio — and also lowered the rating on the bonds backed by First Canadian Place. But there was no suggestion that O&Y might be in trouble. O&Y's paper was still rated as "investment grade." Indeed, DBRS would subsequently come under strong criticism for not having given an earlier warning of the O&Y situation, and then, even when the problems appeared, for not recognizing their severity. Although O&Y would later blame DBRS for what happened next, the bond agency's re-rating hardly represented even a whiff of smoke. The fire started elsewhere.

On Monday, March 2, rumors that a major Canadian company was about to fail, dragging down one of Canada's largest financial institutions, starting buzzing around Tokyo, home of many of the Reichmanns' lenders, and quickly sped down the wires to New York, London, and Toronto. Soon the phones were ringing off the hook. It was these rumors that killed O&Y's commercial paper.

On maturity, commercial paper is usually rolled over, that is, the holder replaces the old issue with a new issue rather than cashing it in, but on Friday, March 6, when Can$40 million of paper came due, O&Y found that holders wanted their money. The company waited until the final minutes before the close of trading to pay out the cash. Word soon went round the market that the Reichmanns were "dragging their feet," that is, they were showing the scariest of all signs as far as lenders were concerned: that they really needed the money.

The same day, DBRS, inundated with calls about O&Y, issued a re-confirmation of its February 13 ratings, pointing out that collateral on the Exchange Tower and Commercial Paper II issues was adequate. A DBRS analyst even suggested that "the rumors about the company have gotten out of hand." But the analyst had no idea what had been going on behind the scenes between the Reichmanns and their bankers. The Reichmanns were begging them for more money and the banks were, for once, saying no.

On March 7, a story in the Toronto *Globe and Mail* declared of O&Y: "It is believed that the company has had ongoing negotiations with its bankers for more than a year. The company is said to have asked the banks to reduce or delay interest payments on its debt." This information was horrifying. It revealed that the Reichmanns were in trouble. Spooked investors began selling O&Y's commercial paper.

In the week beginning March 9, as investors dumped their holdings into a thin secondary market, or demanded cash as their paper reached maturity, it became obvious that O&Y was having to scramble for funds. Just as they had the previous Friday, they were waiting until the end of the business day to pay out on maturing paper. Investment dealer employees who turned up with their clients' paper were being told to come back later for their money. By mid-week, as the word traveled round the market that O&Y was facing a cash crunch, its commercial paper became unsaleable. O&Y suddenly found itself facing the redemption of $1.1 billion of commercial paper within forty-five days.

On Friday, March 13, O&Y received another devastating blow when a London court ruled that it had to pay U.S.$240 million to New York investment banking firm Morgan Stanley under a previous agreement to buy the building that Morgan Stanley had erected at Canary Wharf. The following Monday, O&Y's various commercial paper issues started defaulting as the Reichmanns found themselves without the cash to redeem them.

On March 18, DBRS, responding to what was happening in the market rather than leading it, put O&Y's commercial paper on "rating alert." The following day, O&Y announced that it was withdrawing from the commercial paper market. It had no choice. It had been forced to repay $400 million since the rumors began at the beginning of the month.

Although O&Y continued to blame DBRS for its problems, DBRS was bending over backwards to give O&Y the benefit of the doubt. A DBRS spokesman declared that a proposed refinancing was "quite a do-able deal." He said there was "nothing fundamentally wrong" with O&Y and its commercial paper. He said the market response to the rumors was "totally irrational." But according to a Bay Street money dealer, the DBRS analyst was wrong. "The market," said the dealer, "is perfect." And the market had just announced that the Reichmanns were going down.

On March 22, having been chased from the commercial paper market, and finding its bankers unwilling to make up the resulting cash shortfall, O&Y at last acknowledged to a stunned world that it was forced to "rework" its massive debt. The Reichmanns were on the brink of becoming the largest private financial failure in world history. The deep pockets were empty.

How did this situation come about? The answer lies in the history of an extraordinary man. Unfortunately for his lenders, the most extraordinary thing about Paul Reichmann turned out to be his borrowing ability. Never had one man succeeded in borrowing so much from so many. Paul Reichmann had once been described as a businessman of profound insights, whose learning spanned the ages, a man with a crystal ball. But it turned out that Paul Reichmann was very much a man of the times, times when investors thought real estate inflation was permanent, and bankers threw prudence to the winds.

2

The Road to Morocco

PAUL REICHMANN WAS BORN IN VIENNA IN SEPTEMBER 1930, the fifth child of Samuel and Renee Reichmann, devout Orthodox Jews who had moved to the city two years before. Samuel and Renee had had their first three children, Edward, Louis, and Eva, in Budapest, which sits astride the Danube and commands the approaches to the Great Hungarian Plain. It was in that bustling commercial metropolis that Samuel, after the First World War, had founded a successful egg distribution business, which he transferred to Vienna.

Vienna, which the Hapsburgs had ruled for almost 700 years until the end of the First World War, was a city of great cultural, intellectual, and political importance. The home of Mozart and Freud, it contained the finest examples of baroque architecture. Here the Congress of Vienna had rewritten the map of Europe after the fall of Napoleon. For more than 2,000 years, it had been a meeting place of East and West. In this beautiful city, its skyline dominated by the spire of St. Stephen's Cathedral, Renee gave birth to three sons, Albert, Paul, and Ralph. Meanwhile, Samuel's business grew as he built an integrated operation that took eggs from the farmyard through grading to distribution.

But Vienna was also the cradle of a form of evil of particular danger to the Reichmanns. Vienna's Academy of Fine Arts had a minor employee named Adolph Hitler, who would grow to political prominence in Germany amid the turmoil of the 1930s. The Reichmanns were among those wise enough to flee when Hitler annexed Austria in March 1938. They lived in Paris for two years but fled once again mere hours before German troops arrived, reaching Spain shortly before the border was closed. Continuing south, they wound up in the neutral international port of Tangier.

Tangier, overlooking the Atlantic and the Strait of Gibraltar from the northwest tip of Africa, was very different from Budapest, Vienna, or Paris. Over the 3,000 years of its history, Phoenicians, Carthaginians, Visigoths, Vandals, the Portuguese, the Spanish, and the English had all raided and held it. The strongest mark had been left by the Arabs, but the city also had a long Jewish history. Local Berbers had converted to Judaism as early as 700 B.C., and among the turbans, djellabas, burnooses, and caftans of the bazaar, the dark suits and felt hats of the Jews could be seen on even the hottest of summer days.

When the Reichmanns arrived, the city was renowned as a hotbed of mystery, vice, and skullduggery. But it was also a mecca of commerce. The city and its environs constituted the International Zone of Morocco, which had been created under a statute signed in 1923 by France, Britain, Spain, and Italy. Under the statute, Tangier was granted special status with international municipal administration and no military occupation. Shortly after the Reichmanns arrived, Spanish troops occupied Tangier, abolishing the international administration and extending Spanish laws to the zone. Nevertheless, Tangier remained one of the few free markets for foreign exchange and foreign currencies during the war. Daily quotations were available for dollars, pounds, pesetas, escudos, and Swiss, French, and Moroccan francs. Samuel, with his commodity background, joined the Jewish money dealers who dominated the business in the city.

After World War II, outsiders flocked to Tangier, drawn by low taxes and duties, creating a commercial free-for-all and a frenetic society. "Sodom was a church picnic, and Gomorrah a convention of Girl Scouts" compared with Tangier, claimed a newspaper report of the time. Smugglers used old PT boats to ferry contraband — cigarettes, nylons, soap, whisky, watches, and penicillin — into southern Spain, Gibraltar, Italy or the Mediterranean Islands. Corruption was pervasive and ran to the top. A standard Tangier joke was that the initials C.D. stood not for

Corps Diplomatique but for Contrabandier Distingué. The town advertised in the Paris *Herald Tribune*: "Tangier is waiting for you. Tangier knows no restrictions of any kind." The city buzzed with haphazard construction. The *New York Times* called it a "building contractors' nightmare." *Fortune* described it in 1949 as "a completely uninhibited dream ... everybody's no man's land ... that has no national anthem other than the sweet melody of hard cash."

In Tangier, everybody lived by his wits. There was an anecdote about a wealthy Jewish businessman who, because he was an American protégé, put up an office building two stories higher than the city laws allowed. When the authorities tried to indict him, he noted that local laws did not apply to American protégés. But when his tenants refused to pay their rent and he applied to the Tangier courts for assistance, the authorities reminded him that, as he had pointed out to them, the building did not exist as far as they were concerned. The businessman nevertheless had the last word, for when Tangier tax officials presented him with a bill, he expressed surprise that they should expect to tax property that the courts claimed did not exist! Property development could be a complex business.

Samuel Reichmann was renowned for his mental agility. He could translate American dollars into French francs, or Dutch gulden into Spanish pesetas quicker than it would take to punch the numbers into a computer today. Widely respected, his word was considered good as gold, and in Tangier you could do wonderful things with gold. Following the 1944 Bretton Woods Conference — at which the International Monetary Fund was set up — the world price of gold was fixed at U.S.$35 an ounce, but Tangier was exempted from this restriction. Gold brought up to U.S.$100 per ounce in the International Zone.

Samuel Reichmann strove to insulate his family from the corrupting influences of the city while taking advantage of its commercial potential. The Reichmann children were all brought up in strictly Orthodox fashion, living according to dietary laws and rituals handed down since time immemorial. Renee

Reichmann was a woman who liked to help others. In Budapest and Vienna, she had organized relief for the sick and the poor. From Tangier, she sent relief packages of food and clothing into Nazi concentration camps. Paul and his brothers helped pack these parcels, destined via the Red Cross in Paris for Auschwitz and other centers of horror. Renee would sometimes organize the shipping of as much as 4,000 kilograms of food daily. She also begged the American chargé d'affaires to intercede with the governor of Spanish Morocco to issue Spanish entry visas and papers for Jewish children, thus saving many hundreds of young lives. After the war, she and Samuel arranged for scores of Moroccan children to be sent to France, England, and Israel to study. Renee was instrumental in founding elementary schools that ultimately had 10,000 pupils. Renee and Samuel founded the first modern Jewish educational institution for girls and promoted a similar institution for boys. She was instrumental in bringing instructors from the Sorbonne in France and the Talmudic College in Gateshead, England, to train teachers.

Renee and Samuel's Orthodoxy, their emphasis on continuing the core of Jewish tradition — and hence Judaism — through scholarship, influenced Paul in his first choice of career. He told *Time* magazine in April 1988: "As children before, during and after World War II, we grew up in an environment where the sacrifices and the selfless and total dedication of our parents Samuel and Renee and of our sister Eva taught us forever the differences between material and human, intellectual and spiritual values."

Paul thought he was going to be a teacher. He had been a studious child, remembered by those who attended the Gateshead Talmudic college with him as assiduous rather than academically brilliant. At Gateshead, just outside Newcastle in the northeast of England, Paul Reichmann underwent a rigorous regime of prayer and study that left virtually no free time. Either in lectures or in preparation with another student (Talmudic students often work in pairs), he set about improving his mind. When he finished school, he refused to work with his father, as his elder brother

Albert was now doing. Gripped with youthful idealism, he chose to work instead for a New York–based educational institution out of Casablanca for three years. Then came the revolution in Morocco.

Postwar peace and prosperity ended abruptly on March 30, 1952, when an enormous crowd of native Tanjawis gathered in the medina, then marched through the city demanding Moroccan independence. The police fired on the mob. A wave of fear ran through the city's foreign communities. The riots marked a turning point. Big money began moving to Geneva, Montreal, Caracas, and Montevideo, and the Tangier boom began perceptibly to deflate. Samuel and Renee realized that their family's fugitive life was not at an end.

On August 1, 1955, on a typically hot, bright summer day, a Tanjawi pastry vendor ran amok, killing four people and seriously wounding five. There followed citywide demonstrations on behalf of the sultan, Mohammed V, who had been abducted by the French. An attempt was made on the life of the French puppet ruler. In September 1955, the French bowed to world opinion. In November, Mohammed returned from exile. Morocco's status as an International Zone was abolished. More than 40 tons of gold reportedly left the vaults of Tangier for Geneva. The city disintegrated. The property market fell apart. Anti-foreign sentiments grew. Burglaries and assaults increased. A bomb was placed in the old Jewish cemetery that lay along the eastern wall of the medina. Samuel Reichmann had by then sent family emissaries across the Atlantic to find a new home.

In 1954, Edward, the eldest son, was dispatched to explore North America. By the end of the decade, the whole family had moved, first to New York, then to Montreal and Toronto. For some years, Samuel commuted between Tangier and Montreal. Paul had married a tall and gracious native of Jerusalem, but his wife Lea found the frenzy of New York too much, so she and Paul decided to try Toronto, where younger brother Ralph was already living. They found Toronto, in Paul's words, "a quiet little English town, not unlike Birmingham."

Ralph had taken over an import business started by Edward in Montreal, based on contacts the family had with Spanish tile manufacturers. The business was based in a 4,000-square-foot warehouse in the northwest suburbs of the city. There, Ralph had three employees: a shipper, a receiver, and a bookkeeper who worked half-days. The business flourished. After Paul arrived, he looked for business opportunities in building supplies and started importing metal lath, the sheeting over which plaster was worked, from Europe. The brothers soon realized they needed more space. They bought some land and invited tenders to build a warehouse based on a design by a young architect moonlighting from his job with a bank's building department. Paul decided that the tenders were too expensive, and the brothers undertook to build the warehouse themselves. They put it up for Can$70,000. The lowest tender had been Can$125,000.

The tile business soon outgrew its original location and moved to a site on Toronto's Lawrence Avenue West, where it would eventually become the headquarters of a tile and carpet operation that today occupies 3 million square feet in both Canada and the United States. It not only went on to import tiles and marble from all over the world, but also developed a number of manufacturing subsidiaries that produce everything from terrazzo flooring molds to bathroom fixtures. Olympia Floor & Wall Tile and its satellites would eventually employ more than 1,500 people.

One critical question in any examination of the Reichmann empire is the significance of the family's Jewishness. Paul Johnson notes in his *A History of the Jews* that Judaism, unlike Christianity, "did not polarize piety and prosperity." Riches, according to the Talmud so assiduously studied by Paul and his siblings, were one of seven characteristics that were "comely to the righteous and comely to the world." Jewish laws, notes Johnson, were based on the assumption that "properly conducted trading was not only wholly compatible with strict morality but positively virtuous since it made possible the good works and systematic charity around which the Jewish community revolved."

Johnson also notes that the whole traumatic history of the Jews made them uniquely efficient and enthusiastic capitalists.

Their persecutions and forced movements rendered them expert at concentrating and moving wealth, and forced them to become both more flexible and rational. It also made them masters of negotiation, since they very often had to negotiate for their very lives. Their separateness, meanwhile, made them less attached to particular societies, and thus less concerned with the often sweeping changes that capitalism's process of creative destruction brought about. Their commercial history made them innovators, salesmen, seekers for wide markets, experts at cutting prices, and highly adept at gathering and using commercial intelligence. In this context, the Reichmanns represented the fruit of a long tradition.

In fact, the religious-determinist view of the Reichmanns' success represents a dead end. Their Jewishness certainly determined the way they looked and the way they conducted themselves. It dictated their social separateness. But Judaism cannot be thought responsible for the sheer scope of the Reichmanns' business success. Moreover, the Reichmanns' powerful and pervasive culture should never have been confused with any kind of holiness in their business operations. The brothers would always be very tough businessmen. Charity is an important part of Jewish life, but it is not the basis of business dealings. Conrad Black, chairman of Toronto-based Hollinger Inc., proprietor of the London *Daily Telegraph*, and a longtime associate of Paul Reichmann, said in a 1990 interview, "I suppose elements of the press think it's highly unusual to have businessmen in their position being as religious as they are. Maybe it is. But it's something that should be looked upon with absolute neutrality. It doesn't prove anything."

What made the Reichmanns exceptional was the genius of Paul Reichmann, a genius that first discovered its outlet when the brothers decided to build a little warehouse. From that day forward, his career was a growing love affair with business. He himself had no idea where the affair would take him. The roots of his skill were apparently as much a mystery to his family as to anyone else. Even his own mother, Renee, would be astonished at her son's success.

Paul Reichmann would transform his Talmudically trained

brain into a powerful analytical tool and a commercial weapon. He would turn his studious mind from rumination on arcane points of scholarship to thoughts of how to build a business empire.

3

Gold on the Table

PROPERTY DEVELOPERS COME IN ALL SHAPES AND SIZES, creeds and colors. Their personal styles range from the flamboyance of a Donald Trump to the reclusiveness of a Paul Reichmann. What they have in common is a desire to assemble developments and fortunes. At the highest level, they change the faces of cities, transforming the flows of people and commerce like men moving iron filings with a magnet under a map. They are not necessarily architects or construction engineers or financiers, but their skill lies in bringing these specialties together to satisfy the demands of those who need space to carry on their businesses. They do not draw up blueprints or erect steel or pour concrete, but they cause these things to happen.

Paul Reichmann's supervision of the seminal warehouse and his relentlessly probing mind taught him that there was no mystery in development, but there was lots of profit. The Reichmanns' architect had told them it would cost Can$100,000 to put up the warehouse. The lowest tender had been Can$125,000. Paul had built it for Can$70,000. If he had been building for a third party, he could have undercut the lowest tender by Can$20,000 and still pulled in a net profit of 50 percent.

Paul Reichmann decided to leave the tile and construction supply business to Ralph and move into property development. He started buying industrial properties in the northwest suburbs of Toronto, where the tile warehouse was located, and began putting up simple, single-story industrial buildings for lease or sale. The tile importing business was named Olympia, reportedly because of Ralph's love of the Greek classics. The real estate business was named York Developments, after the Toronto borough. These two companies would form the nucleus of Olympia & York.

Although he quickly mastered the art of real estate dealmaking and construction, one constraint for Paul Reichmann was finance. His scope was increased in 1959 with the arrival in Toronto of the patriarch, Samuel, and Paul's elder brother, Albert.

There has been much speculation over the years about how much money the Reichmanns brought from the family business in Tangier. Paul Reichmann once reportedly admitted that the arrival of his father and brother multiplied the capital available tenfold, but that still did not necessarily represent an enormous amount. According to Canadian writer Peter Newman, a bank manager in North Toronto recalled Samuel and Paul coming in to make a deposit "big enough to choke a horse." According to Newman, the elder Reichmann was rumored to have arrived with "at least $30 million plus much valuable jewelery." But this figure is probably greatly exaggerated. Other stories claim that seed money for the Reichmann empire came from the English branch of the Rothschild family through Renee, whose cousin was David Gestetner, the Hungarian-born British industrialist who invented the modern stencil duplicating process. Certainly, other wealthy Jewish families were involved in the family's early financings, but the fact is that the building of the family business in Canada was a long process, with the bulk of the funds generated internally. Indeed, Paul Reichmann would later claim that until the late 1960s the company was worth only Can$1 million.

Albert joined Paul in real estate, and the brothers began to pyramid an empire on the low-rise base of factories and warehouses in the suburbs of Toronto. The Reichmanns pursued quality and excellence. They worked hard. They listened attentively to their clients. They custom-built and installed attractive landscaping. The rationale was simple: clients would pay for quality; satisfied clients would produce more business and spread the good word about the Reichmanns. By the mid-1960s, there were Reichmann-built warehouses and factories all over the Toronto suburbs.

With their impeccable manners and their sober dress, topped always with their yarmulkes or homburgs, the Reichmanns cut strangely conservative figures amid the rough-and-tumble, concrete and dust atmosphere of the building sites. They would often converse in one of the European languages they spoke in addition to Yiddish. This use of foreign languages was more than just a sentimental harking back to the past. It was a practical way of speaking freely in front of tradesmen, contractors, and even employees without letting them know what you were saying.

The Reichmanns understood that business advantage lay in cornering the market in knowledge as much as in quality control or tight scheduling of projects. They also came from a past in which one did not give outsiders more information than was necessary, because such information could be — and often had been — used against them. Centuries of persecution had bred an inevitable secretiveness. Still, Canada was one of the most tolerant countries on earth. And while Toronto had reminded Paul Reichmann of an English provincial city, there was a very North American attitude toward the entrepreneur. Canada, although it had strong Anglo-Saxon traditions, was a country without stultifying class barriers. It had a business Establishment, but it was a land of opportunity, where immigrants were free to be as successful as their talents and application allowed.

After a decade of building single-story structures, the brothers began looking for opportunities to extend once more the scope of their operation. A form of business genius is to see values where others miss them. The successful real estate developer must also be at least part predator, part scavenger. As success contains the seeds of failure, so failure contains the seeds of success. The Reichmanns' first quantum leap in the real estate field took place in 1965, when they snapped up part of the crumbling empire of one of the most colorful of North American developers, William Zeckendorf.

The Reichmanns would be the heirs of Bill Zeckendorf in a number of ways. They would purchase some of his empire's most valuable lands in Canada. As well, in the late 1970s, they would acquire a major shareholding in the property company that he set up to build his greatest Canadian project, Place Ville Marie in Montreal. They would also inherit many of the real estate techniques that he used. Ultimately, they would follow him into overexpansion and collapse. In the late 1960s and early 1970s, New Yorkers, thinking that a friend, colleague, or member of the family was trying to take on too much, would say: "What are you, the Zeckendorf of the Bronx?" The lesson the Reichmanns failed to learn from Bill Zeckendorf was that a great builder's reach often exceeds his grasp.

Zeckendorf was a 250-pound bear of a man who had risen from being a building salesman to become the world's number-one real estate operator. Born in 1905 in Paris, Illinois, where his father operated a general store, Zeckendorf went to New York University. For thirteen years, he stayed in New York as a real estate and rental agent. In 1938, he joined Webb & Knapp, a conservative real estate firm. The turning point in Zeckendorf's career was his skillful management of Vincent Astor's U.S.$50 million estate while Astor was in the navy. Zeckendorf added U.S.$5 million to the assets, and Astor rewarded Zeckendorf's success with a U.S.$350,000 commission and instructions to "send him a bunch of flowers." Zeckendorf subsequently bought control of Webb & Knapp and took it through a period of dynamic growth.

The developer's reputation was boosted when he sold 17 acres on the East River to John D. Rockefeller, Jr., as a site for the United Nations building. Zeckendorf could have made more money from the parcel, but what he lost in cash he gained in prestige. After hearing that his proposal for the UN headquarters had been accepted, he told his wife, Marion: "We have just moved the capital of the world." Le Corbusier sketched a prototype design for the UN building on the back of an envelope as he sat in Zeckendorf's Manhattan apartment.

Zeckendorf was a showman as well as a salesman. He and his wife would turn up at Manhattan parties with their toy Doberman pinscher sporting a leather wing collar and a silk bow tie. Zeckendorf's girth gave away his favorite hobby; he once claimed that he got all his good ideas from indigestion. He was also superstitious. Each new Webb & Knapp subsidiary was numbered either to contain thirteen or to be a multiple of thirteen.

Through Webb & Knapp, Zeckendorf built a U.S.$300 million conglomerate that included not only real estate but also shipping and oil. After the railroads and the utilities, he was reckoned to be New York's largest taxpayer. He controlled his empire from a strange, windowless, circular hatbox of an office — designed by I.M. Pei — atop Webb & Knapp's Madison Avenue headquarters. The room was equipped with a variable lighting system, reputedly to induce specific moods in his business visitors.

Zeckendorf's greatest asset, and ultimately his heaviest liability, was his vision. Like all great developers and entrepreneurs, his mind was always in the future, in the what-could-be. "If I'm a maverick in my business," he once said, "it's because other people work only with money. I employ imagination."

The 1950s were Zeckendorf's glory years. In 1953, he pulled off the biggest real estate transaction in New York history, buying a U.S.$53 million package of buildings that included the Chrysler Building, the Art Deco fantasy on Lexington Avenue, topped by its six levels of stainless steel arches and its radiator-ornament gargoyles. With his "Wall Street Maneuver" he played a game of musical buildings with the country's largest and most powerful banks. To move clients into new buildings, he would take over their old leases, "like second-hand cars," he said. Olympia & York would use the same technique thirty years later to fill its mammoth World Financial Center in lower Manhattan. There was another strange echo in the very structure of the Reichmanns' World Financial Center, four towers named for their occupants. Bill Zeckendorf had hatched an ambitious scheme to redevelop the approach to the United Nations building. In his autobiography he wrote: "My plan was that the four southern office buildings were to be occupied by four large corporations, and that each building bear the name of its tenant."

Bill Zeckendorf first burst into the headlines in Canada in September 1956. While young Paul and Ralph Reichmann were establishing their little import business in the Toronto hinterland, Zeckendorf unveiled a plan to transform the face of downtown Montreal, one of North America's most cosmopolitan cities. The centerpiece of his plan would be a forty-story, 1.5-million-square-foot development, built in the shape of a cross – Place Ville Marie. The scheme, claimed Zeckendorf, would turn Montreal into a "great city."

Zeckendorf's Place Ville Marie would sit on the cellar dug thirty years before by Sir Henry Thornton, the Canadian National Railways' first president, whose dreams for a similarly bold scheme had been shattered by the Depression. Thornton's plans had cratered in the most literal way. When work stopped in 1932, all that the project had to show was "the world's most expensive hole," the result of moving some 4 million cubic feet of earth.

Donald Gordon, a six-foot-four Scotsman who headed the CNR after the war (the only man Zeckendorf admitted could drink him under the table), began searching in 1952 for private investors to kick-start the development once more, but no Canadian firm had the resources. Zeckendorf heard of the scheme and came to Montreal to look it over. In February 1955, the New York wizard flew over Montreal to inspect the site, then met with Montreal's expansive mayor, Jean Drapeau. Zeckendorf saw that the completion of the Queen Elizabeth Hotel would draw other activity to the area. He envisioned Place Ville Marie as a Rockefeller Center–cum–Grand Central Station. In December 1957, he signed the lease for the Can$100 million project. He raised Can$25 million and immediately spent it on other Canadian ventures, such as the purchase of 277 gas stations.

Besides Donald Gordon and Jean Drapeau, two other men played a critical part in Place Ville Marie: Jimmy Muir, the autocratic head of the Royal Bank, and Lazarus Phillips, the lawyer for Sam Bronfman's hugely successful Seagram distilled spirits empire. They were an odd collection, and Zeckendorf found himself caught up in the intricacies of Montreal's Anglo-French politics. He also had enormous problems finding tenants, but in the end he persuaded the Royal's Muir to move in. Muir was a renowned bully, and Zeckendorf found himself the butt of his bigotry. Muir called Zeckendorf's architect Pei "that damned Chinaman," and he sometimes addressed Zeckendorf as "you — — Jew." But Zeckendorf fulfilled Sir Henry Thornton's dream, and by the early sixties Place Ville Marie had transformed downtown Montreal.

Zeckendorf had also changed the face of Canadian retailing with his huge suburban shopping centers. In May 1964, the opening of the Yorkdale Plaza north of Toronto caused traffic jams on the Trans-Canada Highway. Chartered buses traveled from as far as 100 miles to bring shoppers to the spacious mall.

But as Yorkdale boomed, the Zeckendorf empire was crumbling. Overrapid expansion had left the company short of cash and collapsing under the weight of its debt. In 1965, Webb & Knapp Inc. was put into Chapter 11 bankruptcy reorganization in the United States. Trustees discovered an enormously complex situation, reflecting Zeckendorf's pinball mind and grandiose vision. His moves into hotels and urban renewal schemes had been costly failures, but still Zeckendorf kept pushing into new projects, borrowing money at higher and higher rates. His crucial mistake was a 150-acre amusement park in the Bronx called Freedomland. Freedomland's bankruptcy was the last straw for Zeckendorf. It would eventually be torn down to make way for a huge cooperative housing project. Zeckendorf's empire had already effectively been torn down. Between 1959 and 1965, Webb & Knapp's assets had plummeted from U.S.$300 million to U.S.$22 million. The company had U.S.$100,000 in ready cash and claims from creditors totaling U.S.$84 million. But corporate decay often provides the fertilizer for new ventures, and one part of Webb & Knapp's Canadian empire would prove a critical building block for the Reichmanns. It was a tract of land to the northeast of Toronto called Flemingdon Park.

Webb & Knapp (Canada) and the Rubin brothers, a well-known pair of local Toronto developers, had originally bought the

Fleming estate adjoining the Don Valley in 1958 in what was at the time Canada's largest land purchase. The land was destined to multiply in value because the north-south Don Valley Parkway, which was being built in stages, would eventually link the Trans-Canada Highway, which ran across the north of the city, with the downtown core. Located halfway up the Don Valley Parkway route, Flemingdon Park had been planned as a mixed-use development, combining housing with industrial and office facilities. It was already partly developed and much of the infrastructure of roads and services was under way.

For Paul Reichmann, the value of the land was abundantly obvious. He could not believe that nobody else could see it. At the time he said to Gil Newman, then the Reichmanns' accountant and later one of its senior employees: "There's gold on the table and no one wants to pick it up. Are we making a mistake somewhere? Am I missing something?"

Typically, the purchase was shrouded in secrecy. The final deal was signed in the vaults of the downtown offices of the Bank of Nova Scotia. Present were the Reichmanns, Bill Hay, a dour Scots lawyer who would one day work for the Reichmanns, Lazarus Phillips from Montreal, and representatives of the Oelbaums, another wealthy Toronto Jewish family who reportedly provided part of the deal's finance. The Reichmanns bought the bulk of the 600-acre project, and reportedly recouped their investment in six months by slicing the parcel up and selling a few of the lots.

The switch from industrial to commercial buildings was the result not of a deliberate policy but — like so much else in the evolution of the Reichmann empire — of improvisation in the face of adversity. The brothers had bought a piece of land in the Flemingdon Park area to build a cigarette factory for Rothmans, but then Rothmans had cancelled the project and O&Y was left with the land. Paul Reichmann decided to try his hand at commercial development.

Flemingdon Park literally took the Reichmanns above the ground floor for the first time. The Mony Life Insurance building on the southeast corner of Don Mills Road and Eglinton Avenue was their first multistory building. When they had completed the building, they moved their offices there. The Reichmanns were on the way up.

The brothers decided to bid on a number of commercial ventures, including new buildings for Texaco and Shell, and for the Bell Canada data center. These projects indicated that Paul Reichmann was as skilled and innovative a financier as he was a developer. Having gained Bell's commitment, Paul took the lease to the bond department of an insurance company, for whom a Bell lease was a triple-A investment, as good as Bell bonds. "How much will you cash this lease for?" he asked. They gave him Can$12 million. The Bell building cost Can$6 million to put up. The Texaco building cost Can$3 million, but Reichmann got Can$6 million for the lease. He gave Bell and Texaco an option to purchase the buildings for $1 at the end of the lease. Paul Reichmann viewed the transactions as being financial rather than long-term real estate. Reichmann later claimed these three buildings gave the brothers their first really big money, the working capital with which to expand.

Over the next eight years, the Reichmanns expanded their operations enormously. At Flemingdon Park they participated in the development of several thousand rental and condominium apartment units. They created the largest suburban office center in Canada. By 1974, they had completed thirteen office buildings in the area with a total of 3 million square feet. Meanwhile, they had also acted as a developer or builder for others, either on the client's property or by providing a total package including land, plans, and completed buildings. The Reichmanns greatly favored the "package" method, which gave them higher margins in return for taking the burden of the whole real estate development process — from land assembly through construction — off the client's shoulders. They avoided as far as possible the more traditional tender approach, where a client with a piece of land invites bids from a number of general contractors and the lowest bid usually wins. In Albert's words: "The bidder who makes the biggest mistake gets the job."

The Reichmanns started from the opposite end of the equation. Instead of waiting for a client to come looking for them, they would search out and acquire likely locations, then go looking for customers. Once the package had been sold, it was a matter of putting up the highest-quality building at the lowest cost. The Reichmanns became convinced that, as with automobiles, the premium projects commanded the highest margins. At the cost end of the equation, they emphasized efficiency, which meant squeezing the maximum possible rentable and usable square footage out of a building.

Gross space is all the square footage within the walls of a building. Obviously, not all that space is rentable, and not all the rentable space is usable. The space taken up by facilities such as elevators, service shafts, and mechanical rooms has to be deducted to arrive at rentable space. The Reichmanns soon noticed that architects and engineers did not necessarily share their space-saving priorities. A great deal of time was spent with consultants looking for innovations in areas like elevator systems that would maximize service but take up the minimum floor space. The brothers always took a very close interest in blueprints and layouts. Paul would take home a floor plan, spend the evening mulling it over, and then return the following day having squeezed out another couple of percent of rentable space when it had seemed there was no more to squeeze. Then, once the rentable space had been maximized, they sought to maximize the efficiency of the square footage devoted to elevator lobbies, washrooms, and the like, so that the client got the best use from his rented space.

Flemingdon Park led them into major developments in downtown Toronto, Ottawa, and Calgary. Clients for whom they had built smaller facilities at Flemingdon Park, such as Bell Canada and Shell Canada, were so impressed with the Reichmanns' work that they asked O&Y to undertake larger projects elsewhere. They built the enormous Place Bell Canada for Bell in Ottawa, and, in the latter half of the 1970s, the thirty-three-story Shell Centre in Calgary.

By 1974, the real estate operations were throwing off cash flow of around Can$15 million a year. The tile business had also expanded enormously, and now generated annual sales of more than Can$30 million. Olympia Floor & Wall Tile had moved into manufacturing, and had distribution centers from Quebec City to Vancouver. O&Y had now developed more than 120 industrial and office buildings, but the family was still seen as essentially just another firm of real estate developers. That would change with their next office development.

4

The Flagship

THE INTERSECTION OF KING AND BAY IN TORONTO WAS already Canada's financial center when the Reichmanns decided in 1971 to build Canada's tallest building there. Like so many major intersections across Canada, it had banks on all four corners. But King and Bay was the location the banks had chosen to build their architectural monuments. Two of its corners already sported huge tower developments. On the southeast corner rose I.M. Pei's great silver Commerce Court West, head office of the Canadian Imperial Bank of Commerce. On the block southwest of the intersection were the stark black boxes of Mies van der Rohe's Toronto-Dominion Centre, built for the Toronto-Dominion Bank. The Bank of Montreal's office on the northwest corner, like its neighbor, the Bank of Nova Scotia building on the northeast, had been an imposing edifice when it was built. Now it was a dwarf.

The Montreal, Canada's oldest bank, had adopted a policy of having a major building in each of Canada's main cities. Toronto, as the country's financial capital, had to have something special, a suitably impressive headquarters for a bank with 1,250 offices throughout the world and assets of well over Can$10 billion. First Canadian Place would, in the minds of the bank's management, restore the Bank of Montreal to its rightful place: It would tower over its rivals.

First Canadian Place was conceived as an unprecedentedly massive project within Canada, covering approximately 90 percent of the block bounded by King, Bay, Adelaide, and York. It was to have a mammoth total rentable office and retail space of about 3.5 million square feet. The main building, First Bank

Tower, would have seventy-two stories. A second, smaller tower would follow.

As their principal architects and planners, the Reichmanns chose Bregmann & Hamann, with whose senior partner, George Hamann, they had long had a close relationship. During the previous decade, Bregmann & Hamann had been responsible for many important Toronto buildings, either exclusively or as co-architects. Among these were the Mount Sinai teaching hospital, the Toronto-Dominion Centre, and, more recently, the huge Eaton Centre, a retail-commercial complex. The firm had also designed a number of buildings for the Reichmanns, including their largest project to date, Place Bell Canada in Ottawa. Their style was firmly imprinted on the Reichmanns' developments in and around Flemingdon Park, where they had designed Foresters House, the Texaco building, and the offices for Nestlé and Blue Cross.

The Reichmanns had built their business and reputation on providing what their clients wanted. Buildings were designed to reflect the aspirations of their tenants. First Canadian Place would project quality and prestige because these were what the Reichmanns perceived both their principal tenant and their other, as yet unknown, tenants would want.

The site for the First Canadian Place development was owned 50 percent by O&Y and 25 percent each by the Bank of Montreal and Naloy Properties Limited, a wholly owned subsidiary of North American Life Assurance Company. O&Y's interest was charged to the bank as security. The other 50 percent was to be leased to O&Y. The project was to have two phases. The first would be started in 1973. The second would begin following approval from the City of Toronto. But the City of Toronto was less enthusiastic about the mammoth development than either the Reichmanns or the Bank of Montreal.

In the late 1960s and early 1970s, Toronto was in the throes of a wrenching debate about development and the construction of urban expressways. The diminutive David Crombie swept into office in 1972 as the city's new "tiny perfect mayor." A key plank of Crombie's election platform had been to preserve Toronto's neighborhoods and halt the higgledy-piggledy growth of huge office blocks in the downtown core. A dedicated group of bright young professional planners gravitated to Toronto to become Crombie's Praetorian Guard, caught up in establishing a new destiny for the city. The Crombie team began work on a comprehensive Central Area Plan that would reduce the densities of commercial development while providing a framework for the city's architectural future. To show they meant business, they introduced a by-law limiting the height of new buildings to 45 feet. Anyone who wanted to build higher had to negotiate with the city.

One of Crombie's young lions was an architect named Ron Soskolne. Soskolne, born in South Africa, had come to Toronto in 1969 to study architecture and planning at the University of Toronto. Then he worked as an architect and for a management consultancy firm before joining the city government in 1972, the year David Crombie became mayor. Soskolne took over responsibility for working on the downtown plan that Crombie's group was putting together for Toronto. This soon brought him into conflict with the Reichmanns.

The Reichmanns had received approval for First Canadian Place before the Crombie crew arrived on the scene, but there was a lot of public antipathy to the scheme. This behemoth was the very symbol of everything the new planners were rejecting, a seventy-two-story political lightning rod.

Soskolne's early relationship with the Reichmanns was rough. He opposed them and rapidly tied them down with guerrilla tactics. Paul Reichmann called for a meeting and explained his position. Soskolne discovered that he was not at all the archetypal developer. He was charmed by the soft-spoken Reichmann, who patiently listened to Soskolne's summary of the city's position. The young planner in turn developed a much clearer understanding of the Reichmanns' position, and the two sides quickly came up with compromise plans.

Soskolne and the city planners were impressed with the way the Reichmanns listened to and weighed their recommendations. Most other developers, such as Eph Diamond of the giant firm Cadillac Fairview, were up in arms about the proposed Central Area Plan and the 45-foot maximum. The Reichmanns did not fight City Hall, partly out of deference to the wishes of the democratically elected council; but they were not totally displeased with the planners' anti-development stance. If the city succeeded in its plan of reducing commercial office space densities downtown, First Canadian Place would be that much more in demand. Soskolne, like many of his city planning colleagues, ultimately wound up working for the Reichmanns.

The Reichmanns saw First Bank Tower as dominating Toronto's skyline for the foreseeable future. It would be the tallest office building in Canada and the Commonwealth, and one of the ten tallest in the world. At the base of the tower, and surrounding it, was to be a two-story podium, with a further four levels below ground. The underground concourse level would link into Toronto's downtown climate-controlled network of pedestrian corridors, and the development would bring retail activity to the street level.

The building was to be of steel construction, using the "structural tube" system. That would give First Bank Tower the largest ratio of column-free total office space — around 30,000 square feet per floor — of any tall building in Toronto.

The Reichmanns had initially acquired their reputation and wealth through a combination of quality and efficiency. In First Canadian Place they would demonstrate mastery of another skill that is critical to a developer's profitability: speed. For developers perhaps more than for any other businessmen, time is money. The key to success is to shorten the interval between the start of any development and its tenancy.

The skyscraper reflected both the evolution of building materials — in particular structural steel and cement — and the desire to optimize the use of precious urban space. The developer's aim is to get that steel and cement in place as quickly as possible so he can reap the benefits of that urban space's value. In that respect, First Canadian Place would be a path-breaking development.

The Reichmanns and their construction men — in particular their head of operations, Keith Roberts, an English engineer with public-school training who had joined them before Flemingdon Park and was the linchpin of their building operations — spent a considerable amount of time researching construction methods and devising a plan to put up a huge building faster than had previously been achieved.

One of Paul Reichmann's distinguishing characteristics has been a willingness to challenge precedent. He has always believed that there is a better way. The seed of this project's revolutionary nature was sown when Paul Reichmann and Keith Roberts visited O&Y's York Centre development, just a block from the site of First Canadian Place. They found themselves waiting for an elevator behind a line of workers carrying tools and construction materials. It struck Roberts how much time was lost on a big project while waiting to travel up and down the building, and also how haphazard and piecemeal the movement of materials was. The taller the building, the greater the potential problems. Paul Reichmann also wondered out loud why it would not be possible to finish the lobby of a building before construction was completed. It was difficult to project an image of prestigious office space on a mud floor surrounded by hard hats. A finished lobby would be a valuable tool in selling to future tenants.

Those two observations would be critical in the building of First Bank Tower. Paul and Albert enthusiastically supported Roberts's efforts to formulate a better method of building and took an active part in evolving the plan. They set themselves the objective of saving at least 1 million man-hours. They also hatched a plan to cut out haphazard storage and multiple handling of the 500,000 tons of materials that would go into the building. The bottom line was the bottom line. Saved time meant saved money.

Not only would they finish the lobby before the building was completed, they also planned to start moving tenants into the lower floors before the upper floors were fitted out. Their target was occupancy of the lower twenty-two floors and both lobbies in a period of sixteen months, six months before the building was finished. To do so, they evolved a system for moving men and materials that combined the logistics of a fair-sized war with the timing of clockwork.

At ground level, O&Y set up a 45-ton heavy-duty truck elevator that would remain part of the building's permanent freight system. This elevator, which could handle 100 vehicles a day, took trucks to basement level, where they drove onto a giant turntable. This turntable, the largest in the world, then aligned them with one of eleven unloading bays. From the bays, the pallets of goods were mechanically handled straight to the temporary elevator system, which moved them at once to a preassigned floor.

O&Y's hoist system included two "jumbo jump" elevators whose machinery could be pulled up the shaft as the building rose. O&Y also pioneered the use of "climbing" elevators in self-contained twelve-floor cages. Sixty-ton capacity kangaroo cranes could erect a tier of three floors of steel frame in six days. They also hauled up all the electric ducts, the mesh for the concrete floors, and the huge prefabricated pipe clusters that would carry all the main services through the building. No ladders were used and permanent metal stairs were installed right up to the steel working level. Through the jumping cranes and the jumping elevators, the building effectively lifted itself up by its own bootstraps.

The concrete transportation system, which moved a total of 60,000 tons, was another logistic marvel. The ready-mix trucks would arrive at the site and feed their load into a vertical chute. The chute took the concrete down to a conveyor, which ferried the product to hoppers. These radio-controlled hoppers could deliver concrete at the rate of 130 tons per hour to the thirtieth floor and 80 tons an hour to the seventy-second floor.

Following up the outside of the building, meanwhile, was the double exterior scaffold. The upper scaffold installed the brackets for the Carrara marble that would cover the building, the insulation, and the tracks along which the building's automatic window-washing system would move. The lower scaffold installed the marble. This combination doubled the speed of enclosing the building. While structural core steel was being hauled up and installed at the top of the building, reinforcing steel was following up six floors below. Three floors further down, concrete was being poured. Another six floors down, the upper scaffold was climbing the building with the second scaffolding three floors below. Finally, twenty floors below, the glaziers were installing the windows.

From the computerized control room, all this activity was scheduled and monitored to within minutes. Each truck that entered the project was assigned a time and a delivery route that dovetailed with the tight elevator and crane schedules. All labor movements were computer-orchestrated.

When O&Y outlined its plans to the subcontractors, they were skeptical about the break with traditional methods. O&Y developed a detailed construction manual and gave them frequent briefings. Most important, the company gave them a guarantee of its own performance. As a result, O&Y was able to negotiate more competitive contracts and earlier completion for each trade. In the end, labor time was reduced not by 1 million but by 1.3 million man-hours. Handling time was reduced by up to 90 percent.

The only major problem was a five-month holdup in marble supply when it was discovered, to the horror of the Reichmanns, that the shipments of marble were subtly changing color, moving from grayish white to whitish gray. They were in danger of ending up with a two-tone building. Otto Blau, a purchasing wizard and another linchpin of the O&Y organization, was dispatched to Italy to find alternative sources of supply. Blau secured the marble, and the exterior cladding of the building was finished only a month behind schedule.

The building's 9,000 double-glazed, tinted, heat-absorbing windows and its white marble would be cleaned by an automatic system that ran on rails down the side of the building. The first of its kind in Canada, the system had already been proved on the 110-story Sears Tower in Chicago and the twin blocks of the World Trade Center in Manhattan. First Bank Tower would also have a double-banked system of fifty-eight elevators — again the first of its kind in Canada — to maximize the building's rentable space. There was a sophisticated energy conservation and recycling system by which heat given off by lights, machinery, and people was reclaimed and recirculated throughout the building. The system could provide enough heat for the building until the outside temperature dropped to 16 degrees Fahrenheit, when supplementary heating switched on. The air in the offices was changed every ten minutes. The building was state-of-the-art in every way. Indeed, to call it a mere building seemed short of the mark. It was a climate-controlled, super-sophisticated *environment*.

Building First Canadian Place, however, was less than half the story. More important was finding tenants. The first steel column of First Bank Tower had been erected five floors below King Street on January 15, 1974. Just over a year later, on February 4, 1975, the Toronto Construction Association held its annual general meeting on the fifth floor, attended by over 400 people. The structure by this time was up to the sixty-sixth floor. Shortly afterwards, the building was topped off and on May 18, 1975, on target, the first tenants occupied the finished office space in the lower twenty-two floors. Although the building took longer than expected to fill, the Reichmanns refused to lower their rents, believing that the market would come to meet their expectations. They were correct. The building took four years to fill, twice as long as the brothers had anticipated, and the first year's cash drain was estimated to be Can$20 million. However, the first lessees paid Can$12 a square foot, the last more than Can$40. The Bank of Montreal appeared to have made a real bargain in gaining 450,000 square feet for Can$14 a square foot.

First Canadian Place also took the Reichmanns into retail leasing — an idiosyncratic part of the real estate industry — for the first time. Retail development depends on a subtle blend of knowledge and intuition about which shops should be where, about points of access and flows of people. First Canadian Place would have 600,000 square feet of retailing space on three levels. Once links were established to the underground tunnel system of the

Toronto-Dominion Centre on the south side of the development and to the Richmond-Adelaide Centre on the north side, a great many more people would pass through in addition to the 20,000 who would work in the building. The key to leasing retail space was to persuade store owners that these people would stop. Somebody who went to Yorkdale Plaza was clearly going there to shop, but the lower levels of First Canadian Place were a different matter. A retailing focus had to be built up so that people would make the trip there to shop, and passersby would turn into shoppers. Even with expert consultants to guide them, the brothers still had to feel their way in this new area. There was also a constant fight over who would pay the costs of building the underground links to the north and south of the building.

Once the first phase was developed, and many of these problems had been ironed out, a more serious problem emerged with the Reichmanns' principal tenant. Although both parties typically tried to suppress information about the wrangle, a storm blew up between O&Y and the Bank of Montreal over the development of the second tower.

During the demolition of buildings that used to be on the site, the National Bank of Canada had been given an option on space in the new development. However, the Bank of Montreal understood that it was to be the only bank in the project, and objected strongly when the presence of a National Bank branch in the second tower was announced. A legal dispute blew up, based on whether the second tower of the development was technically linked to the first and whether the whole development thus represented one project.

Caught in the middle of this dispute was Sun Life Assurance of Canada, which was meant to be the second tower's principal tenant. Sun Life had planned to purchase a 45 percent interest in the land on which the tower would be built, and to take 400,000 of the 1 million rentable square feet of office space within it. But then, when construction was under way, the Bank of Montreal filed an objection to the plans and work was halted.

Sun Life, in the end, did not move into the building, which acquired a new identity. It became the Exchange Tower when the

Toronto Stock Exchange agreed to transfer its operations there. The Reichmanns' financial interests meanwhile were little damaged by Sun Life's withdrawal. In fact, the market firmed up and they wound up with higher rents.

The spat with the Bank of Montreal soured relations between Paul Reichmann and Bill Mulholland, the bank's brilliant but autocratic chairman. Over the years there were also wrangles over the sharing of the building's profits, in which the Bank had a share as holder of a quarter of the ground lease. The dispute over the National received little or no publicity. Nevertheless, it indicated that the Reichmanns were sticklers for detail and squeezed every possible advantage from a deal. If there was a debatable point, they would sit at the bargaining table until they had won. Nevertheless, the bank would remain one of their two "relationship" banks, along with the Canadian Imperial Bank of Commerce.

Despite all these problems, First Canadian Place, in particular First Bank Tower with its acres of white marble, was now the Reichmanns' flagship and showpiece. The brothers loved it. Said Albert: "Half the money in Ontario is within a few blocks of this building." From the luxurious penthouse offices and dining rooms of Bill Mulholland at the top, through the corporate, law, accounting, and investment offices in the middle, to the throb of retailing activity in the basement, First Canadian Place would become a microcosm of Canadian business life. Filled with its list of blue-chip tenants, it would also provide both the stage and the dramatis personae for the corporate soap operas that the brothers would help script in the mid-1980s.

The Reichmanns disliked personal publicity but they loved it for their projects. *The Guinness Book of Records* was contacted and First Bank Tower was duly listed, at 935 feet, as the world's tallest bank building, replacing the Chase Manhattan Building in New York City. The stylized, illuminated symbol of the Bank of Montreal also became the highest advertising sign in the world, overtaking the RCA sign in New York's Rockefeller Plaza. Other bankers pooh-poohed the 20-foot-high blue sign as a piece of crass bad taste on the part of the bank; the whole point about such gigantic structures was that they were meant to speak for themselves. But that was what the bank wanted, so that was what it got.

5

The "Deal of the Century"

THERE IS A SUBTLE TRANSITION BETWEEN SKILL AND GENIUS, between reputation and mystique. For the Reichmanns, that transition occurred as the result of a deal consummated in New York in 1977. The groundwork for a mystique had already been laid by a combination of natural reclusiveness, business skill, and management style.

The Reichmanns' natural reclusiveness was part and parcel of their devout religious beliefs. Despite, or perhaps because of, their strict adherence to Orthodox Jewish beliefs, they were not well known even in the local Toronto Jewish community. Their strictness kept them apart from the business community as well and lent some unusual twists to their business practices. Although they employed various races and creeds within their business empire, their religion dictated a ban on work on the Jewish Sabbath, from sunset on Friday to sunset on Saturday. Their organization also closed for all the Jewish holidays, which could lead to the loss of as many as fourteen working days in some years. Jewish dietary laws did not permit them to enjoy — or endure — business lunches. Adherence to these laws, however, did not mean ascetic abstention. (At one time, Paul Reichmann chain-smoked Lark cigarettes and enjoyed social drinking, although he ultimately gave up both.) Nevertheless, the brothers could never have lunch at a club just to shoot the breeze. The Reichmanns recognized the dangers inherent in their separateness. Nevertheless, they saw no good reason why their business activities should lead to access to their private lives. In this they were hardly exceptional. Successful businessmen do not as a rule hold open house for the inquisitive.

Paul Reichmann claimed that his religious studies had had a

profound influence on his business outlook. He said he had received the key to much of his business success from the Talmud, the compilation of Jewish law and tradition that is meant to provide guidance for every life situation. Paul Reichmann expressed puzzlement about the role and usefulness of business schools, but his assessment, not untypically, perhaps said too little about his own extraordinary talents and gave too much credit to the influence of the Talmud.

The Talmud is the summary of oral law that evolved after centuries of scholarly effort by sages who lived in Palestine and Babylonia through the early Middle Ages. It is regarded as a repository of thousands of years of Jewish wisdom. According to Adin Steinsaltz's *The Essential Talmud*, it is "a conglomerate of law, legend, and philosophy, a blend of unique logic and shrewd pragmatism, of history and science, anecdote and humour." Talmudic study creates a questioning mind and a proclivity to painstaking and thorough analysis of words and meanings. It deals always in the concrete rather than the abstract, and teaches through practical examples and models drawn from life. In an interview in 1988, Paul Reichmann claimed: "With the Talmud, you have texts written two, three thousand years ago, with each generation adding its own commentaries. In general studies, law or engineering, for example, a student usually ends up specializing. The Talmudic student doesn't have that luxury. He must deal with a multitude of subjects; none is ever exhausted."

Seeking to explain his motivations, he quoted a commentary in the Book of Genesis: "A literal translation from the Hebrew reads that on the seventh day, God 'rested from all his work that God created to do.' Commentators struggle with the meaning of the last two words. Ibn Ezra [a 12th-century commentator] says that in God's creation, the seeds were there for everything that will ever be. Thus God finished the world in six days and gave it to the people as the raw material 'to do,' to create with. In other words: 'Here is the material, now you people take it and develop it.' "

The Talmud often deals with what appears trival, or obscure, or even bizarre. In ancient times it also raised issues that assumed later significance. According to Steinsaltz: "One of the subjects of Talmudic debate, the 'tower floating in the air,' was cited for centuries as an example of the degree to which the human imagination could run riot. The sages certainly never dreamed that mechanical methods of constructing flying towers would someday be developed, nor were they particularly intrigued by the problem. But since one of their number happened to raise the question of what would happen if a tower should float in the air, they settled down enthusiastically to clarify all the possible aspects of the problem." Now, generations later, a Talmudic scholar was in the business of building such "towers in the air."

Although the Talmud might have trained its students' minds, the business skills of the Reichmanns were honed by hard work, experience, and what would soon begin to look like almost superhuman insight.

The Reichmanns' mystique also flourished within their own company. Their management style was that of benevolent despots. Paul and Albert would always seek advice, but they did not share decisionmaking. When asked, employees would contribute their opinions or knowledge; the brothers, usually Paul, would make the final decision. These decisions were not to be questioned, nor did the Reichmanns feel any compulsion to explain them. They were good employers, and they were dealing with their own money. What explaining was there to do? After all, the principles on which they were building their empire seemed remarkably simple. Paul Reichmann would sum them up in aphorisms as arresting as they seemed obvious. For example: "You build on cost and you borrow on value."

The Reichmanns took such simple principles, which had long been basic tenets of the real estate business, and developed them into a fine art. They had, from the beginning, paid close personal attention to maximizing the "efficiency" of their buildings, squeezing out the greatest possible rentable and usable space. This helped cut costs. But at the same time they emphasized quality and service. Thus they could command top rents. These rents determined the value of the building, and it was this value that they could take to the banker as collateral against loans for further ventures. The greater the gap between the cost of a building and the amount they could borrow against it, the more funds they had for growth. By adding the most value, the Reichmanns established the best collateral and thus had the most funds to expand. But it was not the availability of funds per se that made their next deal so remarkable. It was that it seemed to be such a gigantic risk. It was not a piece of development but a simple deal. It put at their disposal borrowings almost beyond the dreams of avarice.

In 1976, following the completion of First Bank Tower, Paul Reichmann called some Bank of Montreal executives, apologizing for having had to cancel a meeting. "I'm sorry I couldn't see you last week," said Reichmann, "but I had to go to New York. We're just picking up a few buildings."

Reichmann's portrayal of the deal in hand was typically low key. When one of the bank executives discovered the nature of the transaction, he and his colleagues were, in his own words, "slack-jawed." The Reichmanns were taking what looked like the risk of their lives. They were committing more than U.S.$300 million to Manhattan real estate at a time when most developers feared that the island was about to sink.

During the late 1970s, Canadian developers had made a rapid penetration of American real estate markets, but New York City was one area of which both they and their U.S. counterparts steered clear. The New York authorities had spent and borrowed themselves into a hole from which there seemed no escape. Martin Mayer, author of the bestseller *The Bankers*, summed up the problem plainly and devastatingly: "On the simplest level, the story of New York's financial collapse is the tale of a Ponzi game in municipal paper — the regular and inevitably increasing issuance of notes to be paid off not by the future taxes or revenue certified to be available for that purpose, but by the sale of future notes. Like the chain-letter swindles, Ponzi games self-destruct when the seller runs out of suckers, as New York did in the spring of 1975."

Manhattan-based corporations had found themselves paying more and more in local taxes to get less and less in city services. The municipal government was seen as bloated, self-serving, and anti-business; the city's unions as rapacious. Businesses responded to the deterioration in the environment by voting with their offices. Many moved to the green and pleasant suburban satellites of lower New York State, New Jersey, and Connecticut.

New York's financial decline and "intransigent irresponsibility" were, according to former secretary of the U.S. Treasury William Simon, a microcosm of the potential disaster awaiting the whole country unless it mended its fiscal ways. In 1975, the city teetered on the brink of bankruptcy. The possibility of a stop to welfare checks brought visions of a city in flames.

Edward Minskoff was an almost archetypal New York investment high flyer, from the solid gold Rolex on his wrist to the Steinberg cartoons on his wall. He was whip-smart, well connected, and, most important, hungry. With his slicked-back hair, lean good looks, and flashy suspenders, he couldn't have appeared more different from the somberly clad Reichmanns. But he had known the brothers for half a dozen years and had developed an enormous respect for them. Minskoff had been a senior vice-president with the investment bankers Lehman Brothers and had become involved in the financing of some of the Reichmanns' earlier projects. Then he had quit Wall Street and begun to buy and develop for his own account.

The Reichmanns had already undertaken U.S. real estate projects in Dallas and Los Angeles, and had by now accumulated total real estate assets estimated at close to $1 billion. They were hardly small fry, but the New York real estate pond was about as shark-infested as the business got.

Minskoff brought the brothers' attention to a mammoth group of skyscrapers known, after their builders, as the Uris package. Harold and Percy Uris had been bankrupted in the 1930s but had returned to become among Manhattan's most active builder-owners. In 1973, the assets of the Uris Corporation had been sold to National Kinney Corporation, which had made its mark in funeral chapels, parking garages, and commercial cleaning services. Kinney in turn was 40 percent owned by Warner Communications. Warner chief Steve Ross had decided that he wanted out of real estate, in particular New York real estate. Most big investors felt the same way. In the words of Harold Grabino, the National Kinney executive who negotiated the deal with the Reichmanns: "Most of the institutional buyers who could afford this kind of deal had already drawn a big red line around Manhattan Island. They were afraid of it."

Real estate investors from all over the world, from The Hague to Hong Kong, had looked at the package, which then consisted of nine buildings. Minskoff went to Paul Reichmann and pointed out that the price of the buildings was considerably less than their replacement cost, while their rentals, averaging around U.S.$10 per square foot, were 40 percent less than market levels. There were also low-cost loans on 80 percent of the portfolio, mortgages of U.S.$288 million with interest rates ranging from $5\frac{1}{8}$ percent to $8\frac{3}{4}$ percent.

The Uris brothers were not renowned for the quality of their work, but the buildings were situated on some of the best real estate in the city. The package consisted of two giant towers on Park Avenue, at 245 and 320, which housed, respectively, the head offices of American Brands and IT&T; 10 East 53rd Street, the head office of publishers Harper & Row; 850 Third Avenue; the Sperry Building on the Avenue of the Americas; and 1633 Broadway. Downtown, there was 2 Broadway and the RCA Global Communications building at 60 Broad Street.

There had been a ninth property in the Uris package, the J.C. Penney building at 1301 Avenue of the Americas. But Penney exercised its option to match any offer for the building. A half-interest in the Sperry Building was held by the Rockefeller real estate interests, but the Reichmanns closed on the Rockefellers' 50 percent before the deal was signed on the other seven and a half buildings in the Uris package.

The tower at 245 Park Avenue sat cheek by jowl with what had once been the headquarters of New York Central Railroad but was now the Helmsley Building, property of Harry Helmsley, one of New York's most spectacularly successful developers. Built in 1967, the Uris building was described by *New York Times* architecture critic Paul Goldberger as "ruthless" in its "disregard of the ideas that made Park Avenue such a remarkable lesson in urban design." Both 245 and 320 were "head and shoulders" buildings in the boxlike International Style. But the brothers were not primarily interested in aesthetics. Park Avenue was, and in their minds always would be, one of the world's prime addresses.

The same went for the downtown locations. Wall Street and its environs, the Reichmanns thought, would always be the financial capital of the world. Their purchase at 2 Broadway occupied an entire blockfront in the financial district and towered over one of the world's most famous streets. Almost all of its thirty-two floors, embracing a total of 1.6 million square feet, offered panoramic views of New York harbor and historic Bowling Green. The thirty-nine-story tower at 60 Broad Street had more than 1 million square feet.

After Minskoff had drawn their attention to the Uris package, Paul and Albert traveled to New York and toured the buildings, chatting to the concessionaires in the lobbies and approaching a number of the tenants. They quickly became convinced that the land on which the buildings stood was worth more than the U.S.$320 million asking price. Also, because of existing mortgages, the cash portion of the deal was only U.S.$50 million. Like many great business moves, the Uris purchase was based on a simple premise. The Reichmanns looked beyond the heated political debate over city finances that pitched fiscal conservatism against reckless "liberalism" (although the Reichmanns were clearly on the side of the conservatives). They saw through the panic and were confident that New York would make a comeback. "A boom in New York rents wasn't a hope," said Paul, "it was a conviction."

Two weeks after first visiting the buildings, the brothers decided to buy. Warner-Kinney negotiator Grabino was a little taken aback when he first met the Reichmanns. He wondered whether these two guys from Toronto, with their skullcaps and their dark suits and their gentlemanly ways, were in a league to make a deal like this. Nor did the negotiations run entirely smoothly among Minskoff, the Reichmanns, and Grabino. They started talking at the end of October 1976 and signed a contract in March 1977, but it took until September to close the deal.

On Friday, September 19, 1977, the deal was signed in the Park Avenue law offices of Paul Weiss Rifkin Wharton & Garrison. In the afternoon, following confirmation of the wire transfer of U.S.$50 million in cash, the Reichmanns acquired the empire it had taken the Uris brothers a lifetime to build. At a stroke, they acquired 10 million square feet of office space and 1,200 tenants and leaped into the position of Manhattan's second-largest landlord after the Rockefeller interests. Soon they would be number one.

The purchase was seen at first as a staggering gamble, but in fact the timing could not have been better. The outlook for the city changed almost overnight. Compromise was reached with Washington and the banks on the city's finances, and real estate developers began to realize that the Big Apple wasn't so rotten after all. Ronald Nicholson, a New York developer (and also the son-in-law of Bill Zeckendorf), said: "The Reichmanns bought these buildings like twenty minutes before the real estate market turned around. They had a great buy — whether they were brilliant or lucky or whatever. Every sharp guy in New York had looked at those buildings and turned the deal down. I can't believe the Reichmanns were smart enough to anticipate what was going to happen. Rents went from ten bucks a square foot to twenty overnight. Nobody could have anticipated that."

The deal would soon look shrewd. In another couple of years, it would look brilliant. In four years, it would be called "the deal of the century," ranking in real estate mythology right up there with the Louisiana Purchase.

The Reichmanns established their New York headquarters in the American Brands building at 245 Park Avenue in October 1977 and proceeded to make a number of other deals. In particular, they bought a majority interest in a huge building at 55 Water

Street, facing the East River and dominating a 4-acre "super-block" of the financial district, two blocks from Wall Street. Again, *New York Times* critic Goldberger had some hard words for Water Street as a whole, describing the block on which the building sat as a "row of horrors." But for the Reichmanns, 55 Water Street was more important for its statistics than for its aesthetics. Its fifty-three-story tower and fifteen-story wing offered a mammoth 3.5 million square feet, as much as all the office space in both blocks of First Canadian Place.

The Reichmann brothers set about upgrading the Uris buildings and establishing the reputation for quality that they had acquired in Canada. Lobbies were refurbished, services were improved. As a showpiece, they also refurbished a site at the side of the Helmsley Building and named it Park Avenue Atrium. The building was gutted down to the structural steel and given five additional floors and a twenty-four-story atrium with stainless steel and glass terraces and balconies, dripping with greenery and flowers, rising 300 feet to the skylights above. Somehow, the building provided an inner calm from the Manhattan turmoil without. From a financial point of view, meanwhile, the atrium was far from wasted space. It meant that inward-facing offices, with their pleasant prospects, could command rents as high as those on the outside of the building.

As New York recovered and the United States boomed, rentals increased along with the value of the Uris package, providing an enormous boost to the brothers' equity, equity against which they could borrow. The Reichmanns became one of the most powerful forces in New York real estate, but they were still not known personally. The Real Estate Board of New York, the exclusive group of top developers, waited for the brothers to turn up and present themselves for approval, but the Reichmanns did not want or need approval. This attitude, of course, only deepened their mystique. An article in the *Washington Post* called them "the Rothschilds of Canadian realty." They were now seen both by the business community and by the press as possessors of almost superhuman commercial wisdom. They had achieved the *ne plus ultra* of real estate speculation. For their next trick, they would pull off the world's biggest commercial real estate development.

6

Grand Designs

ONE DAY IN THE FALL OF 1980, PAUL REICHMANN WAS SHOWN
into the Manhattan office of Richard Kahan, the man appointed to
bring to fruition the long-frustrated attempts to develop Battery
Park City, a 92-acre landfill in lower Manhattan. The location, on
the Hudson River below the World Trade Center, had been
viewed as a white elephant almost since New York State had
created the Battery Park City Authority in 1968. Various developers had broken ground in the 1970s but had always abandoned their plans. In 1979, the authority had been absorbed by the
New York State Urban Development Corporation, of which
Kahan was the chairman and chief executive officer, and he had
received the mandate from Governor Hugh Carey to get the
project off the ground. One of the main problems was the source
of the ground.

Much of the Battery Park landfill had come from excavations
for the World Trade Center, whose huge twin towers had been
the most spectacular example of an intensive building boom in
lower Manhattan between 1969 and 1973. The boom had flooded
the market with an additional 28 million square feet of office
space. The World Trade Center had cast a 110-story shadow over
both lower Manhattan and the real estate market. Downtown
vacancy rates had soared to 13 percent, with a corresponding
softening in rents. It had taken the rest of the 1970s to absorb the
space.

Kahan's job had been made somewhat easier by the improved
economic environment. By 1980, New York had survived its
crisis and there had been a resurgence in Wall Street and the
financial service industry. When Kahan announced a new com-

petition to develop Battery Park, a dozen top developers, including O&Y, presented proposals. Paul Reichmann came that autumn day to make his pitch. He lobbed a slow ball that offered Kahan the opportunity to hit a homer.

While other contenders had come to Kahan with grandiose architectural visions for the site, Paul Reichmann came with a single, folded, blue sheet of paper. The sheet contained not an architectural outline but a series of numbers. The numbers were the repayment schedule on the U.S.$200 million of bonds that the authority had floated some years before. "If I were to guarantee these bond repayments," asked Reichmann, "would I be on the right track?" Kahan reportedly felt an urge to plant a kiss on the Toronto developer's bearded cheek. Here, at last, was a man who understood. Reichmann had gone straight to the heart of the official's most pressing problem: the threat of default on the bonds.

Kahan had introduced a novel method of competition for the project. Usually in such circumstances, public agencies announce a "request for proposal" under which they invite developers to submit both a design and a financial plan. In this case, Kahan had called in a prominent firm of designers, Cooper, Eckstut Associates, to draw up a detailed set of planning and architectural guidelines to which the bidders had to adhere. Kahan thus hoped to accelerate the process in order to generate income with which to pay off the bonds.

While other developers were still treating the project as a normal development, Paul Reichmann had seen that the required solution was not architectural but financial. He offered an iron-clad set of guarantees. If there was a delay in construction, letters of credit ensured that O&Y would still pay the U.S.$50 million in ground rent and taxes it would owe if the buildings were finished. He also undertook to build the project much faster than any of the other contestants, in five years. Again, the attraction to the city of that approach was the speedier generation of municipal revenue.

Of course, by taking the pressure off Kahan, Paul Reichmann was putting it on O&Y. He was committing to finance, build, and lease the world's largest commercial development in record time and in one of the world's toughest building environments. "New York," in the words of an O&Y construction supervisor who had worked there all his life, "is a snake pit."

When Olympia & York got the job, some who had been watching Battery Park's snail's-pace progress thought the Reichmanns would wind up abandoning the project as their predecessors had. Others saw the potential for the men who had made the deal of the century to experience the blunder of the decade.

The Reichmanns had always hired away talent that they came across in the course of their business. Although it had taken them almost fifteen years from the first time they met him, they now employed Bill Hay, the Scots lawyer who had negotiated the Flemingdon Park deal with them, and then gone on to be president of Trizec. They hired Malcolm Spankey, who had been the Bank of Montreal's day-to-day overseer of the progress of First Canadian Place. In January 1981, they snapped up Ed Minskoff, the sharp ex-banker and real estate broker who had brought them the Uris package. They had also hired some of their most radical opponents from Toronto. These men, Mayor David Crombie's young lions, would all play a critical role in the New York development.

Ron Soskolne, the architect who had locked horns with the Reichmanns over First Canadian Place, had developed a respect for them in the course of negotiations. After Toronto's Central Area Plan was completed in 1978, Soskolne decided to move back into the private sector. He went to Paul Reichmann and was immediately offered a job.

Initially, Soskolne was hired to gain approval for a Boston project with which O&Y was having a lot of trouble. Called Exchange Place, it had become bogged down in a dispute with the city about the demolition of historic buildings. With his combination of planning experience and architectural skills, Soskolne was able to come up with a scheme that incorporated the best of the existing buildings into the new project. The Reichmanns were impressed. The young architect soon became influential as their in-house "taste-maker." He was also instrumental in bringing in other bright young men, in particular one of his most radical former colleagues, Michael Dennis.

Dennis, a lawyer by training, had been an adviser to Mayor Crombie, and had then been appointed the first head of the city's new Housing Commission. One of the Crombie group's priorities was the creation of "affordable" — that is, subsidized — housing. The counterpoint of the planners' desire to reduce downtown commercial densities was to put this subsidized housing in the heart of the city. Dennis became the driving force behind the St. Lawrence Market development.

Although he came from a family of developers, Dennis seemed an unlikely developer himself. Radical, cocky, and abrasive, Dennis enjoyed shaking up the Establishment. When he went to visit a friend's newly purchased house in the heart of Toronto's posh Rosedale district, he came armed with, and blowing, a hunting horn.

Dennis had left the Housing Commissioner's office shortly before Soskolne had quit the planning department. When he heard that Soskolne had joined O&Y, he called and asked if the Reichmanns would have any use for him. In fact, they were looking for someone just like him who could combine legal expertise with that of planning and development.

Dennis was soon assigned to New York, where he became one of O&Y's most influential executives. Toronto's former champion of social housing would wind up virtually running the world's biggest property development for the men who would soon be acknowledged as the world's biggest property developers. Perhaps the switch was not so much a classic example of gamekeeper turned poacher as it was the natural result of the widespread belief that the Reichmanns really *were* different from other developers. Or perhaps Dennis realized that whereas the city of Toronto had been the place to work in the early 1970s, now the place to work was for the Reichmanns.

The last of the Toronto city group to join O&Y was Tony

Coombes, whom Soskolne had succeeded as chief city planner. When O&Y won Battery Park, Soskolne was given the responsibility for finding an architect and supervising the design, which he did by organizing a competition. Coombes had gone off to form a consulting firm, Coombes Kirkland Berridge, and Soskolne called him in to help with the competition. Coombes went on to play a vital role in working with the Battery Park City Authority to gain the myriad municipal approvals needed for the development. Then, when the detailed design development work began, Coombes was hired to play a full-time coordinating role.

This core of former city planners — whose convictions had been tempered fighting developers in the cauldron of city politics — now set out with similar conviction to demonstrate what enlightened developers could do. New York held no dread for them. In fact, they were convinced that they had a few things to teach the Big Apple.

Soskolne chose a number of leading architects to submit plans for the Battery Park site based on the Cooper, Eckstut guidelines. Some, like Hellmuth Obata & Kassanbaum, were enormous established concerns. Others, like Kohn Pederson Fox, were smaller firms picked by Soskolne for the promise of their recent work. He gave the seven firms just three weeks to produce a rough proposal. From the submissions, three finalists were chosen: the entries of Kohn Pederson Fox, Mitchell/Giurgola, and Cesar Pelli & Associates.

O&Y's original request to the architects was for a three-tower design. However, after the first stage, the Reichmanns decided to change the massing of the buildings and come up with a fourth tower. They added the requirement for some form of gateway leading in from Liberty Street to the development so that it would better "address" the existing downtown area. Based on these new parameters, the three finalists were asked to make fuller submissions, complete with scale models.

When Cesar Pelli, the dean of Yale's School of Architecture, arrived at 245 Park Avenue to make his presentation — at which Albert Reichmann was present — he was dressed in a tuxedo, even though it was only four o'clock in the afternoon. In fact, he was not trying to be smooth; it was just that he had a function to attend that evening and would not have time to change. From Soskolne's point of view, Pelli's attire was appropriate. His design stood out as the classiest.

Kohn Pederson had produced four identical towers with a rounded facade facing southwest. Mitchell/Giurgola had come up with a more sensitive treatment of the location, but their buildings looked a little boxy and dull. Pelli's four towers, by contrast, were arresting.

Born in Argentina, where his family had immigrated from their native Italy more than a century before, Cesar Pelli had studied architecture at the Universidad Nacional de Tucumán and later taught design there. After a scholarship to the University of Illinois, he had joined the firm of Eero Saarinen and Associates in Bloomfield Hills, Michigan, in 1954.

Saarinen had caused a professional uproar in 1956 with his eaglelike design for the TWA terminal at Idlewild Airport (now Kennedy) in New York. He was considered beyond the pale by the purist purveyors of the steel, concrete, and glass boxes of the International Style, which dominated corporate and civic architecture in the postwar period. The Finnish architect had an enormous influence on Pelli, who spent ten years with Saarinen's firm.

In 1964, Pelli moved on to Daniel, Mann, Johnson and Mendenhall in Los Angeles, where his craft was further honed by tight budgets and schedules. In 1968, he joined Gruen Associates in Los Angeles. There, he was responsible for the city's Pacific Design Center and for the U.S. Embassy in Tokyo. Under his leadership, Gruen's designers in 1969 won the competition for a new United Nations Organization Headquarters and Conference Center in Vienna. In 1977, Pelli was appointed dean of the School of Architecture at Yale, where his commissions included the expansion and renovation of New York's Museum of Modern Art.

Two of the requirements of the Cooper, Eckstut Battery Park City master plan had been that the design integrate with the New York architectural "vernacular," and that the material of the buildings change color as they rose. Pelli's reference to the New York vernacular was clear. His buildings were computer-age descendants of the great crowned skyscrapers of the 1930s and 1940s. His interpretation of the change-of-color requirement was considered brilliant. As they rose, the buildings would "peel" back and the surface area would shift from predominantly granite to predominantly glass.

Pelli's design was at the crest of a new wave in architecture. A backlash had developed against the boxes of the International Style, whose intellectual source lay in the teachings of Walter Gropius, founder of the German Bauhaus school. Even as the Battery Park competition was being held, the International Style was being satirized by author Tom Wolfe in two articles in the June and July issues of *Harper's* magazine.

In these articles, subsequently published in book form under the title *From Bauhaus to Our House*, Wolfe maintained that American architectural clients had for decades been held in thrall by the intellectual bullying of the Bauhaus gang. America had been subjected to a sea of "functional" buildings and gigantic, ugly cubes based on "revolutionary" theories that had no place in the United States.

"Every child," wrote Wolfe, "goes to school in a building that looks like a duplicating-machine replacement-parts wholesale distribution warehouse . . . Every new $900,000 summer house in the north woods or on the shore of Long Island . . . looks like an insecticide factory . . . Every law firm in New York moves . . . into a glass box office building with concrete slab floors and seven-foot-ten-inch-high concrete slab ceilings and plasterboard walls and pygmy corridors — and then hires a decorator and gives him a budget of hundreds of thousands of dollars to turn these mean cubes and grids into a horizontal fantasy of a Restoration townhouse."

Although many architects rejected Wolfe's lacerating attack as simplistic, the fact was that almost everybody else agreed with him. Perhaps he failed to take sufficient note of corporate and developer complicity in the International Style; after all, it had also been dubbed "balance sheet architecture." Boxes were the most efficient way of putting useful space within walls — but the worm of taste was turning. In fact, a good part of the impetus was now coming from corporations who realized that they could hardly be strongly identified with their head office monuments if they all looked like cornflake boxes. The age of the cornflake box was drawing to an end.

"Postmodernism" was the catchall for the new architectural styles. One branch went off in almost bizarre pictorial directions, such as Philip Johnson's Chippendale AT&T headquarters on Lexington Avenue. Another main branch harked back to the great New York and Chicago skyscrapers of the 1930s. This direction was the one taken by Pelli. His buildings had the subtle stepping of the classic traditional skyscrapers, such as the Woolworth Building, not the huge, ugly steps of postwar Park Avenue, which gave buildings what looked like long, skinny heads on massive padded shoulders. Pelli's granite-to-glass transition was also both subtle and effective. And, although they did not have the fabulous spires that had made structures like the Chrysler Building world-famous, his towers were crowned with four different geometric shapes. If you wanted to be irreverent, you could call them "hats." In fact, the whole point was that the mood of the time *was* irreverent.

Taken by themselves, Pelli's buildings were elegant and graceful. But standing so close to the World Trade Center they were almost *fun*. They would look like cute, expensively dressed, preppie kids standing beside strait-laced, pitchfork-toting parents straight out of *American Gothic*. Compared with Pelli's design, the World Trade Center looked square in every sense.

The Reichmanns had set up a committee consisting of Soskolne, Dennis, Coombes, and construction chief Keith Roberts to oversee the choice of design. The committee soon sold itself on Pelli's plans. Its next task was to sell the Reichmanns.

One Sunday morning at eight o'clock, Ron Soskolne got a call at home in Toronto. It was Paul Reichmann in New York: he and Albert had some time free and they would like the committee to come down and run them through the Battery Park plans. Roberts, Coombes, and Dennis were called. By noon the whole group was in the Park Avenue office.

At first, Paul and Albert had some problems with Pelli's design. It seemed less than revolutionary to them. In fact, they thought it looked a little old-fashioned. Their concern with building design, as ever, was not so much with aesthetics as with image. They looked at buildings from a marketing standpoint and tried to see them through the eyes of their clients. How would the head of a large corporation view the building? Would he want it for his head office? The Reichmanns' experience over many years had given them a clear idea of a prestige office building: it was an elegant tower with clean lines and high-quality materials. They were already experimenting with the new styles — for example, the pyramid-topped Fountain Plaza they were building in Portland, Oregon — but Battery Park was no place for experimentation. Why, they asked, were they going back to the past? Why were the buildings not more like First Canadian Place?

Soskolne had his case well prepared. His argument was that, taking a long-term view of the architecture of office buildings, the ones that had best stood the test of time were those built in the 1930s. Lever House and the Seagram building, although excellent examples of the International Style, would ultimately appear — indeed, already were appearing — dated. He sold his bosses on the basis that O&Y was anticipating a trend. But the buildings were more than just a trend. Their architecture would prove timeless. Moreover, they would cater to the growing corporate demand for more individualistic and identifiable headquarters. By six that Sunday evening, the Reichmanns had been convinced. Pelli's design was given the nod.

The two brothers soon had evidence that their choice was a wise one. Pelli's concept drew rave reviews from critics, those of the *New York Times* in particular. Ada Louise Huxtable, the architecture correspondent, described it as "a co-ordinated and architecturally first-rate urban complex of the standard, significance and size of Rockefeller Center, that will add a spectacular new beauty to the New York skyline. There has been no large scale development of comparable quality since the 1930's."

In his book, *The Skyscraper*, the architecture critic Paul Goldberger declared, "This complex seems destined to become the major keeper of the New York skyscraper tradition in our time."

Pelli had given his clients a design that promised them a place alongside the builders of the world's great pieces of architecture. But the Reichmanns had more immediate concerns than posterity. They had to get the project built, and, even before that, they had to begin finding tenants.

7

Bell Cows and Brass Knuckles

REAL ESTATE DEVELOPMENT IS, AT THE BEST OF TIMES, A business of frustrations. Even at Battery Park City, where there was a financially strapped state authority eager to push the development, progress still faced a vast array of obstacles. There were city authorities, who, although they wanted the revenues that the new complex would generate, also wanted to give away as little as possible in tax incentives; there were other developers, who, fearing Battery Park as a rival, put roadblocks in its way; and finally, there were the New York building unions, which many reckoned were the toughest in the world. Then, of course, there were the prospective tenants. Naturally, a developer could hardly refer to them as obstacles, since their leases would provide the collateral for financing the project. But the wooing process was long and difficult, and they often demanded handsome dowries.

Both Paul and Albert Reichmann were, as always, closely involved in all aspects of the project, from making design modifications to courting lessees. One of the city authority's requirements was a "Winter Garden" as a public showpiece for the site. The brothers chose a 120-foot-high crystal palace of vaulted glass that would provide the focus for the site's retail, restaurant, and entertainment facilities.

Paul also introduced a number of modifications to the overall plan, based, once again, not primarily on aesthetics but on image and leasability. For example, the site was designed like a compound, with the buildings grouped around gardens facing the Hudson. Architecturally, the "entrance" was formed by the twin octagonal towers of the gateway, but in fact almost everybody would enter the area via two pedestrian overpasses spanning the busy West Side Highway. Paul Reichmann was concerned that people driving down the highway would think they were looking at the backsides of the buildings; therefore he had additional entrances placed on the highway side.

The West Side Highway, meanwhile, was itself a source of problems. For a number of years there had been debate over the construction of a new highway along the old West Side route to link midtown Manhattan with Wall Street. O&Y was concerned that the construction of the new road would cut Battery Park City off, at least temporarily, from the rest of the financial district. The West Side Highway was already a significant barrier. It was therefore essential that overpasses be built to carry pedestrian traffic, whether the new highway went ahead or not. But the main crosswalk was linked to the World Trade Center complex, whose owners saw the Battery Park complex as an obvious rival for their leasing space. Thus they were less than accommodating.

There was a year's delay between "winning" the deal and completing all the documentation. Negotiations with the city over "pilots" (payments in lieu of taxes) and ground rents were very complicated. There was also controversy over tax abatements that O&Y wanted from the city. Abatements had been one of the methods used to lure real estate investment back into New York after its near collapse. Now, however, many critics were saying that, in the healthier real estate environment, abatement was no longer necessary.

Richard Kahan's regard for Paul Reichmann increased during the course of the negotiations. Opposition lawyers constantly tried to pick holes in the verbal agreement between them. But if Kahan said that something had been agreed, Paul Reichmann went along with it. Later Kahan said, "My faith in this project comes from Paul." Kahan joked that if Reichmann would stop chain-smoking, the project would require less security. He was, said Kahan, "the biggest crapshooter this town has ever seen."

While they were still struggling with final approvals for the deal, the Reichmanns and their staff had already begun an intensive search for tenants. The 14-acre section of the landfill site that

O&Y had committed itself to develop would have a whopping 8 million square feet of space, of which 6 million would be office space. They needed not just tenants but big tenants.

The Battery Park site was off the beaten track. Even though it was off by only a few blocks, those few were important. The Reichmanns, Minskoff, and Dennis had to make Battery Park an "address." Lower Manhattan, the southern tip of the island, has a "golden triangle" of property bounded on the north by Wall Street, on the west by Broadway, and on the east by Water Street. This area, the traditional financial heart of Manhattan, contains mainly buildings of 1930s vintage. North of it is the insurance district; to the east, along the East River, is a predominantly banking area; to the west, between the triangle and Battery Park City, lies the World Trade Center and the old shipping district, which had moved into decline along with its principal industry. North of the World Trade Center lay the "back offices" of the financial core.

A counterbalance to Battery Park City's location problem was that much of downtown Manhattan's space was unsuitable for the new demands of the financial industry. The older buildings did not have adequate wiring; the ceiling heights could not accommodate trading floors; and they did not have the large floor spaces necessary to handle modern business. The 1930s buildings were obsolete when it came to coping with fiberoptic cables and other modern communications developments. Also, the growth of many financial institutions had caused staff to be scattered among a number of buildings, so another selling point for Battery Park City was that the new tenants would be able to consolidate their space requirements in a single address.

Dennis and Minskoff drew up a "hit list" of dozens of potential tenants, then began knocking on executive doors. Each of the four towers, ranging from thirty-three to fifty-five stories, offered an average floor space of 40,000 square feet. "Look at the quality and size of these buildings," the O&Y executives told clients. "Any financial institution worth its salt has to think seriously about taking a big piece of space in Battery Park."

If the executive replied that his company was quite happy

where it was, the O&Y pitchman would change tack. "What would it cost you to move?" they would ask. "Three million dollars? Fine. We'll factor that in. You're moving at no cost. Now, what about the costs of fitting the space to your requirements? Do you want more elevator capacity, or underfloor ducting, or special security arrangements? Whatever the cost, we'll factor that in too. Any other problems?"

"Well," the prospect might say, "the fact is that we've already got a long-term lease." "So what's the cost?" O&Y would ask.

"Well," the tenant might respond, "we're paying twenty dollars a square foot and we're signed up for ten years." "No problem," would come the reply. "We'll just take that lease back from you. All you have to do is just sign here on the dotted line."

The prospective tenant, faced with a free move, unburdened of his old lease, and offered the prospect of state-of-the-art, custom-fitted premises, would have to think pretty fast for reasons *not* to sign on the dotted line. But of course there was a price to pay: Battery Park rents reflected the quality and status of the buildings. O&Y was the IBM of property developers, but as with IBM, top service meant top dollar. Securing a first tenant to sign a big lease was very important. O&Y needed to attract a "name" into the development as a "bell cow" that would lead other tenants in. To do so, they were prepared to provide additional accommodations. The bell cow was brought to them by a well-known Manhattan real estate broker named John C. Cushman III.

When Cushman came to see Minskoff in the summer of 1981, he was trying to sell O&Y a skyscraper at 59 Maiden Lane, three blocks north of Wall Street, owned by City Investing — a conglomerate with $8 billion of assets and interests ranging from air conditioning equipment and insurance to printing and budget motels. The asking price was $175 million. The insurance giants Prudential Assurance and Equitable Life — both mammoth holders of real estate — had already turned him down. O&Y also rejected a straight purchase. But then Minskoff and Cushman came up with a deal based on a variation of Bill Zeckendorf's old "used car" technique: O&Y would buy 59 Maiden Lane if City

Investing would sign a long-term lease on a big enough chunk of Battery Park.

The first face-to-face meeting between Paul Reichmann and George T. Scharffenberger, chairman and chief executive of City Investing, was reportedly a less than scintillating occasion. Neither man specialized in small talk. Seeking to break the ice, Scharffenberger asked what plans Reichmann had for the building's lobby. Reichmann suggested that it would be lined with shops. Scharffenberger was less than impressed; that didn't sound very good for the company's image at all. "Oh, don't worry," Reichmann said. "It will be very, very dignified."

The negotiations proved tough, but they also had a time limit: the proposed enactment of a new city sales tax on real estate purchases that would have added U.S.$15 million to the cost of Maiden Lane. Racing to beat the clock, O&Y and the City Investing negotiators worked virtually round the clock for six weeks. In November 1981, just a week after the final agreement had been concluded with the Battery Park City Authority, a deal was announced under which City Investing would take nearly 700,000 square feet of space. According to a rare O&Y press release, it represented "one of the largest tenancies, in dollar volume, in New York City's history." The release made no mention of the actual dollars, but the lease was reportedly for thirty-five years at U.S.$35 a square foot, which fitted in with reports of an "$850 million deal." But of course that sum referred to the total stream of lease income, which was a very different thing from the deal's present value. Discounted at 10 percent per annum over its thirty-five-year life, it was worth about U.S.$240 million. No mention was made in the release of O&Y's purchase of Maiden Lane. O&Y announced that construction of the "City Investing Building" at Battery Park would begin almost immediately. It was to be finished by 1984. In fact, City Investing never did move into Battery Park City, and wound up, with some irony, having to negotiate an expensive lease to stay in the building at 59 Maiden Lane, which now belonged to the Reichmanns. There were no press releases about that development.

At the time, however, O&Y seemed to have its bell cow, but it was really just a bell calf. City Investing's lease took only 11 percent of the Battery Park space. Minskoff and Dennis continued to make the rounds of financial giants with offices scattered throughout Manhattan, firms that might want to consolidate in one building. As it happened, the financial giant they wanted came to them as a result of a chance meeting.

Minskoff was walking home one evening up Park Avenue when he ran into Sandford (Sandy) Weill, chairman of the newly merged Shearson/American Express financial conglomerate. Minskoff had known Weill for many years, and as they chatted, he said, on the spur of the moment: "Why don't we buy your headquarters? You can take the capital gain [as City Investing had done] and consolidate all your operations in the Battery Park." Weill said he would think about it. A month later, serious negotiations began.

For American Express, the idea of realizing the capital gain on their headquarters was particularly attractive as it would help them solve another business problem. They had a bond portfolio that had declined considerably in value. If it were sold, large write-offs would damage profits. But if O&Y bought Amex's office block, the real estate write-up would more than offset the portfolio write-off.

O&Y's proposal was outlined in a simple two-page letter from Paul Reichmann to Weill. O&Y was helping Amex solve its particular problem, but Weill was also well aware that he was helping Reichmann solve his: once Amex had taken a big chunk of Battery Park, the place was "made." American Express, formed in Buffalo, New York, in 1850 from the merger of rival freight companies, had first leaped to prominence with the invention of the traveler's check in 1891, and had really boomed after the Second World War with the expansion of the travel business. Its green card became the fantastic plastic. Its gold and platinum cards would become the status symbols of the yuppie 1980s. In 1977, James Robinson III had taken over as chief executive and led the company into an acquisition binge, starting with the almost

U.S.$1 billion purchase of investment giant Shearson Loeb Rhoades Inc. Although Robinson would later run into severe problems, his move was lauded on Wall Street as a bold step toward creating a financial services conglomerate. In the early 1980s, Amex was the darling of both Wall Street and the media. Once Amex had signed up, the Reichmanns could lure other tenants at higher rents. Just as travelers had come to believe that you should not leave home without Amex, many big companies would feel more inclined to leave their homes if they saw that the prestigious company had moved into Battery Park.

O&Y agreed to pay U.S.$240 million for Amex's building, giving Amex a U.S.$180 million capital gain to cope with its portfolio loss. In return, and after some hard bargaining between Reichmann and Weill over rent, American Express signed a lease on the biggest of the buildings, the planned fifty-one-story structure on the northeast corner of the site, the one with the pyramid-shaped "hat." The lease on the American Express building, when it was announced in March 1982, was touted as "the largest real estate transaction in history," worth U.S.$2.4 billion over its thirty-five-year life.

With its second major tenant announced, and half its office space rented, Olympia & York renamed its Battery Park development the World Financial Center. Many sage voices had said — privately, of course — that the Battery Park development would depress the Wall Street real estate market for many years and that the Reichmanns were tying themselves to a white elephant. But now, with the City Investing and American Express leases signed, doubts were muted.

Said Henri Alster, one of Manhattan's leading real estate consultants: "They not only have confirmed what many said a year ago would be impossible: that is, to fill half of the office space at the $1 billion mixed-use complex in six months. They have done what William Zeckendorf did when he established the United Nations building on the East Side in the early 1950s — created an address and wound up with all the land surrounding it. An extremely intelligent move."

However, the project was still some way from being sewn up. Half the planned space still had to be leased. And the project had to be built — in record time.

Buildings have many meanings for those involved with them. Architects view them aesthetically; construction workers see them as a place of macho camaraderie; corporate chieftains look at them in terms of prestige and costs; developers regard them as so much collateral and cash flow.

For most people, a building comes into existence only when it is completed. For the people who put them up, by contrast, their interest often ceases when the process of creation is at an end. For those in charge on the site, buildings are not so much physical entities as a series of struggles against the forces of obstruction and chaos, against Murphy's Law writ large.

By the time Governor Hugh Carey broke ground for the project in December 1981, the logistics of the enormous development were already well into the planning stage, under the supervision of construction chief Keith Roberts. The blueprints had to be transformed, via the organization of thousands of men and hundreds of thousands of tons of materials, into a huge, granite-clad, concrete-and-steel reality. Over the next four years, Roberts would spend an average of two or three days a week in Manhattan. But the man who held the hands-on responsibility for the physical construction of the project was John Norris, another Englishman who had been with the Reichmanns for a dozen years.

Norris was a British bulldog. Short and stocky, with a square, pugilistic face and a jutting jaw, he looked like the rugby player that he still was. Norris had joined O&Y in 1968, the year he came to Canada. In England, he had been an area manager for British property magnate Charlie Clore. When he joined O&Y, its construction side consisted of Keith Roberts and purchasing manager Otto Blau. The company had been mainly involved in the Flemingdon Park development and was just beginning to move to larger downtown projects in Ottawa, Toronto, and later Calgary. Norris took over the site management at many of these major projects, such as Place Bell Canada and the Esplanade Laurier in Ottawa, and also at the Shell and Esso buildings in booming Calgary. Norris had developed with the company and had been closely involved with the innovations for building First Canadian Place, in particular the computer control system.

Norris had found the building styles in North America very different from those in the United Kingdom. The Reichmanns demanded as much from their staff as they demanded from themselves, and that meant both quality *and* speed. Norris soon learned what "fast-tracking" meant: that is, literally designing a building as it was being put up. This method — to generate rentals as quickly as possible — put a lot of pressure on supervision and quality control, and it put a lot of pressure on people. John Norris was appointed to be the source of that pressure. That, in turn, put a lot of pressure on him.

Norris was a hard man. He knew how to make subcontractors jump, and he was not above using an expletive or two to get his point across. His style inevitably led to some problems with the New York unions. They could be pretty tough, too.

Manhattan's bustling character and the sheer cost of its real estate had created a peculiarly rich environment for the construction industry. Buildings had to be put up fast because of the potentially crippling carrying costs of real estate financed with large amounts of borrowed money. The implications were not lost on the building unions. They were renowned for driving hard bargains and for securing the maximum overtime. (During a later New York State inquiry into construction industry work rules, it was revealed that one of the union representatives on the Battery Park site pulled in an annual salary of $570,000, much of it while on holiday, and partly through the supernatural feat of working twenty-six-hour days.)

At first, Norris's uncompromising style did not sit well with the unions. Both sides were used to giving ulcers rather than getting them. Dealing with the unions, said Norris diplomatically, was "like a game of chess." About as much like a game of chess as a pool hall brawl in Harlem. It was also a rare game of chess where you had your life threatened, but that, on several occasions, happened to Norris. Nevertheless, an accommodation was eventually reached and the local unions developed a grudging respect for the O&Y vice-president.

Norris was hardly easier on his own construction staff, whom he used to gather for six o'clock breakfast meetings to plan the day's campaign. They were sometimes on the receiving end of his short fuse, but they suspected there was a heart of gold under that crusty exterior. Somewhere. You always had to have a sense of humor. One staff member found a magazine picture of a 2,300-pound great white shark, printed "John Norris" on it, and duly sent it on the rounds of the in-trays.

To supervise the nuts-and-bolts construction of the building, a more diplomatic approach was needed. That was where local experience came in, particularly in the form of men like Dan Mernit.

Dan Mernit, a bespectacled, avuncular figure with a bald head, tinted glasses, and a trimmed mustache, looked more like a friendly storekeeper than a builder. But he had spent the best part of forty years erecting skyscrapers in New York City. He had put up twenty-story buildings with the help of just a timekeeper and a labor foreman. There had been no electrical or mechanical engineers in those days, none of the "brain surgeons," as he called them, on the sites. But the increasing specialization of the building industry had made men like Mernit, who could take in the big picture, all the more important.

Ironically, Mernit had spent many years working for the Uris brothers. When he turned up at the Toronto offices of O&Y to be interviewed for the Battery Park job, he was taken aback because all over the walls were pictures of *his* buildings, like 245 Park Avenue. It was only then that he found out that the Reichmanns had, with a small flourish of the pen and a gigantic leap of faith, acquired a thousand times his lifework and much more besides.

After his Uris years, Mernit had worked on such major projects as Detroit's Renaissance Center and Walt Disney's Epcot Center in Florida. He had seen enormous advances in equipment and materials, from the kangaroo crane to dry wall. The technology within the buildings had also evolved beyond recognition. They still consisted of walls and floors, but those walls and floors were now alive with a multitude of sensitive systems that made the buildings "smart." They could automatically turn lights on and off; they could regulate heating and air conditioning; they could put you in touch with the rest of the world.

Looked at another way, however, the building business had not changed at all. It was still about human nature. Each building presented new problems, but essentially they were variations on a theme. Whatever happened, Dan Mernit had been there before. Now he was given the job of superintending the biggest commercial development in the world in record time. He, too, discovered what O&Y's "fast-tracking" meant.

The first employee on the Battery Park site, Mernit began to put in the roads and infrastructure on the flat barren ground. Rapidly, Norris hired people to take over specific site tasks, such as security and transport supervision. At the height of activity, 3,000 people worked on the site. Within Mernit's trailer, with its metal stacking chairs and its Styrofoam coffee cups, the walls were covered with notices, memos, and blueprints interspersed with those cute signs saying things like "It's tough to soar with eagles when you work with turkeys." There, Mernit received a constant stream of calls and visits about problems and progress on the site: an area needed the electricians to put in more light; a group of tradesmen had not turned up; part of one of the buildings had a structural problem.

Often he would sally forth, walkie-talkie holstered at the ready, like some tough but kindly local sheriff, to deal with the workers and subcontractors. Everybody loved Dan. He had a comforting cliché for every situation. One of his favorites was "We have met the enemy and it is us." He even had it pinned up on his wall. Each morning at five-thirty he would be on the site, ready to take on the problems one by one, and each day, as the Circle Line Tour ferry plowed past between the site and the Statue of Liberty, progress was made.

Many of the techniques introduced in First Canadian Place were refined for the World Financial Center. In particular, a more advanced system of computerized control for the movement and monitoring of men and materials was introduced and put under the supervision of Torontonian Dan Frank, one of O&Y's "Romanian Mafia," whose charter member was Otto Blau.

The system, designed by former NBC man Joe Weinstein, president of Autocomp Systems Corp., still required three full-time staff to spend most of their time on the phones to suppliers and subcontractors, but the program allowed them to coordinate schedules for deliveries and use of hoists very rapidly, and the computer's ability to spit out paper saved huge amounts of time.

For Mernit and those who worked with him, the Reichmanns were a mystery. Just as his vision embraced the work of literally thousands of individuals, from the laborers to the "brain surgeon" specialist engineers, so Mernit realized that, somewhere up there, the Reichmanns' vision embraced his. They were, he would say with a shake of his head, *swift*. He would see them at ceremonies, such as the groundbreaking, or he would get a call from their office or from John Norris telling him that one or both were coming for a site inspection. Then he would be waiting for them at the gate when they turned up in their limo, with their undertakers' suits and their homburgs, and he would take them around. He had little doubt that their basic questions had deep meanings. Compared with them, he felt that he was a simple man. He daydreamed about scuba diving or flying. He felt he could not begin to guess what weird and wonderful things went on in Paul Reichmann's mind. Dan Merrit had his own capsule comment on the Reichmanns' mystique: "They make their deals in the clouds."

The City Investing and Amex leases had accounted for half the space at the World Financial Center, but that still left almost 4 million square feet. City Investing had been the bell calf, American Express the bell cow. Now came the "thundering herd," Merrill Lynch & Co. Inc.

Merrill Lynch, the world's largest investment company, with

40,000 employees worldwide, was an obvious candidate to consolidate its office space. It had eleven head office and administrative facilities scattered throughout Manhattan. Over many months of negotiations, the Reichmanns, Michael Dennis, and Ed Minskoff worked on Merrill Lynch management, and a complex deal was finally worked out in which the investment company would occupy two of the World Financial Center's four buildings, which it would partly own as a joint venture with O&Y. The two buildings, one of thirty-four stories and one of forty-four stories, would have a combined space of 3.9 million square feet.

Once again, on the basis of the "used car" technique, O&Y agreed, in a separate transaction, to buy Merrill Lynch's existing headquarters, the 1.8-million-square-foot One Liberty Plaza, which was a mere stock certificate's flutter up Liberty Street from its new offices.

The deal was announced, with much fanfare, on August 24, 1984. Press releases were issued containing the usual computer-generated executive remarks, only in this case, they came from some very high level sources. William Schreyer, Merrill Lynch's freshly appointed president and chief operating officer, stated, "This major undertaking will assure that Merrill Lynch remains a major corporate presence for years to come in New York City, which is truly the financial capital of the world."

Paul Reichmann declared, "We are delighted that Merrill Lynch, an industry leader, shares our great confidence in New York and its future."

Governor Mario Cuomo got to the real nitty-gritty of the transaction as far as the city was concerned. "Today's action," he said, "will result in the creation of thousands of construction, office and retail jobs, guarantee redemption of Battery Park City Authority bonds and repayment of State advances with interest from the 1979 financial rescue plan, and permit the Authority to proceed with development of another 12,000 housing units on the 92-acre landfill site."

Mayor Ed Koch, with a little more color, noted, "Merrill Lynch's spectacular headquarters and operations project insures that the city of its birth and nurturing will remain the financial capital of the world. This is a real New York story."

No figures were released.

The realities of the deal were inevitably somewhat tougher than the sweetness and light of the announcement. At the end of the lengthy negotiations, a Merrill representative informed Paul Reichmann that he would be expected to pay a U.S.$6 million leasing commission to Merrill Lynch's in-house real estate brokerage arm. Landlords usually pay the brokerage commission. In this case Paul Reichmann felt that it was inappropriate. He turned with a look of displeasure on the unfortunate emissary and said, "You take that message back to your principals and ask them if they really meant you to deliver it."

The brokerage fee was not mentioned again.

The leasing of the World Financial Center was now substantially completed. Elsewhere, the Reichmanns felt that real estate had plateaued for the time being.

Even as the four towers of the World Financial Center were beginning to rise above the mists of the Hudson, Paul Reichmann was plotting deals that would make the heads of even the most financially sophisticated observers spin. Paul Reichmann's restless ambitions moved on to new challenges. There seemed to be few, if any, left in real estate.

8

Bumping into the Bronfmans

WHEN PETER NEWMAN'S SEMINAL BOOK *THE CANADIAN Establishment* appeared in 1975, the Reichmanns scarcely rated a mention. They were consigned to a listing of "the $50 million group," and garnered a footnote for having capitalized on executives' desire for corner offices by building the York Centre in Toronto with eight corners per floor. But in the latter half of the 1970s, their corporate profile rose dramatically.

The Reichmanns' apparent lack of concern about being part of any Establishment only increased their fascination for the Canadian business community. Newman defined the business Establishment by its associations and its trappings, but the Reichmanns were almost impossible to pigeonhole. They did not buy hockey or baseball teams; they did not belong to clubs; they did not play golf or ski or fish. In fact, all they appeared to do, when they were not with their families or studying the Talmud, was work. The results of all that work were phenomenal.

Their real estate business was like a giant cash register, relentlessly ringing up millions of dollars each week in revenues. Equally important, the empire, in particular the Uris properties in New York, had become a growing collateral base against which the bankers and the other financial institutions were virtually begging the Reichmanns to borrow.

As for their wealth, their refusal to comment upon it merely whetted the appetites of the press and the bankers. In a 1978 interview with the Toronto-based *Executive* magazine, the following exchange took place between the magazine's Dean Walker and Albert Reichmann:

Question: As a private company you do not have to reveal any figures but I would like to give some indications of the size of this enterprise. Are there any sorts of figures you are prepared to give me?

Answer: No.

Question: I have seen one published guess, putting the assets at $1.3 billion. Do you care to comment on that?

Answer: We'll leave it at a guess.

Astonishingly, such secrecy appeared to make them all the more attractive to lenders. In the 1970s, "asset growth" had become the name of the bankers' game. A bank's assets are its loans, and success was increasingly measured by how much you could persuade your clients to borrow. The rapid expansion of Canadian developers into the United States in the 1970s had been made possible by their Canadian bankers. They could lend their individual clients far more than most American banks, whose exposure was restricted by law. As the value of the Reichmanns' property portfolio moved into the billions, so the funds available to them multiplied. The brothers were held in awe, even in Manhattan, because they could pick up the phone and arrange a U.S.$300 million credit in less time than it took to order a pizza.

The availability of funds supported accelerated expansion within real estate and diversification outside it. That expansion and diversification inevitably led the Reichmanns to run up against other Canadian moguls. In 1979, they collided with the junior branch of the Bronfmans, just as that branch was casting off its junior status.

In 1979, the Reichmanns' attention was drawn to English Property Corporation, Great Britain's third-largest developer. Since English Property controlled a considerable stake in Bill Zeckendorf's old vehicle, Trizec, which was now controlled by Edward and Peter Bronfman, the Reichmanns' move inevitably stirred Bronfman fears that it was really Trizec the Reichmanns were after.

Edward and Peter were the sons of Allan Bronfman, the youngest brother of Sam Bronfman, the larger-than-life founder of the mighty Seagram distilled spirits empire. The main Seagram inheritance had passed to Sam's sons, Edgar and Charles, but Edward and Peter had made a shrewd move in acquiring two smart advisers to nurture and expand their holding company, Edper Investments: Trevor Eyton, a large, gregarious, and slightly rumpled partner in the Toronto law firm of Tory, Tory, DesLauriers & Binnington, and Jack Cockwell, a whip-smart South African–born chartered accountant who joined the Edper organization in 1969 from Touche Ross.

The keystone to the success of the Edper group was its 1976 acquisition of control of Trizec, the company founded in 1960 to complete Bill Zeckendorf's Place Ville Marie. When his empire foundered, Zeckendorf lost control of Trizec to Britain's Eagle Star Insurance. Zeckendorf was succeeded as head of Trizec by James Soden, a tough Montreal lawyer. Under Soden, Trizec grew rapidly through both development and acquisition. By 1968, with assets of Can$241 million, Trizec ranked as the largest publicly owned Canadian real estate company. By 1972, following a number of acquisitions and mergers, one of which gave the Bronfmans 9 percent of Trizec's equity, Trizec had become the largest publicly owned real estate company in North America.

Toward the end of 1975, Peter Bronfman approached Soden and asked if he would be sympathetic to a move by the Bronfmans to "Canadianize" Trizec. Canada had witnessed an increase in economic nationalism in the early 1970s, most clearly demonstrated in the creation of the Foreign Investment Review Agency (FIRA). The majority of Trizec's equity was still controlled by Eagle Star Insurance through its minority-owned property arm English Property Corporation. English Property's management, feeling the chill in Canadian attitudes toward foreign investment, helped hatch a complex plan under which English Property would continue to hold the majority of Trizec shares, but control of Trizec for FIRA purposes would pass, via a new holding company, Carena Properties Inc., into the hands of the Bronfmans.

Once the deal was done, the Bronfmans moved quickly and ruthlessly to shake up Trizec. They injected cash and installed

Harold Milavsky, a hard-nosed accountant, as president and chief executive. Under Milavsky's guidance, Trizec became both larger and financially stronger. By 1979, its assets had reached the magic Can$1 billion mark. Then the Reichmanns suddenly appeared on the scene.

In the middle of January 1979, Paul and Albert Reichmann traveled to London to visit English Property executive Stanley Honeyman. They told him that they were interested in buying control of his company. The Bronfmans and their advisers were horrified, fearing that it was really Trizec the Reichmanns were after. They regarded the Reichmanns' actions as unfriendly. One analyst predicted "one terrible fight." Edper executives claimed that Olympia & York would not be an acceptable partner for publicly owned Trizec because of potential conflicts of interest with O&Y's privately controlled real estate empire.

English Property became the subject of a many-sided bidding war in which the Reichmanns, now dubbed "the shy Canadians" by the British press, appeared the favorites. English Property's Gerald Rothman was quoted as saying that the situation between the Reichmanns and Bronfmans was now "a game of corporate poker and bluff." The battle was billed as one for control of the Canadian development industry.

The Reichmanns had no direct contact with the Bronfmans. Nevertheless, Paul Reichmann told a newspaper: "There has been a very mistaken notion in the press that we are unfriendly bidders. It is not Trizec we are bidding for but English Property. Before we entered, the bid was 37 pence a share. I would say that at 60 pence ours is a very welcome bid. It was made in full cooperation with the management of English Property."

But if there was a "mistaken notion," it certainly had not arisen in the press. It was firmly implanted in the minds of Edward and Peter Bronfman by Paul Reichmann's lack of communication. Asked what he would do if the Bronfmans started a fight, he said: "I am not worried about any battle, because I don't see the potential of a fight in the future. I can think of many reasons why they would not want us to be in English Property, but I don't see any problem if we acquire it." Clearly, Reichmann did not consider the Bronfmans' problems his problems, although he said, "Trizec is a very well run company and if our offer is accepted for English Property we anticipate doing nothing to change its management structure." But Reichmann's supposedly calming words seemed to have the opposite effect on the Bronfmans.

In March, Edper decided to enter the bidding war for English Property. A team of six financiers and lawyers, headed by Harold Milavsky, Trevor Eyton, and Jack Cockwell, was dispatched to England to evaluate the company. But the day before they were due to launch their rival bid, Milavsky and Eyton spotted Paul Reichmann in a London hotel lobby. Milavsky suggested they should pay their respects. Recalls Eyton, "It's the Canadian way at the very least to be courteous, so we went over to shake his hand. He obviously liked that and he obviously didn't want a public fuss, so he said, 'Why don't we go inside and talk.' And so Paul Reichmann and Harold and myself and Jack Cockwell sat in the lobby and in a period of ten minutes we came to a general understanding which we translated into agreements about a week later in Montreal, which is the basis for our agreements and our understanding and our association in Trizec today."

At those subsequent meetings in Montreal, Eyton was impressed because Paul and Albert did not have a lawyer. He admired the Reichmanns' speed and facility of decisionmaking. Whenever they reached a difficult point, Paul and Albert would excuse themselves and step outside the door. Sometimes they would return in less than a minute, declaring with a smile that they had just had a board meeting, and here was their answer or proposal.

The Bronfmans agreed not to challenge the Reichmanns' bid for English Property. The Reichmanns in turn gave the Bronfmans an option to increase their ownership of Trizec. The brothers approved existing Trizec policies and management, and also gave an undertaking to avoid conflicts of interest in partnership dealings with Trizec.

The accommodation over Trizec was of great importance in

establishing links between the Reichmann and Edper empires. The critical link was not between the Reichmanns and the Bronfmans, but between the Reichmanns and Trevor Eyton and Jack Cockwell, who would go on to guide the Edper holdings through a dazzling array of acquisitions, and create a corporate web of almost impregnable complexity.

In the subsequent expansion of both the Reichmann and Edper empires, a key financial éminence grise was Jimmy Connacher, the aggressive head of Gordon Securities, a secretive Toronto investment house that concentrated on "block trading," that is, buying and selling large chunks of corporate stock. This specialization put Gordon center stage during takeovers, when the speedy, secret acquisition of a large position in a company could prove the critical factor in victory. The Gordon men made a point of knowing where all the shares were buried.

Connacher played more than the role of middleman. Sometimes he would accumulate blocks in anticipation of a takeover, and even act as a financial *agent provocateur*, precipitating the battle by peddling the block. Paul Reichmann admired people who shot from the hip and were prepared to back up their words with actions and money. Jimmy Connacher — whose nicknames included "the Piranha" and "the Barracuda" — ranked very high on both counts.

Edper's critical acquisition was Brascan, a sprawling Toronto-based company which had started out running mule-drawn trams in Sao Paulo and wound up electrifying, and then owning, large parts of Brazil. Under Edper control, Brascan went on to seize mining giant Noranda, which in turn controlled MacMillan Bloedel Limited, Canada's largest forest products company. Between them, O&Y and Brascan would account for a large portion of the Canadian business news in the 1980s. Jimmy Connacher was always somewhere close behind the headlines.

Another key link between the Reichmann and Edper/Brascan empires was forged as a result of a controversial episode that went into Canadian corporate history as "the Royal Trust Affair." The imbroglio would also bring Paul Reichmann into contact with Robert Campeau for the first time.

In August 1980, Campeau, a mercurial French-Canadian property developer, approached Ken White, the crusty, Establishment chairman of Royal Trust, Canada's largest trust company, to sound him out on acquisition. Like many others, Campeau believed that Royal was too staid and conservative, and that it was not utilizing its business assets to the best advantage. White expressed indignant displeasure at Campeau's suggestion (the proposal was made at White's farm and White immediately marched Campeau off the property) and subsequently lined up a business Who's Who to fight off the bid.

White's defensive strategist Austin Taylor, the head of Toronto broker McLeod Young Weir, decided to approach Paul Reichmann. The ironies of the Toronto Establishment turning to Orthodox Jews to fight off upstart French Canadians were duly noted. Reichmann responded, not out of any desire to save the financial Establishment or to become part of it, but because he saw Royal Trust as an attractive investment. In fact, he responded more enthusiastically than the Establishment wanted, saying that he was prepared to come in for 50 percent of Royal Trust. When his suggestion was politely rebuffed, he countered by committing to buy 10 percent of the institution with a view to increasing that stake over time to 20 percent. As a condition, however, Reichmann demanded seats on the Royal Trust board, plus a commitment that the trust company's dividend increases would continue. Olympia & York then purchased about 9 percent of the trust company's equity. Albert later was invited onto the board.

Campeau's bid foundered, although he sold the stake he had accumulated to the Reichmanns for a Can$2 million profit. But the whole affair provided a somewhat embarrassing example of the Canadian business Establishment's clubbiness. It became the subject of an inquiry by the Ontario Securities Commission, which subsequently issued a report harshly critical of White and other Bay Street worthies.

The greatest irony was that Royal Trust was gobbled up by those supposedly brought in to "defend" it. Trevor Eyton was chosen by Paul Reichmann to be the final instrument of retribution for the Royal Trust management. Reichmann turned up at

Eyton's office and suggested that Edper match the Reichmanns' stake in the trust company, and that Eyton and Cockwell should manage the investment for both parties. As Eyton tells it: "He came to us and said, 'I would like you to be a partner in the Royal Trustco investment and I'd be happy for you to manage the investment' ... We took it as a great compliment ... So we bought stock up to their position."

The brothers subsequently brought their stake up to 23.3 percent. By June 1981, Edper held 17.4 percent.

According to Trevor Eyton: "I think Ken White lost control of all of the fences. He appointed Austin Taylor and others and they went running around and said, 'OK, we've protected you from the big bad wolf,' but Ken White probably never thought to ask, 'What about the big bad bear?'" Once Paul Reichmann, "the big bad bear," had been invited into the Royal Trust compound, the consequences were inevitable.

"And so it was," wrote Rod McQueen in his book *The Moneyspinners*, "that Ken White gained his Pyrrhic victory. Less than ten months after he marched Campeau off his property, Royal Trust had gone from a widely held company with 6,600 shareholders to one owned 40 percent by the Reichmanns and the Bronfmans."

The Reichmanns' financial bonds with the Edper-Brascan empire were further cemented when, in 1983, they exchanged their Royal Trustco shares for cash and a stake in Trilon Financial Corporation, an insurance and financial services company set up by Brascan the year before.

Brascan had a controlling interest in London Life Insurance, the largest insurance business in Canada, and it seemed clear to Eyton and Cockwell merely from looking across the U.S. border and seeing the financial conglomeration at companies like Sears and American Express, that the same development was bound to happen in Canada.

Trilon's formation, as Patricia Dest and Ann Shortell pointed out in their book *A Matter of Trust*, "gave the Bronfmans a running start in the race to create financial conglomerates in

Canada." Their action did not please the banking Establishment, but it seemed like the wave of the future. And the Reichmanns had a piece.

The Reichmans' enormous money power and reputation made it inevitable that the business Establishment would wish to embrace them, but that desire seemed inversely proportional to the Reichmanns' desire to belong. It was not that, like Groucho Marx, they did not want to be a member of any club that would have them. It was just that they did not join clubs.

Although the Reichmanns had little desire to be embraced by society, their low-key, behind-the-scenes approach was the very essence of the Canadian way of doing business. You didn't get involved in knock-'em-down, drag-'em-out fights. You didn't get involved in formal agreements. You just whispered a word in the right ear. And things got done.

The Reichmanns were not interested in Establishments. They were interested in making money with money. That desire would now take them beyond real estate. But it would also eventually lead them into a knock-'em-down, drag-'em-out fight.

9

Image and Reality in a Changing Empire

BETWEEN 1979 AND 1981, THE REICHMANN EMPIRE WENT through a fundamental realignment. Since that first warehouse back in 1956, the geometric progression of the family's business growth had taken place in real estate. Low-rise industrial build- ings had led to Flemingdon Park and multistory office blocks. Multistory office blocks had provided the experience for the building and financing of the O&Y flagship, First Canadian Place. Buying and selling real estate had culminated in the 1977 New York "deal of the century." Battery Park City had provided both the greatest challenge, and the greatest achievement, that real estate had to offer.

The Reichmanns' success — borne on a tide of real estate inflation — had created another challenge: what to do with all the money thrown off by the property empire. Paul Reichmann real- ized it gave him the opportunity to buy other companies on a grand scale. His first moves were opportunistic, but eventually a pattern would form: he would build a conglomerate based on the indus- tries for which Canada was most famous — paper and petroleum. But he would also grab any other likely-looking corporate morsel that came along. He would prove to be a relentless acquisitor. During 1980 and 1981, Paul Reichmann spent more than Can$1 billion on corporate acquisition. Most of the decisions were made off the cuff. The first big one was Abitibi-Price.

In 1978, Andy Sarlos, a Hungarian-born Toronto investment guru, and Maurice Strong, a fascinating hybrid whose interests embraced both greenmail and the Third World Green Revolu- tion, staged an assault on Toronto-based Abitibi-Price Inc., the world's largest newsprint manufacturer. The contention of Sarlos and Strong was that Abitibi's stock was undervalued, largely as a result of staid management. With financial backing from Peter Bronfman and Paul Nathanson, the reclusive heir of the Famous Players cinema fortune, they accumulated Can$31 million of Abitibi stock in a five-day spending spree.

Backed by institutions holding another 12 percent of Abitibi, Sarlos and Strong demanded management and financial reforms. They wanted higher dividends and representation on the board. Tom Bell, Abitibi's chairman, told them that board membership was out of the question. Canada's seventeenth-largest industrial corporation, with sales of well over Can$1 billion, did not take instructions from financial wheeler-dealers. However, Bell hoisted Abitibi's dividend from 95 cents to $1.50.

Sarlos and Strong sold out at a profit, but their assault had stirred the interest of larger potential acquisitors, including the Reichmanns. During the summer of 1980, the Reichmanns started picking up Abitibi stock. By the beginning of 1981, they had accumulated almost 10 percent of its shares and found themselves in the middle of a takeover battle with a number of rivals, the most powerful of which was Thomson Newspapers — owner, among many other assets, of the *Times* of London — whose chairman, Ken Thomson, sat on the Abitibi board.

A full-scale bid for Abitibi was not originally part of the Reichmanns' plan, but they did not want to be left with a minority stake, so David Brown, a gentlemanly investment dealer with Burns Fry who had earned the Reichmanns' regard in earlier financings, suggested that they should cut the nickel-and-dime stuff and just go for the whole company. Like Livy's Hannibal, they would conquer the world in self-defense. The Canadian Imperial Bank of Commerce and the Bank of Montreal were only too pleased to put up the funds. O&Y simply blew its competitors out of the water, bidding Can$32 for all of Abitibi's shares in one of the largest takeovers in Canadian history, worth well over Can$500 million.

Abitibi's conservative management, which had been less than friendly to outsiders, now had to succumb to the one power that transcended all tradition: sheer, naked money. Paul Reichmann met with Abitibi's chief executive, Bob Gimlin, and assured him that O&Y wanted Abitibi to continue under its existing management. He also asked Tom Bell, the chairman, to convey to the directors that he wished the whole board to stay. He approached Ken Thomson and his chief lieutenant, John Tory, and after he outlined his good intentions, they, too, agreed to remain as directors.

From the point of view of the business establishment, the Reichmanns' Abitibi victory seemed to indicate a profound shift in Canadian corporate power. An article in *Maclean's* quoted a Bank of Montreal executive as saying: "In terms of traditional Canadian wealth and resources, it wasn't long ago that you'd expect Abitibi to be doing the takeover, not the other way around. That's how much things are changing."

The Abitibi takeover swelled the Reichmann myth. They had taken on the Thomson empire, which was not accustomed to losing corporate battles, and they had not merely outbid it, but co-opted it, making peace with Ken Thomson and persuading him to stay on the Abitibi board. There had been no master plan behind the Abitibi purchase. Paul Reichmann had done it simply because he could, although, of course, he had plenty of advisers to tell him it was a good deal. Even Paul Reichmann himself admitted that in the Abitibi battle he had "only reacted to the bidding." Reichmann also bought stakes in a number of oil and gas companies, including Canada Northwest Land, Brinco Oil & Gas, and Bow Valley Industries.

He explained his diversification rationale simply and somewhat coldly: "Over time, we have accumulated shares in many Canadian companies, particularly natural resource companies. And when the opportunity to buy control is available, we have moved. We are not only interested in the company and its value, but in the quality of people who operate it. In Brinco and Abitibi, and any other investment we make, we depend on their existing management to run the business. . . . If we did not have faith in their ability to handle crises, we would not have invested. But if we are wrong, other people can be found."

He freely admitted the opportunistic nature of his deals and acknowledged that they were based on gut feelings rather than exhaustive calculations. In an interview with the *Globe and Mail* in 1981, he said, "It is a myth that corporations decide where they will go. They move where they will by being at the right place at the right time." At around the same time, he was quoted in the *Financial Times of Canada* as making the extraordinary statement, "You can go broke if you depend too much on numbers."

Paul Reichmann could not have stated his motivations and goals more clearly; the nature of the brothers' wealth could not have been more obvious; their personal lives — although they refused to answer questions about them — could not have been more straightforward. They were devoutly religious family men who applied themselves relentlessly to business success. The intuitive genius behind their success was Paul.

The brothers were time and time again described as "reclusive" and "private," but they gave far more interviews than the average senior corporate executive. The brothers were in fact far less reclusive than any average multimillionaire. What they were was secretive. When they spoke to the press, they had a very clear idea of what they wanted to promote and what was off limits. Until it suited their corporate purposes, money had always been off limits.

In her 1981 book, *Men of Property*, Toronto-based writer Susan Goldenberg wrote: "Publicity is rare for the Reichmanns who have become legendary not only because of their astute deals, but also because they are an enigma. In the real estate world, there are the Reichmanns and then there is everybody else. . . . They are the deans of the real estate development world, possessed of infinite patience and down-to-earth common sense and practicality."

They received this accolade despite the fact that when Goldenberg asked how acquisitions were financed, Albert Reichmann said that was an issue he "would like to leave out. We work with banks and financial institutions and use leverage."

Again, Paul, when granting an interview to *Maclean's* magazine shortly after the Abitibi takeover, said, "We have always preferred to remain private in our affairs. . . . That's always been our way, long before our company became big or we became rich. Surely no one can begrudge us that."

Most pieces about the Reichmanns were not even so impolite as to address the crude question of money. A lengthy and breathless profile in the *Globe and Mail* in 1981 claimed: "From where they stand at the pinnacle of the Canadian development industry, the Reichmann brothers are in danger, their modesty and reticence notwithstanding, of becoming a legend. . . . [They] have left the path behind them strewn with complex myths born of their passionate desire for privacy and the sense of awe they have inspired in people who watched them build their empire bloodlessly, calmly, systematically.

"It is said that in an industry the public generally considers ruthless and disruptive, the Reichmanns offer stability and reliability.

"It is said they consummate deals worth millions with a handshake and then keep their word even when, in time, the deal becomes less advantageous to them.

"It is said their business acumen is second to none."

And if the Reichmanns were a little reticent about their business skills, there were plenty of those close to them who were prepared to sing their praises. Ron Soskolne, their architectural taste-maker, was quoted in *Maclean's* as saying, "They're like grocery shopkeepers out at the market every morning at 6 a.m. squeezing and choosing the fruit and vegetables themselves personally." In another article, he called Paul Reichmann "the Wayne Gretzky of money."

Paul Reichmann, meanwhile, could pooh-pooh all the interest in him. In still another interview with the *Globe and Mail* in 1981, he said, "I have never believed that anyone reads, remembers or cares about all that silliness that is published about where we come from or who we are. Your readers are not interested in that. As people, we are no different from any other of the three million people around this city."

The Reichmanns were just your regular old self-made multibillionaires!

What made the Reichmanns run? The Reichmanns' fabulous success and obvious religiosity were treated by the media almost as some kind of paradox. To minds bred on the New Testament and conventional liberal wisdom — filled with images of camels struggling through the eyes of needles and rapacious robber barons — there was a direct contradiction between the two. Paul Reichmann's extraordinary charm was also a factor in ensuring that the brothers were for a long time given an extraordinarily easy analytical ride by the press.

The *Globe* article went on to say, "Mr. Reichmann displays thinly veiled revulsion at the suggestion that there might well be an interest in personal material on a family with the accomplishments of the Reichmanns. 'If you're a movie star, I suppose there is some value in being bandied about, but frankly . . .' "

But gradually, it seems, Paul Reichmann came to realize that a carefully cultivated mystique could be worth money. Press connections might also skillfully be used to burnish the image of unimaginable wealth.

Mid-1981 marked the peak of both the resource and the real estate booms. Interest rates suddenly climbed through the stratosphere and the bloom fell off the resource rose. Developers, too, were suddenly fighting for their lives and people began to realize how much damage the banks had done by lending money to all and sundry. By the spring of 1982, Canadian publicly quoted real estate companies had suffered a stock market bloodbath. While the Toronto Stock Exchange 300 Composite Index had fallen 34 percent from its high of November 30, 1980, the developers' and contractors' index was down 71 percent. The property management index (which included Cadillac Fairview and Trizec) was down 46 percent from its July 1981 high.

The Reichmanns successfully promoted the view that they lived in another development world. According to *Maclean's* magazine of April 5, 1982: "Olympia & York Developments Ltd., that market enigma, is seen as forging ahead against the common industry wisdom. It's expanding, analysts say, in spite of present conditions and the losses it has felt on major recent acquisitions such as Abitibi-Price. . . . [I]t's also succeeding in leasing its large New York development in spite of a slowing Manhattan office market."

The deal referred to was the one with American Express on the largest tower of the World Financial Center. But the climate soon led to a change in that deal. American Express agreed to buy the leasehold on the tower for about U.S.$600 million, while the price that O&Y paid for the Amex headquarters was hauled down from U.S.$240 million to U.S.$160 million. Amex's purchase of the tower led to a massive change of construction priorities on the World Financial Center site. Dan Mernit, the general superintendent, found his job suddenly complicated not merely by the accelerations of the Amex building but also because American Express brought in its own contractors to fit out the building. They inevitably clashed with O&Y's contractors. But the men on the site did not grumble too much. They just shrugged. They knew they were seeing the down-to-earth results of another deal done "in the clouds."

In 1981, Paul Reichmann had said in an interview with the *Financial Times of Canada*, "If we run short of money, we are luckier than an industrial company. It can't sell off a few machines. But we could always sell a building if necessary."

Now, a year later, O&Y quietly put parts of the Uris package on the market, but the Reichmanns reacted strongly to any suggestion that this had anything to do with their running short of money. They denied problems either with the state of the property market or with the more than $1 billion they had borrowed for their diversifications the year before.

The Reichmanns wanted to raise at least U.S.$500 million by selling or refinancing at least two of the Uris buildings, but they were also quoting a figure of U.S.$2.5 billion for anyone who wanted to buy the whole lot. Knowing the Reichmanns' penchant for tungsten-hard bargaining, U.S.$2.5 billion would obviously have been the top price. Nevertheless, suddenly the press started bandying about the Reichmanns' asking price as the buildings' value. It looked so good, so *mythical*, when set up against their U.S.$320 million cost.

Meanwhile, even as the renegotiations with American Express were going on at the World Financial Center, the costs of the project were undergoing a dramatic upward revision. Suddenly, without any explanation, the "U.S.$1 billion project" became the "U.S.$1.5 billion project."

O&Y found itself arranging long-term mortgages at high rates, while it also tried to get some U.S.$1.4 billion secured against the U.S. buildings then under construction, including the World Financial Center. Nevertheless, the company claimed that it still had considerable collateral left on the Uris buildings.

The empire had other problems. The building markets in Dallas, where it had completed a U.S.$100 million office tower, and in Calgary, where it had three huge developments either built or under way, were very soft. Paul Reichmann was obviously getting a little concerned about all these rumors of real estate problems and bad investments. In the spring of 1982, he gave a lengthy interview to *Fortune*.

In large part, he succeeded in persuading the magazine (which repeated the journalistic shibboleth that the Reichmanns had "a passion for privacy") that O&Y was somehow not subject to the economic laws that were laying waste to real estate and resource companies everywhere else. "O&Y," declared the article, "can afford to play the epic contrarian, but many of its rivals cannot ... O&Y is an anomaly, a venturesome developer with the deep pockets of a big insurance company."

The question was, just how deep were the pockets? Paul Reichmann professed to come clean. "Disclosing key financial data for the first time, Paul Reichmann told *Fortune* that O&Y's assets, largely carried at cost, are valued on the books at U.S.$7 billion. That's more than double the assets of another big Canadian developer, Cadillac Fairview, which has the most of any publicly held real-estate company in North America."

The magazine estimated that the market value of O&Y's assets was U.S.$12 billion and that O&Y was "so conservatively leveraged" that it could sell off its assets, pay its debts, and still wind up with U.S.$5 billion, "a figure Paul Reichmann concedes is close to the mark. It is a safe bet that few families have ever had so grandiose a net worth. The company's cash flow, says Paul, is U.S.$233 million a year."

But if, with assets worth U.S.$12 billion, it could pay off its debts and still wind up with U.S.$5 billion, that meant its debts were U.S.$7 billion, a phenomenally high figure. Moreover, by Reichmann's own admission, the book value of O&Y's assets was U.S.$7 billion. Looked at as U.S.$7 billion of assets with U.S.$7 billion of debt, the empire took on quite another complexion, particularly at a time of high interest rates and jittery bankers.

As the director of one of Canada's major chartered banks pointed out in an interview, it was getting "pretty hot in the kitchen" for the Reichmanns. There were heavy carrying costs attached to the diversifications, which were not doing well. O&Y's paper loss on Abitibi alone was around Can$200 million. It was down more than Can$100 million on its other investments. Nevertheless, the Reichmanns shrugged off losses, claiming, as ever, that they were in for the long haul and that they were convinced of the value of their petroleum and newsprint holdings, whatever Wall Street or Bay Street said.

At the same time, for 1982 and a good part of 1983, the Reichmanns were concerned with putting the empire on a more solid financial basis. The two smallest of the Uris buildings — 850 Third Avenue and 10 East 53rd Street — were sold for U.S.$225 million. O&Y remortgaged 245 Park Avenue, its headquarters, with Aetna Life for U.S.$308 million. In the middle of 1983, the brothers sold their 7 percent stake in Bow Valley at an after-tax profit of Can$14.5 million.

Paul Reichmann obviously took umbrage at the notion that

O&Y could ever be in real financial trouble. Nevertheless, the stories kept coming. In October 1982, *Business Week*, in a long story entitled "End of the Office Boom," wrote: "Another episode that has distressed an increasingly skittish investment community involves Olympia & York Developments Ltd., the biggest — and reputedly indomitable — Canadian developer. Olympia recently sold off part of its interest in some big residential properties near New York City. The action set off rumors that even Olympia was strapped for cash and would soon be putting more properties on the block. Olympia asserts that the sale was misread and was in fact part of its plans, and it denies that there will be a wave of distress sales of any of its properties."

Paul Reichmann became visibly annoyed when he read such stories. He vented his feelings to a *Globe* reporter at the end of 1982. The story said of Paul Reichmann, "Yesterday, he expressed noticeable exasperation about the latest reports that the company is being squeezed. He said he would put out a press release to correct the 'distortions,' if he can find the time."

But O&Y was not, like other developers, merely retrenching from the excesses of the past, it was tidying up its financial condition for the next leap forward. In March 1984, O&Y stunned the financial community with a highly original, and as usual unprecedentedly large, financing. It raised almost U.S.$1 billion through a unique issue of fifteen-year floating rate notes, secured by another three of its New York buildings, 2 Broadway, 1290 Avenue of the Americas, and Park Avenue Atrium. The U.S.$970 million deal, organized by the financial wizards at Salomon Brothers, was the first nonrecourse, marketable security of its kind. It was also the largest mortgage of any kind. The money was raised via a private placement to more than forty institutional investors, mostly savings and loan associations. American Savings & Loan took U.S.$350 million of the issue.

With the U.S.$970 million Salomon mortgage, O&Y had the funds available for its next big move. *Business Week*, after getting yet another exclusive interview with the "reclusive," Paul Reichmann, wrote in August 1983: "According to Paul Reichmann,

O&Y's long-term strategy for investment in other companies is to take a 'substantial position where we can have an influence on the affairs of the company.' As more of O&Y's real estate matures and is sold and surplus funds become available, the company plans to increase its corporate investments, either through its holding company or through subsidiaries. For example, as a buffer against the cycles of the forest-products industry, the Reichmanns might diversify Abitibi-Price into other natural-resource activities such as oil and gas."

While other real estate companies were coming back from the traumas of 1982-83 licking their wounds, if they were coming back at all, O&Y was about to come back like a three-stage rocket.

To understand what happened after the retrenchments of the early 1980s, it is first necessary to step back and look at the nature and structure of the Reichmann empire, at its strengths and its weaknesses, at its philosophies and its attitudes.

The Reichmanns had developed an unparalleled reputation, but that reputation was based entirely on the quality of their real estate activities. The 1977 New York property deal had given them an almost superhuman aura of business wisdom. They were the men who took what seemed like great risks, but turned out to be no risks at all. Observers thought the Reichmanns had a crystal ball.

The very success of the real estate operations, and the collateral provided by the New York properties, had made diversification almost inevitable. They had picked resources because they thought resources were like real estate: you held onto them and in time their value was bound to increase. Just as they were not making any more prime real estate (give or take a little landfill here and there), they were not making any more petroleum either. Forest products were renewable, but it took a long time to grow a forest. The value had to be there, too, whatever the short-term problems. The Reichmanns were seen as being the ultimate in "patient money."

But the Reichmanns were not superhuman, and they were not

infallible. Moreover, the reality of their organization was almost frighteningly thin. Getting to the heart of the Reichmann empire was a little like reaching the end of the Yellow Brick Road: when you drew back the O&Y curtain, it was virtually a one-man show. That was not to say that it did not have talented executives, but these tended to be on the real estate side, and real estate was just where the money was made. The main emphasis now was on where that money, or rather the borrowings against the real estate collateral, was being invested.

The Reichmanns had proved adept at using the press to promote their projects or correct "misapprehensions" about their financial condition. Paul had successfully promulgated the notion that the three brothers were equals in business affairs and virtually interchangeable when it came to decisionmaking. Such assertions were based less on reality than on a sense of family loyalty. Albert tended to be more involved in land acquisition, financing, leasing, and building design, but Paul was always in on the major real estate decisions. Albert in turn was always closely involved in diversifications, but the strategic thrust came from Paul.

The relationship between Paul and Albert was critical. The brothers' personalities and tastes were quite different. Albert was considered a lot "looser" than Paul, but he was also Paul's closest adviser and sounding board. The constant interplay between the two brothers was described by one of their executives as being almost like a process of osmosis. They interacted informally and frequently, and were always in each other's offices, tossing ideas back and forth. Their offices in fact clearly reflected the contrast in their tastes. Paul's was more "classical," with traditional furniture and Persian carpets. His walls were decorated with paintings of Venice. His architectural tastes were also different. He liked simple, elegant, masonry buildings. First Canadian Place was very much a "Paul" building. Albert was more "modernist" in his leanings. His office sported contemporary furniture, and his walls had paintings by Marc Chagall. O&Y's Exchange Place in Boston — an irregular tower with glass curtain walls — was more his architectural preference.

Albert was more of an operating man, interested in the marketplace, the costs, and the structures. Paul was always mentally on the move, looking for the next step. He lived at a much more conceptual level. His obsession was how to increase yields, how to structure deals. Said Bernd Koken, who had now taken over as chief executive of Abitibi, of Paul: "He's lots more than a chief financial officer or a corporate developer or a treasurer. He's some super-version of all of these things combined. He's a deal creator. He is *always* thinking. He's an extremely intellectual guy. When Paul talks at a meeting, he's usually seven steps out in front."

One of the critical features about O&Y was that it was very much a family company controlled by a particularly tight-knit family. To work at Olympia & York was to be under no illusions about who the bosses of the company were. Some who had worked with the Reichmanns considered them insensitive to others' ego requirements. Employees were paid well but had to realize that they were essentially corporate servants whose expertise was there to be fed into the master equation that existed in Paul's head. Albert was one of the very few individuals who might suggest variations in the equation. Others were there merely to feed in the variables.

Said one senior employee: "They deal very sensitively with people in the organization, but they expect them to understand that it's their prerogative to exercise judgment and not have to explain it. The people who are successful in working with them are those who understand that they are here to support the Reichmanns in what they do, and that requires a degree of ego-subordination. On the other hand, it enables one to experience in an exhilarating way the sense of shared achievement when one's judgment is engaged as part of their process."

Another real estate consultant who worked for them said: "Their management style is based on accepting information from a number of sources and then acting. Once they have made a decision, they do not return to explain why any particular recommendation has been rejected." If the consultant ever questioned a decision and went to one of the brothers for an explanation, the brother would give him one — and inevitably one that made sense — but would seem surprised that the consultant's ego might have been bruised.

The Reichmanns paid, and paid well, for people's brains. They were not interested in egos. According to a former employee: "They ruffle lots of feathers because they are unaware that they're ruffling feathers. In Paul's case, it's almost a kind of naivety."

More than one O&Y employee compared Paul to a computer. When a decision had to be made, he would draw on many sources. When an outside or inside adviser was summoned into Paul Reichmann's office, he never knew how long he would be there. Sometimes counsel was sought for ten minutes and then he was politely shown the door. Sometimes he would find himself still there four hours later as his mind was relentlessly probed for the key piece of information, the crucial insight, that Reichmann was seeking. And then, when all the input was in, Paul Reichmann would switch off the outside world.

Said one former senior employee: "You all feed your little bits in, then he takes it and churns it around and he comes out with an answer. And sometimes he tells you his conclusions and sometimes he doesn't. Sometimes you will tell him something very forcefully about what should or shouldn't be done and you'd think that he wasn't listening, but then you'd find out that he'd followed your advice."

Nevertheless, this view of Paul Reichmann as corporate automaton, as a great number-crunching brain, was also misleading. The essence of genius is the intuitive mental leap that is a mystery even to the brain that makes it. So many enormous deals start with boxcar numbers and feelings about a particular individual or management group. Paul Reichmann's intellectual churning was piggybacked on his intuition. Then, often to the wonder of those around him, the answer popped out, and everyone would marvel, "Why didn't I think of that?"

Olympia & York revolved around the mind of Paul Reichmann, and Paul Reichmann's mind revolved constantly, almost obsessively, on diversification, reinvestment, and growth.

Bill Zeckendorf had noted in his autobiography that "the secret of any great project is to keep it moving, keep it from losing momentum." Real estate was a business peculiarly susceptible to loss of momentum. Its most famous exponents always used their last building to help finance their next effort. This pyramiding process tended to make real estate companies rather like sharks, not in the predatory but in the purely physiological sense: if they stopped moving, they were in danger of sinking, or being swallowed by their own debts.

The Reichmanns' momentum had now carried them beyond real estate. Bulging real estate funds had been used to buy minority positions in resource companies. These would in some cases be built into majority positions and control. The acquired companies in turn would be used to buy other companies. The only question was: Where would it all end?

Toward the end of 1983, Paul Reichmann began to think about the family's next quantum leap. They had tested the water with the acquisition of stakes in several small- and medium-sized oil companies. It was now time to consider a larger acquisition — the largest oil company acquisition in Canadian history.

10

Drawing a Bead on Gulf

BY THE LATE 1970S, INVESTMENT DEALERS AND BANKERS WERE clamoring to see Paul Reichmann either to peddle deals or to lend him money. He spoke to all those he thought had something worthwhile to sell — or from whom he could learn. Paul Reichmann loved free advice, and nobody had more available to him than a billionaire who wanted to spend money. More and more of the deals being put to him were about oil.

While the Reichmanns had been quietly and inexorably building their real estate empire throughout the 1970s, the province of Alberta had been turning out a virtual stampede of Canadian corporate success stories based on an oil and gas boom of unprecedented proportions. The Calgary-based boom could be traced directly to the OPEC crisis of 1973 and the subsequent surge in oil and natural gas prices. A new pantheon of Canadian business heroes had emerged virtually overnight.

Before the boom, Western oilmen had found their visits to the bastions of Toronto's Bay Street to be exercises in frustration. They had more luck selling their investment dreams south of the border. But the OPEC crisis had bestowed wondrous new charms on the West and its oil producers. Now the Eastern bankers came begging the oilmen to take money. Toronto investment dealers and financial carpetbaggers flew in, their briefcases bursting with a cornucopia of fancy financing schemes.

In the latter half of the 1970s, the most obvious sign of the boom was the volume of Calgary construction. By the beginning of 1979, the value of office buildings either under construction or planned for Calgary passed Can$1 billion. The golden crescent of the city's downtown core — bounded on the south by the railroad tracks below Ninth Avenue and on the north by the slow curve of the Bow River — was sprouting skyscrapers like weeds. Fittingly, O&Y was deeply involved. It had built the thirty-three-story Shell Centre and had a huge twin-tower development planned for Fifth Avenue that would house the headquarters of Esso Resources, the exploration arm of Canada's largest oil company, Imperial Oil. Now the brothers decided to become more directly involved. For a family of devout Orthodox Jews, the role seemed a little unusual; but for anybody looking to be where the Canadian business action was, the Reichmanns' next move was almost inevitable: they had to join the ranks of Canada's Blue-Eyed Sheiks.

The brothers had a lot in common with Calgary's aggressive entrepreneurs. Like the Reichmanns, the biggest crapshooters in Calgary had in most cases founded the companies they headed, and many were still the largest shareholders. And like the Reichmanns, they rejoiced in the flexibility and speed that only proprietorship gave. There were other similarities between oil and gas and real estate. The fabulous success of both the oilmen and the real estate moguls was ultimately based on rapid inflation in their basic product.

Having dabbled in smaller oil holdings, Paul Reichmann now planned one of the most complex and controversial takeovers in Canadian history.

Gulf Canada, the 60.2-percent-owned subsidiary of Gulf Oil Corporation, was Canada's second-largest oil company. Its parent was the smallest of the Seven Sisters. The 1970s and early 1980s were a time of turmoil for all the major oil companies, which were suspected of having manipulated the OPEC crisis for their own corporate ends. For Gulf Oil Corp. and its Canadian subsidiary, the political and business turmoil created by OPEC was greatly exacerbated by internal corporate problems.

In 1973, Gulf Corp. was revealed to have made major illegal contributions not only to Richard Nixon but also foreign politicians and parties, including President Park of South Korea. Gulf was also embroiled in a furor over an international cartel accused of attempting to fix world uranium prices. These revelations of

U.S. corporate skullduggery would have come as no surprise to Albert Leroy Ellsworth, the man who, in 1906, had founded British American Oil Company Limited (BA), the company that eventually became Gulf Canada. Ellsworth had a profound distrust of Americans. His negative feelings were obviously not without foundation. He had spent ten years working for the granddaddy of them all, John D. Rockefeller's Standard Oil, in Buffalo.

With the spread of the automobile in the first half of the twentieth century, British American had expanded across Canada. In 1934, it opened a refinery in Moose Jaw, Saskatchewan. The Moose Jaw refinery developed a special significance for British American, and later Gulf Canada. The no-nonsense engineers who were recruited from the University of Saskatchewan to take their first jobs at Moose Jaw, and later went on to higher executive positions, were dubbed the "Moose Jaw Mafia."

After the Second World War, Gulf Oil Corp. acquired a 20 percent interest in BA. In 1951, BA president William K. Whiteford, an American, was invited to join Gulf in Pittsburgh. He eventually became president and chairman of Gulf, and Gulf took control of British American, which became Gulf Canada in 1969.

Under a talented chief executive, Jerry McAfee, Gulf Canada produced the outstanding performance among the Canadian majors in the early 1970s. Between 1970 and 1974, the company quadrupled its earnings to Can$176 million and raised its return on capital from the lowest to the highest among the "Big Four" Canadian integrated companies — Imperial, Gulf Canada, Shell Canada, and Texaco Canada. As a result, Pittsburgh called Jerry McAfee to clean up the head office. When McAfee left for Pittsburgh, his colleagues in Canada presented him with a T-shirt. On it were emblazoned the words "Mr. Clean."

McAfee's departure led to major problems at Gulf Canada, which became embroiled in uncertainties over management succession and corporate direction, leading to a proliferation of bureaucracy and the onset of inertia. Then Gulf began to get lucky.

The first major success — or so it seemed at the time — was

Gulf's participation in the 1979 find at Hibernia, 200 miles off-shore St. John's, Newfoundland, which was pronounced capable of producing 20,000 barrels of oil a day. Here, it was claimed, was another potential North Sea. To add to its apparent exploration blessings, Gulf Canada was also involved with Dome Petroleum in the Beaufort Sea in what Dome claimed to be major finds. The two pieces of news sent Gulf shares soaring. But just when it seemed that the oilman's greatest asset, luck, would haul the company from its prolonged identity crisis, on October 28, 1980, something far less pleasant appeared on Gulf Canada's business horizons: the National Energy Program.

The NEP, hatched secretly by a group of staunch Canadian nationalists and economic interventionists within Prime Minister Pierre Trudeau's ruling policy elite, painted a threatening picture of foreign-controlled oil companies in Canada. Soaring oil prices would mean that foreign-controlled multinationals like Gulf would wind up owning an inordinate amount of the national wealth. According to the NEP — a program made up of equal parts of economic incomprehension, paranoia, and xenophobia — finds like Hibernia, far from being a cause for congratulation, were a source of fear. Three-quarters of the field would be owned by foreign oil companies, who would use its proceeds to increase their hold on the Canadian economy. Such companies had to be stopped in their tracks.

The NEP introduced hefty new taxes and a discriminatory system of exploration grants designed to take money from the multinationals and the main producing province of Alberta and funnel it toward exploration in the Canadian frontiers. The not-so-hidden agenda of this policy was that foreign oil, faced with this crippling array of taxes, discrimination, and expropriation, would sell out.

For Gulf Canada, which was not merely predominantly foreign-owned and controlled but also had its most attractive assets in the Canadian frontiers, the NEP was a disaster. The walls in Gulf's executive suite in Pittsburgh rang with denunciations of the Canadian federal government's perfidy. They would be damned if they were going to be blackmailed into selling.

Although Gulf Canada's management and board also despised the NEP, the prospect of "Canadianization" was not repugnant. After all, most of them were Canadians, and proud of it. More important, there was suddenly lots of money — in the form of the new discriminatory Petroleum Incentive Payments, or PIP grants — in being officially stamped with the Maple Leaf. If they could not get their hands directly on the highest levels of PIP grants, which offered a mouth-watering 80 percent of frontier exploration expenditures, they could at least take a bold initiative that would indirectly benefit from the grants. They would build a massive drilling fleet to carry out PIP-funded drilling in the Beaufort Sea.

The Beaufort Sea had first come into the exploration spotlight following North America's largest oil and gas find, at Prudhoe Bay in Alaska in 1968. That single field, with over 10 billion barrels of oil (more than all of Canada's proven reserves), sparked a landrush in the Canadian onshore and offshore lands to the east: the Mackenzie Delta and the Beaufort. But the Beaufort presented unprecedented exploration difficulties. For most of the year the sea is a slow-moving sheet of ice, grinding clockwise with the polar ice pack at about three miles a day. As the twenty-four-hour dark of winter gives way to the twenty-four-hour light of summer, the ice melts, allowing a brief but hazardous three-month marine drilling season.

The history of Beaufort exploration had been more a case study in politics than geology. It all started with the "northern dream" of Dome Petroleum's uniquely persuasive chairman, "Smilin' Jack" Gallagher. Gallagher went to Ottawa in the mid-1970s and sold the Liberal government on the concept of "superdepletion," that is, very high tax allowances, for drilling high-cost frontier wells.

The soft-spoken Manitoba native, who delivered his low-key Beaufort slide-show to the investment faithful, politicians, and bureaucrats almost like a holy rite, sold these write-offs to Ottawa by painting an alluring picture of huge Beaufort finds, massive tax revenues, insulation from uncertain world oil markets, and independence from Alberta. In fact, Dome's main reason for peddling superdepletion was that they had bet the company on building an Arctic drilling fleet, which was not finding enough business.

Gallagher's lobbying was a classic example of a private entrepreneur attempting to gain public funds to further his own corporate ambitions. Businessmen all over the world attempt to gain benefits from governments in the name of the national good, but Canada's particular fears about freezing in the dark, and its paranoia about foreign ownership, created a unique environment for exploiting the public purse. Paul Reichmann was well aware of this political background when he eventually moved on Gulf Canada.

The bottom line of Gallagher's highly successful piece of lobbying was that federal tax dollars wound up paying for virtually all Beaufort drilling. There was an inevitable surge in exploration activity, and Dome did not fail to take advantage of its monopoly position. Those forced to use Dome's facilities did not see Gallagher and his belligerent president, Bill Richards, as visionaries; they saw them as pirates. Gulf Canada was constantly frustrated either by Dome's attempts to drive hard bargains for the fleet's use, or simply by its unavailability. The NEP, somewhat ironically, offered Gulf Canada the opportunity to build a rival fleet. Gulf Canada spent Can$674 million on one of the most elaborate drilling fleets ever assembled. But the drilling fleet soon began to appear to be a bold move in the wrong direction.

In 1983, a number of Beaufort exploration agreements were announced calling for some of the most expensive wells in history. The projected cost of one of Gulf's PIP-supported wells was a mind-boggling Can$214 million. Gulf's exploration partners began to kick and scream, while the nine-digit well costs also set off the alarm bells in Ottawa. Gulf had the rates for its drilling system forced down by Ottawa, threatening its profitability. Meanwhile, the 1983 Beaufort drilling season had to cope with the worst summer ice in memory.

The political controversy surrounding PIPs — whose multi-billion-dollar costs were far higher than those projected by a naive government — made it clear that the grants were a far from long-term proposition. Meanwhile, a pronounced weakening in world oil prices undermined Beaufort economics. Once again, it appeared, Gulf Canada had blown it. Once again, a corporation had been the victim of perverse government policies. And yet ironically, given the intentions of the NEP and the company's own managerial shortcomings, Gulf in 1983 seemed safer from takeover than ever.

The NEP had declared a holy war against foreign-controlled oil. It had led to an orgy of corporate acquisition in the name of Canadianization. When the party was over, most of the Canadian acquisitors were left with terminal financial hangovers. Companies like Dome Petroleum — which, typically, had made the most ambitious and expensive acquisition — were put on life support systems by banks too scared to face the consequences of their demise. Most ironic of all, none of the majors had been Canadianized. Indeed, in the wake of the NEP, they appeared more firmly entrenched than ever.

Pittsburgh meanwhile retained its powerful objections to being blackmailed into a sale of one of its prize assets. In the end, change of control at Gulf Canada was brought about neither by its own managerial ineptitude nor by political blackmail, although politics would still play a major role in the company changing hands. Canada's ill-advised post-NEP takeover spree was followed by an even more aggressive bout of acquisition fever south of the border. That was how Gulf Canada finally came on the auction block.

In March 1984, following a takeover battle precipitated by renowned corporate crusader and greenmailer Boone Pickens, Standard Oil of California (Chevron) bought Gulf Corporation for U.S.$13.2 billion, at the time by far the world's most expensive takeover. This suddenly made Gulf Canada's future very uncertain.

Gulf Canada would either be absorbed into Chevron's Canadian subsidiary, Chevron Canada, or it would be sold. The former alternative held few attractions for Gulf Canada's management. Pittsburgh had always been a relatively passive major shareholder and had allowed Gulf Canada to go its own way. Chevron's head office in San Francisco was felt to have a much tighter grip on its Calgary-based Canadian operation, which had been spectacularly successful in the 1970s. Gulf Canada would much rather be bought by a Canadian who was not in the oil business.

Gulf Canada was a valuable company, with earnings in 1983 of Can$218 million and revenues of more than Can$5 billion. The company had strong reserves and promising exploration acreage, particularly on the Canadian frontiers.

Gulf Canada was estimated to be worth around Can$5 billion, so Chevron's 60 percent would cost around Can$3 billion. Within the Canadian private sector, there were few companies that could manage an acquisition of that magnitude.

Business Week, referring to the likelihood of a sale of Gulf Canada in the wake of the Chevron takeover, opined that "no Canadian buyers with the resources to take on such a deal are apparent, and foreign companies are likely to be no happier than [Chevron chief executive George M.] Keller with the prospect of relying on Gulf Canada's modest dividends to pay off a massive investment." But *Business Week* was obviously unaware of the Reichmanns.

Following the establishment of the National Energy Program, investment dealers had quickly seen that there were big bucks to be made from Canadianization. Gordon Securities' Jimmy Connacher had gone to Gulf Canada and offered to help put the company under the Maple Leaf flag. Close to the top of his list of potential buyers was Paul Reichmann. In 1981, Reichmann had gone to Bill Wilder, president of Hiram Walker Resources, in which O&Y had just taken a significant stake, and suggested that the two companies might stage a joint assault on Gulf Canada. Reichmann had been impressed by the strategy used by Dome Petroleum to take control of Hudson's Bay Oil & Gas from its parent, Conoco. Dome had bought Conoco shares and then swapped these for Conoco's stake in HBOG. Reichmann suggested to Wilder that O&Y and Hiram Walker might jointly purchase Gulf Corp. shares with a view to swapping them for control of Gulf Canada. However, Hiram Walker's board had turned the idea down.

While Gulf Corp.'s battle with Pickens had been in full swing in the final months of 1983, Paul Reichmann had several times had meetings with Gulf management in Pittsburgh with a view to buying its Canadian subsidiary. His plan had been to acquire Gulf Canada via Abitibi for a combination of cash and Abitibi shares, but the two sides could not agree on price. Following Chevron's takeover, Reichmann had spoken to Chevron's investment advisers, but they, too, had wanted more than Reichmann was prepared to pay. But Paul Reichmann had both Gulf Canada and Canadian politics on his side.

Paul Reichmann did not like hostile takeovers, and he liked his targets to be standing still, so for him Gulf Canada seemed perfect. The company, which would rather be taken over by almost anybody than rolled in with former rival Chevron Canada, provided the Reichmanns and their advisers with all the data they needed. Gulf had a sophisticated computer model through which it could run projections of what various petroleum price levels, tax changes, and other variables meant in terms of the company's future cash flow and value.

As usual, all final decisions were made by Paul, but a number of advisers were crucial over the long and complex negotiations of the following year. Within O&Y, apart from Paul and Albert, much of the load was carried by Gil Newman, the bulky, bespectacled former chartered accountant who was both the Reichmanns' chief number-cruncher and corporate tough guy. Also, in November 1984, Reichmann hired David Brown, the investment dealer from Burns Fry who had done much business for the Reichmanns over the years, including the Abitibi purchase.

Among the Reichmanns' outside advisers were Howard Blauvelt, the former chairman of U.S. oil company Conoco, which had now been acquired by chemical giant Du Pont, and Garfield "Gar" Emerson of the Toronto law firm of Davies, Ward & Beck.

Deeply involved too, although their presence was less obvious, were several of the financial hit men from Gordon Capital, including Jimmy Connacher, Bob Fung, and Neil Baker. Connacher and Fung had for several years been working on the potential sale of Gulf Canada.

The Chevron side was represented by Salomon Brothers and Wood Gundy. Salomon's Ron Freeman already knew the Reichmanns from earlier discussions about Gulf Canada, and from Salomon's huge real estate financings for the brothers. Ted Medland, the white-haired head of Toronto's Wood Gundy, was also well acquainted with the Reichmanns since he was on the board of Abitibi.

Paul Reichmann's fundamental concern when looking at the Gulf Canada acquisition was the same as when he considered a real estate development: how could he minimize the cost and maximize the value of the investment?

Howard Blauvelt told him that he should certainly steer clear of Gulf's refining and marketing activities. These, like all such facilities, had suffered from overcapacity and offered a low return. When considering how to dispose of them, Paul Reichmann's immediate solution was to sell them to the Canadian state oil company, Petro-Canada. His advisers thought that this might be very difficult, given the arrival in power in September 1984 of a new Tory federal government that had no love for Petro-Canada and presumably little desire to see it expand. Nevertheless, Paul Reichmann felt that a deal could be worked out. Another key government-related part of his strategy was to take advantage of a tax loophole worth almost Can$600 million.

Then there was the role of Abitibi-Price. Since Reichmann had bought the newsprint giant in 1981, he had toyed with the idea of using it to expand into oil and gas. Now, instead of having Abitibi buy Gulf, as he had originally planned, he would have Gulf buy Abitibi. Then he would use the funds to help pay for Gulf. It was a classic example of both having and eating one's corporate cake. Not all his advisers thought that it was a good idea, and Abitibi's management was less than enthusiastic, but that was what

Paul Reichmann wanted, and so that was what he got. The final part of Reichmann's strategy was to have Gulf buy out its own minority shareholders, thus saving the Reichmanns the expense of doing so.

The components of this plan, which were modified in the course of negotiations, had to be carefully orchestrated. But they were a good deal more than merely complex, they were also highly controversial. Paul Reichmann's plan called for the use of a great deal of other people's money, much of it funneled from the taxpayer. That inevitably caused problems both with and for the Tory government. The Reichmanns' takeover of Gulf Canada would, in the end, prove a particularly telling example of the destructive role of politics in Canadian business.

11

Paul and Bill Do the Bump

BILL HOPPER, THE PUDGY, EBULLIENT, AND MACHIAVELLIAN chairman of state-owned Petro-Canada, had long lusted after Gulf Canada, but he had never been able to muster political support from the previously Liberal government. It seemed less than likely that he would receive it from the new Tory government, which had been badly burned in a bungled attempt to disband Petro-Canada in 1979.

The Tories returned to power in 1984 determined to take a firm line with their old nemesis, but they were almost immediately faced with a dilemma. If they wanted to Canadianize Gulf, the only candidate was Paul Reichmann, and Paul Reichmann told them that part of the price was "participation" by Petro-Canada. The other multinationals might be prepared to look at acquiring Gulf's downstream assets, but Reichmann realized they were unlikely to pay as much as Petrocan, where empire-building had always taken precedence over value-for-money.

Tory cabinet members like Pat Carney, the new minister of energy, mines and resources, who was suspected of being a closet economic nationalist, were particularly keen for the Reichmann acquisition. Taking an active role in encouraging this largest of all Canadianizations would deflect any suggestion that the Tories, although they had dismantled the NEP, disagreed with its nationalist principles.

Toward the end of April, Paul Reichmann went to Bill Hopper's Ottawa office and asked if Petro-Canada would be interested in taking Gulf Canada's downstream off his hands. Hopper declared that he was primarily interested in Gulf Canada's refining and marketing operations west of Ontario, where Petrocan had a relatively small share of the market. Pat Carney, however, wanted Hopper to take more, not for commercial, but for political reasons. There was a concern among the Tories that Petro-Canada would be perceived as having been merely used by the Reichmanns to pick up the choice upstream assets of the Gulf. After months of hard bargaining, Petrocan finally settled on a package consisting of all Gulf Canada's downstream. The cost was a whopping Can$1.8 billion.

Chevron had, in the meantime, accepted the Reichmanns' offer of $3 billion for its 60.2 percent of Gulf Canada. However, the offer was conditional, not on Petro-Canada's involvement, but on tax rulings from the federal government. Those tax rulings were part of the price the people of Canada had to pay for Gulf's Canadianization.

For every new budget, governments tinker with the tax system in an attempt to encourage or discourage some form of economic or social activity, or in pursuit of "fairness," or merely to correct the faults of previous tinkerings. The result is a jungle of fiscal complexity through which sharp-eyed tax lawyers and investment advisers prowl.

The Reichmanns knew all about the tax angles. Property development financings were always structured with an eye to the tax system. One of Paul Reichmann's corporate imperatives was to avoid taxes. With an eye to the Gulf acquisition, the tax jungle had been thoroughly charted and an enormous loophole had been found. Nicknamed "The Little Egypt Bump," after a famous Chicago striptease artist of the 1890s, it was based on the "partnership step-up" rules put on the law books in 1971 to eliminate double taxation on the liquidation of business partnerships. However, astute lawyers had discovered how the law could be used simply to avoid taxes. Where there was a large difference between a company's "book value" and the value of its assets in the market, the value of the bump became potentially very large. This was the case with most oil companies.

When Paul Reichmann first went to see Bill Hopper to discuss

Petrocan's role in the Gulf takeover in April 1985, he brought up the bump because he knew that Hopper had experience of the fiscal sidestep. Petrocan had used it in the controversial takeover of Petrofina Canada in 1981. The role of the deputy minister of finance Mickey Cohen in either bringing this loophole to the attention of Paul Reichmann, or in discussing it with him, would later cause considerable controversy when Cohen went to work for the Reichmanns.

When O&Y's tax lawyers turned up in Ottawa to strut their stuff before Revenue Canada, the Revenue Canada audience did not applaud. In fact they booed. In their view, the Reichmanns had simply come to snatch the public purse. Then political problems erupted.

When the Tory caucus discovered the nature and extent of Petrocan's proposed involvement, they were outraged. This storm broke over the prime minister's office just after the order pemitting Petrocan's huge expenditure had been passed by the Cabinet. Prime Minister Brian Mulroney gave the order to pull the plug. Hopper was told to call Paul Reichmann and tell him Petrocan was out of the deal.

A couple of days later, after flying to Washington to meet with Chevron's chairman George Keller and explain what had happened, Paul Reichmann apparently walked away from the deal, forfeiting a U.S.$25 million deposit he had put on the table. The deal had apparently foundered on the shoals of politics and the prime minister's perfidy. But it wasn't quite that simple. In fact, it looked as if Reichmann had seen it coming all the time and was quite prepared for it. Pulling the plug turned out to be less a betrayal than a golden opportunity to negotiate a better deal.

Reichmann had been growing increasingly concerned about the weakening of world oil prices in the course of 1985. He had spoken many times with Bill Hopper about his concerns. But Reichmann was in any case not entirely happy with the original deal with Petrocan. He had never been enthusiastic about selling any of Gulf's upstream, and he wanted to gain further concessions.

The story of Mulroney's vacillations was rapidly leaked to the press, which reported that the duplicitous prime minister had counted on Paul Reichmann being far too much of a gentleman to "blow the whistle." It apparently never occurred to the press to ask themselves, if Paul Reichmann was being so reticent, how they were getting the stories. In fact, Reichmann's advisers had no compunction about blowing whistles. They cleverly worked the press to paint Mulroney's behavior in its worst light. "Deep throats" close to the Reichmanns suggested to journalists that they might like to call former Liberal cabinet minister Jean Chrétien to get his comments on the issue. Chrétien poured scorn on Brian Mulroney. He neglected to mention, however, that during the Gulf deal he had been working as a consultant for Gordon Capital.

There was more controversy when it was announced that Mickey Cohen was joining Olympia & York, having been invited to do so by the Reichmanns the previous February. The controversy arose because Cohen had been deputy minister of finance during the whole period that the negotiations were going on over the Little Egypt Bump.

Cohen, a lawyer by training, had represented the Reichmanns before he moved to Ottawa in 1970. He had emerged as a powerful force in the nation's capital. Following the first OPEC crisis, he had been at the center of the Liberals' energy policy formulation and had rapidly moved to the heart of Pierre Trudeau's technocratic machine. He had held three deputy ministerships, the highest bureaucratic level in any department. The most controversial of these had been his stint as deputy minister of energy during the formulation of the National Energy Program. Somehow, however, Cohen had managed to sidestep any responsibility for that disastrous policy and had moved on to be deputy minister of finance. In the words of one senior oil executive, "Mickey Cohen makes Houdini look like a piker."

Now, some more subtle sidestepping was required. Cohen explained to the press that he had had nothing whatsoever to do with the Little Egypt Bump. He said that as soon as Paul Reichmann had approached him, he had told both Brian Mulroney and his minister at Finance, Michael Wilson, of the offer. Cohen told the *Globe and Mail* that it was Industry Minister Sinc Stevens who first informed him that the Reichmanns were going to make a bid for Gulf Canada. "He started to talk to me about it," Cohen was reported as saying, "and I turned him off, went to Wilson and said, 'Look, I can't touch this deal,' and from that day forward I was out of it. . . . It was all kind of comical, because I kept saying to everybody in the place, 'Look, I'm busy' — it was right around the budget — 'I just haven't got the time, you guys look after this, leave me out of this.' "

Sinc Stevens said that he had no memory of talking to Cohen.

But given that Cohen did successfully stay away from the issue of Petro-Canada and the Little Egypt Bump, that still leaves another intriguing issue: Paul Reichmann obviously knew that he was going for one of the biggest tax breaks in Canadian history when he approached the deputy minister of finance to offer him a job.

For O&Y, a highly secretive company, the allegations about the Little Egypt Bump brought an unfamiliar and unwanted publicity. Suggestions of impropriety led to public refutation. "The tax rulings," declared a release from Gulf Canada, "which have not involved any special Government concessions, confirm the application of existing laws to the facts of the proposed transaction." Reichmann pointed out in another of his exclusive interviews with the *Globe and Mail* that allegations by opposition leader John Turner of a $1 billion giveaway figure were way off. The deal would save only $500 million in taxes over five years, "with another $50 to $90 million saving after that time."

Reichmann said that the Little Egypt Bump ruling — which he of course did not refer to by that name — "is simply an interpretation of law. It is nothing given." Asked about concessions he had been seeking from the government, Paul Reichmann decided that that point did not need clarification: "I think I'll stay away from the details of those discussions because they'll only get me in hot water . . . [T]hese questions are irrelevant because they were rejected in the end." It was not clear what concessions Reichmann was referring to, or *could* have been referring to. He had already received about every concession imaginable.

The Gulf Canada purchase negotiations were like a three-ring circus, with Paul Reichmann as ringmaster. In one ring, tax lawyers and government officials snarled at each other over Petrocan's participation and the Little Egypt Bump. In the second ring, Chevron waited sedately, like an elephant, to receive its financial peanut. In the third ring was Gulf Canada perched like an expectant, attentive, and slightly nervous performing seal, waiting for Paul Reichmann to teach it new tricks.

In most straightforward takeovers, the acquisitor makes an offer for the target company, and the target's management and board have to decide whether to accept or reject it. If they reject it, they usually have to come up with an alternative, or a defensive strategy. The Gulf Canada situation was quite different. The company knew that, one way or another, it had to change hands. Paul Reichmann had two tricks in particular that he wanted his new acquisition to perform: the purchase from him of Abitibi-Price and the buyout of its own minority shareholders.

Within Gulf Canada, the realization that the company was being sold and split up, and that many employees would finish up with Petro-Canada, or with no jobs at all, inevitably created severe morale problems. Nevertheless, anything was at first considered better than being rolled in with Chevron Canada.

Keith McWalter, who had taken over as president of Gulf in April, found himself immersed in a baptism of fire. For most of 1985, he worked seven-day weeks at the head of a key management group that he described, with some irony, as the "Happy Gang." McWalter, who, like his predecessor, John Stoik, was a member of the Moose Jaw Mafia (he had been born in the city) was also, like his predecessor, somewhat stone-faced. However, he privately gave vent to his frustrations at being kept in the dark by the secretive Reichmanns. On one occasion he said of the brothers: "They're like flies. They land, shit, and take off again."

The Reichmanns' demands also put heavy pressure on Gulf's board. Insofar as the Little Egypt Bump had reduced Gulf's tax burden, the fiscal dance met little opposition from Gulf's director. There were also more general advantages in a buyout by a Canadian-owned company. Reichmann ownership would mean an extra Can$100 million of PIP grants. But the Gulf board was inevitably concerned about the Reichmanns' proposal to sell them Abitibi. The big issue was the price.

Alf Powis, chief executive of Brascan subsidiary Noranda and chairman of the committee of independent directors of Gulf Canada, was deputed to deal with the Reichmanns. Powis had plenty of his own problems at Noranda, which was saddled with a hefty debt load due to a number of expensive diversifications. He was grateful for the fact that the Reichmanns worked on Sundays. That was the only way he was able to fit the Abitibi negotiations in with his own corporate burdens. Powis found Paul Reichmann a tough negotiator.

Paul Reichmann produced an opinion that said that Abitibi was worth at least Can$26 a share. Powis, for his part, got a fairness opinion that put an upper value on the newsprint giant of Can$21.50. But he did not want to announce that opinion because then Reichmann would be justified in asking Can$21.50, which Powis thought was too high.

For Powis, another worrying aspect of the deal was that Abitibi's share price had risen sharply in the early months of 1985 while Gordon Capital had been aggressively buying the stock. Gordon was deeply involved in the Gulf takeover. It was clearly in the Reichmanns' interest for the Abitibi share price to be high, otherwise they would be accused of corporate rape. Gordon had started buying in February and the stock had moved, in the first quarter, from Can$11 to Can$19.

Powis was squeezed by Reichmann into paying Can$21 a share for 90 percent of Abitibi. Compared with Can$11, that looked very expensive. Compared with Can$19 it did not look too bad at all. Powis, with admirable candor, said, "I wasn't particularly proud of my negotiating prowess." However, he felt that he could justify the price in terms of the other financial "goodies" that Reichmann was bringing to the takeover party.

"The price that we ended up paying for Abitibi had to be viewed in the context of the overall transaction," said Powis, "because my personal view was that we were paying too much for it. But on the other hand, if Paul could realize a similar amount of money on the downstream, then it wasn't so bad. In my view, a reasonable price to pay for Abitibi would have been $17 or $18 a share. Paul wanted $26. We finally settled on $21 and I was able to say to the Gulf directors that we could justify that in terms of the context of the overall transaction, including the tax deal and the sale of the downstream."

Asked about the movement of the Abitibi share price as a result of Gordon's buying, Powis said in early 1986: "It bothered me too. I don't know anything about it. I can't comment on that. I guess all you can say is that the whole thing is vindicated by the fact that they are doing a very large share issue at $26." In March 1986, Abitibi issued a prospectus to raise Can$137.5 million through the issue of common shares and warrants at a price per common share and per half common share warrant of Can$27.50. Once again, the move was preceded by pronounced upward movement in the share price.

Although Powis maintained that the Reichmanns' package was fair from the Gulf shareholders' point of view, which was his main concern, his comments raise broader issues. Looked at another way, Gulf could afford to overpay for Abitibi (it cost them Can$1.2 billion versus the Can$560 million O&Y had paid for it) only because Petrocan was overpaying for most of Gulf's downstream, and because the Canadian taxpayer was subsidizing the deal through the Little Egypt Bump.

On August 2, 1985, O&Y signed the new deal with Chevron under which it would pay the American company Can$2.8 billion for its Gulf Canada shares. Gulf's purchase of 90 percent of Abitibi was also set in motion. On August 31, the Little Egypt Bump partnership was signed. On September 30, the sale to Petrocan of Gulf's Ontario and Western refining and marketing assets was made official and, effective January 1, 1986, a deal was concluded with British-controlled Ultramar for the remainder of Gulf's downstream assets. But that still left the question of the minority shareholders.

The Reichmanns had obtained an exemption from the Ontario Securities Commission from making a follow-up offer to Gulf's minority when they had made their first offer to Chevron. When the deal had cratered and been revived in July, the Reichmanns went back for another exemption. O&Y told the OSC that it would "use its reasonable efforts" to get Gulf to offer its minority shareholders a cash deal similar to that given to Chevron. This arrangement placed the burden of financing the other half of the Reichmanns' takeover on the takeover itself. The Reichmanns seemed to be treating Gulf as if it were already part of their private family fiefdom. There were no squawks from investment authorities.

Under a complex plan of arrangement revealed toward the end of 1985, Gulf's minority shareholders could opt either to take a cash and debenture deal, or switch their old Gulf shares for shares in a new Reichmann-controlled Gulf. The circular nature of the deal made it difficult to assess. The more shareholders who opted for new shares, the stronger would Gulf's balance sheet be. The more who opted for the cash and debenture alternative, the greater would be Gulf's debt burden.

The Reichmanns were hoping that shareholders would be persuaded to swap their old Gulf shares for shares in the new, reformulated Gulf. However, just as the plan was being formulated, the OPEC price began to collapse. As the world oil price weakened, it seemed that the cash and debenture offer was the more attractive option. As a result, the Reichmanns in December persuaded the Gulf board to "sweeten the pot" by adding a Can$5 preferred share for those who agreed to take a share in the new Gulf for a share in the old Gulf. This of course included the 60 percent of Gulf shares owned by O&Y, so the greatest beneficiaries of the preferred shares, which would further weaken Gulf's financial position, would be the Reichmanns.

At the meeting to ratify the plan of arrangement, in the concert hall of Toronto's Royal York Hotel on January 31, 1986, nobody questioned any part of the plan. The Reichmanns were conspicuously absent. The vote was, in any case, a formality, since all that was required for the plan to be approved was for the Reichmanns and 6 percent of the remaining shareholders to vote for it. Once that arrangement was ratified, shareholders had until 5 P.M. on Monday, February 3, to opt for the cash and debenture offer.

Gulf Canada's own directors were firmly convinced that the overwhelming majority of shareholders would opt for the cash and debentures. They even had a betting pool among themselves to guess how many shares would be left outstanding after the shareholders' options had been exercised. Most predicted that 80 percent or 90 percent would go for the cash. In the event, only 62 percent did. Says Powis, "We were amazed at how many people stayed in. Why didn't people tender? I don't know. Inertia? Capital gains? There were also a bunch of people out there saying, 'Well, we'll stay with the Reichmanns. They know how to make money. . . .' "

Given the oil price collapse, this amounted to a tremendous act of faith in the Reichmann reputation, which was still being burnished by a gushing press. In July 1985, the editor of a prominent Canadian business publication had written of the Gulf deal: "People who can pounce on bargains like this must be real tigers, one-dimensional workaholics with telephones extending from their ears. Somehow they have to be objectionable, right? Not so. The Reichmanns are the antithesis of Sammy Glick: quiet, courtly men who keep their own counsel and whose word is their bond. In an era when you can't trust your banker, they're the exception. Budding entrepreneurs should use them as role models, because sometimes, the biggest are the best."

In mid-January, an analyst was quoted in the *Globe and Mail*: "Investors will be looking at the outlook for Gulf, comparing it with other investments and asking themselves, 'Does Gulf have something the others don't? . . . Gulf's biggest edge is that it is owned by Olympia & York. . . . Hopefully, some of that profit-making ability will show up at Gulf.' "

An act of faith was also being strongly recommended by the

investment dealers. In the weeks before the deal, many brokers recommended shareholders to go for the share swap. This was hardly objective advice. One Bay Street observer said: "They paid every dealer on the street to do fairness opinions. Burns Fry, Merrill Lynch, and McLeod Young Weir were paid millions and I suspect that they were all on the phone that last week. The Reichmanns certainly wanted everybody to stay in. That's the way the street works and really the investors who stayed in should not complain of lack of disclosure." Most of those who stayed in were smaller shareholders who believed their brokers when they said: "Stay with the Reichmanns. They know how to make money."

The completion of the deal left the Reichmanns with 80 percent of the new, more heavily indebted Gulf. In the weeks following the plan of arrangement, the world price of oil dived further, hitting a low of less than U.S.$13 and forcing Gulf, and indeed all oil companies, to cut back drastically on planned expenditures.

For the Reichmanns, meanwhile, the financing of their own share of the Gulf takeover had not been completed. They had planned a Can$1 billion preference share issue — typically, the biggest in Canadian history — in order to finance most of the acquisition cost not covered by the sale of Abitibi to Gulf. Market conditions had forced that issue to be shelved.

Shortly after the minority deal had been completed, Alf Powis, who remained on the Gulf Canada board, said: "Sure, they've had to borrow from the banks for this deal, but I don't think they are in an uncomfortable position. The banks aren't uncomfortable. . . . But it is obviously a cash drain. Even when and if they did the preferred it would still be a cash drain. Whether debt or preferred, it's still a negative carry. Over time, they are counting that Gulf will be worth a lot more than they paid for it. . . . Gulf will survive at $12 oil but they won't be nearly as profitable. But if you have faith that owning oil and gas in the ground is a good thing, then it's a good deal."

Alf Powis didn't sound convinced.

To most knowledgeable observers, Gulf looked like a disaster.

"Can you imagine what price we'd get for Gulf now?" asked Chevron Canada's head, Gerry Henderson, in the first quarter of 1986. Still, many refused to believe that the Reichmanns' crystal ball had cracked. "Just remember the New York deal," they said. Some of them even imagined that the Gulf Canada deal was *like* the New York deal, that the Reichmanns had snapped up oil and gas assets at the bottom of the market. In fact, they had missed the bottom by a mile. During the year or so it took to pull the convoluted parts of the takeover together, the world oil price halved. After the deal, it dropped another third.

The reason the Reichmanns *weren't* in more trouble was the structuring of the deal. At one level, the Gulf takeover could be viewed as a strategic masterpiece, pulled off in the most difficult circumstances. But at another, it had been a game of tax smoke and market mirrors, an exercise in the art of corporate arm-twisting, political manipulation, and the exploitation of bad tax policy. The Canadian public paid as much toward the Reichmanns' takeover of Gulf Canada as the Reichmanns.

Their complex maneuverings also seemed somehow out of character, or at least out of the character they had so successfully nurtured. But the Gulf deal was not out of character at all. Those who had dealt with the Reichmanns knew they were the toughest negotiators around. In Manhattan, the real estate community told a story that, if you were negotiating with the Reichmanns and there were ten points of contention, then the brothers would stand tough on five and give on five. At the end of the day, you would feel pretty happy with your skills. But the next day the Reichmanns would be back to go over the five points that you had won, and they would perhaps let you have two and a half, but they would stand firm on the other two and a half. And you'd begin to wonder. And then the next day, the Reichmanns would be back again. . . .

They had always squeezed every last drop out of negotiations and played their cards close to their chest, keeping those they dealt with in the dark as much as possible. They showed no particular sensitivity toward shareholders. Fellow shareholders were a relatively new phenomenon for them. Abitibi's minority had been largely dormant since the Reichmanns had acquired control of the company. The inevitable redundancies in personnel when Gulf Canada's downstream operations were sold — including the closing of its Montreal refinery — appeared to be of little concern to them.

Paul Reichmann now seemed almost obsessed with corporate growth, despite staunch denials that such was any part of his motivation. Also, perhaps he *was* like a great corporate automaton. He was relentless and he was brilliant, but he had blind spots. Soon those blind spots would become glaringly apparent.

It seemed reasonable that, given what had happened to oil prices, a period of retrenchment might now be appropriate for Olympia & York. After all, they had executed the biggest takeover in Canadian history in the most complex and trying of circumstances. However, one of the Reichmanns' rationales for the Canadianization of Gulf was that it would enable Gulf to be acquisitive, and Paul Reichmann was not going to let a little thing like the collapse of world oil prices stop him. In fact, he could not afford to stop. The momentum had to be kept up.

Otherwise, like the shark, O&Y might sink.

12

The Reichmanns Are Coming!

BUD DOWNING, THE CHIEF EXECUTIVE OF TORONTO-BASED conglomerate Hiram Walker Resources, was on holiday at Rancho Santa Fe in Southern California when he was jolted awake just after 5 A.M. on the morning of Wednesday, March 19, 1986, by a call from his secretary in Toronto. She told him that Albert Reichmann had just called and asked Downing to return his call immediately. Downing was puzzled. He had first met Albert Reichmann three years before, in connection with the Reichmanns' 10 percent stake in HWR. He liked Albert. But what could Albert want? There had been concern for some years about the Reichmanns' intentions with regard to Hiram Walker, but Downing had spoken recently to Albert, and Albert had told him that O&Y might take its stake to 20 percent, but would let him know before doing so.

Downing dialed Reichmann's Toronto number. Albert Reichmann came on the line and asked Downing to wait while he put Paul on the extension. Then he told Downing that Gulf Canada would, that morning, be making a "floor bid" of Can$32 a share for 38 percent of Hiram Walker's shares. Downing knew that such a bid gave Hiram Walker a limited time to respond. He said the bid put a lot of pressure on Hiram Walker. Paul Reichmann gave a nervous laugh and said: "That's why we're doing it."

Albert said that he had spoken to Hiram Walker directors Bill Wilder and Allen Lambert and that they had said they thought the Reichmanns' offer was reasonable (Lambert subsequently strongly denied this). He also said they had spoken to Dick Haskayne, chief executive of Hiram Walker subsidiary Home

Oil. Albert said they wanted the offer to be friendly; they liked the management of Hiram Walker, in particular that of Home Oil.

Downing said he could not comment on fairness until he had studied the offer, but he said that if it was to be a friendly affair, then he would as soon it was Olympia & York as anybody else. He pointed out that no management liked to be taken over, but his main concern and responsibility was to maximize the value of any offer to his shareholders. Entrenchment of himself or his management would not be a consideration.

Albert thanked him and hung up. Bud Downing started making calls. Dick Haskayne called from Calgary and offered to send Home's corporate jet to take Downing back to Toronto. Downing said he could make it back on Air Canada.

The Reichmanns' bid for Hiram Walker would open a corporate Pandora's box whose whirlwinds were felt around the globe. What started as an issue of power and pride in Canada's ruling business elite turned into a worldwide business war with few precedents. In Canada, deep and bitter rifts were created between companies that had hitherto been allies. Internationally, the reverberations were felt in stock markets from Toronto to Melbourne, from New York to London.

At the local Canadian level, Bud Downing and the old guard would, in the end, go down, but they would not go without a fight. They were carried off the field clad in the armor of righteousness, because they could unequivocally claim that they had done their duty toward their shareholders. They would also expose a relentless and almost ruthless side of Paul Reichmann. Part of the reason for that at times naked aggression was that Paul Reichmann believed that Hiram Walker had not given him the respect he deserved.

Paul Reichmann had started buying Hiram Walker stock five years before, in the spring of 1981. Since Hiram Walker's head office was in First Canadian Place, Bill Wilder, whose Consumers' Gas had recently been merged with Hiram Walker, often ran into the Reichmanns. In the spring of 1981, he received a call from Paul Reichmann saying that he wanted to come for "a brief chat."

Reichmann did not specify his purpose, but Wilder knew what he wanted to talk about. As Reichmann walked into his office, Wilder thought he would try to put the developer at ease with a touch of humor. "Have you come to collect the rent, Mr. Reichmann?" he asked.

Reichmann did not laugh. "No," he said, "I checked before I came and it's fully paid." It was not at all clear whether he was joking.

Reichmann outlined his intentions of taking a "friendly" minority stake in Hiram Walker. After he had left, Wilder told Hiram Walker's chairman, Clifford Hatch, Sr., about the conversation. Flippantly, Wilder said to Hatch: "You'd better dust off your homburg." Clifford Hatch did not laugh either. An investment analyst would later ask Hatch what he thought of the Reichmanns' move. Hatch just could not bring himself to say what he should have said: that he was delighted to have attracted the confidence of such a worthy investor. He just snapped back, "What would you have me think?"

By the fall of 1981, Paul Reichmann had taken O&Y's stake in Hiram Walker up to 10 percent. Reichmann believed that a holding of that magnitude should entitle the family to representation on the board, but Paul Reichmann did not want to be seen to be asking for a seat, and he certainly did not want to be seen being turned down. But no offer was immediately forthcoming. Also, when he had approached Hiram Walker through Bill Wilder with a proposal to stage a joint assault on Gulf Canada that same year, he had been rebuffed. Those perceived slights made Paul Reichmann angry. Paul Reichmann was not a man to anger easily. Or to forget. When he and Albert were finally invited onto the Hiram Walker board in 1985, they turned the seats down. By then, Paul Reichmann had determined that he was justified in carrying out a form of corporate action in which he had claimed he would never become involved: a hostile takeover.

Hiram Walker was a conglomerate with its roots and heart in the distilled spirits industry. Hiram Walker–Gooderham & Worts (HW-GW), based in Windsor, Ontario, across the river from Detroit, was a company with a long and intriguing history. When the Reichmanns made their bid for its corporate parent, Hiram Walker Resources, HW-GW's chief executive, Clifford Hatch, Jr., was the third Hatch to occupy that post. His grandfather, Harry Hatch, a tough Canadian entrepreneur, had made a fortune selling liquor to American bootleggers in partnership with his brother Herb during Prohibition. They had marshalled a fleet of marine rumrunners that became known as "Hatch's Navy." Harry had parlayed those essentially clandestine skills — which were nevertheless widely admired, and at least tacitly supported by the Canadian government — into a legitimate business empire, gaining control first of Toronto-based distiller Gooderham & Worts in 1923, and then, in 1926, amalgamating it with the larger Hiram Walker to form Hiram Walker–Gooderham & Worts.

Hiram Walker produced Canadian Club whisky, one of the world's first great brands. The company's eponymous founder, an American entrepreneur and philanthropist, had moved his fledgling distilling operation across the river from Detroit partly because of the threats from a powerful temperance movement in Michigan. He created Walkerville — then east of, now part of, Windsor — as a model community and constructed a magnificent headquarters, based on a sixteenth-century Renaissance villa, on the Detroit River. The building was — and remains — a showpiece of polished brass and delicately carved and sculpted classical references. In the 1920s, the refinement of the building stood in marked contrast to the skullduggery surrounding its business.

During Prohibition, the "Windsor-Detroit Funnel" became one of the major transshipment points for illicit liquor imports into the United States. Much of the highest quality liquor was produced by Hiram Walker. Canadian governments at every level either turned a blind eye to, or blatantly took advantage of, the illicit U.S. market. As long as liquor bought in Canada for export had a B-13 customs document with a non-U.S. destination stamped on it, that was fine with Canadian authorities. Elliot Ness of "Untouchables" fame called the B-13 form "The Canadian Print Job."

Hiram Walker executives could sit in their wood-paneled, bay-windowed offices, each with its replica of a palatial Italian marble fireplace, and watch boats large and small, with export papers for Cuba or some other unlikely destination, head off for some secret location across the Detroit River. In winter, liquor-laden jalopies would crawl across the frozen river like ants. Overhead, Al Capone's fleet of converted bombers made their frequent hooch runs.

Harry Hatch demonstrated even greater business genius after Prohibition. Like Sam Bronfman, his counterpart at the other great Canadian liquor company with its roots in Prohibition, Seagram, Hatch had high-quality, aged stock to release onto the parched U.S. market. He had also shrewdly acquired the agency rights for many overseas wine and spirit brands. He built the world's largest distillery in Peoria, Illinois. He developed strong links with the Scotch whisky industry, with whose top-hat-and-tails aristocracy he shared a love of horse racing. When the giant Distillers Company, lord of the Scotch business, threatened in the late 1930s to cut off supplies of grain whisky which HW-GW used in the production of its Ballantines brand, Hatch, to Distillers' chagrin, built a replica of Peoria at Dumbarton to manufacture his own whisky. During the Second World War, he visited Argentina and started distilling there. He also acquired Argentinian thoroughbreds like Siete Colores and Kandahar, whose bloodlines ran through some of the finest racing stock in North America.

Harry Hatch died in 1946, but his son, Clifford, Sr., was by then working his way up the company. Cliff, Sr., having worked first for his father's private wine company, T.G. Bright, had joined Hiram Walker in 1937, when he was twenty-one. During the war years, he became a naval commander, hunting U-boats in the North Atlantic. Afterwards, he returned to Walkerville and rose through the ranks until he became president in 1964, the year the company acquired the Courvoisier and Kahlúa brands.

Cliff Hatch's philosophy was to build a core of quality brands — the great assets of the liquor business. Under him, Hiram

Walker become an even more international company. Its products were marketed all over the world, although its primary emphasis remained North America.

The company became an increasingly important institution to the growing town of Windsor. The Hatches became Windsor's first family. Cliff Hatch, Sr., established himself as a pillar of the community. A man of modest tastes and frugal habits, he was universally respected and admired, not merely within Hiram Walker but within the whole industry. His attitude was that there was room for everybody, and that although he and his competitors might fight in the market, that did not mean they could not sit down and have a few laughs over a long lunch or dinner. But he had the good fortune to preside in times when such attitudes were possible. His years as head of Hiram Walker–Gooderham & Worts were the fat years for distilled spirits. Fueled by the continuing postwar industrial boom, markets were growing everywhere.

As he approached retirement at the end of the 1970s, a dramatic change was coming over the liquor market. Liquor was an easy tax target for cash-strapped governments; there was mounting concern about drinking and driving; and fitness was in. Taxes, neo-Prohibitionism, and the Spritzer Generation suddenly threatened the hard stuff with hard times.

Hiram Walker–Gooderham & Worts was still a very rich and attractive company, with hefty profit margins and little debt. But it was also a vulnerable company. Most people in Walkerville assumed that the Hatch family owned at least a controlling block of the company's stock. But in fact the Hatch family had never held more than 10 percent of the company, and by the late 1970s that share had dwindled to less than 2 percent. It was seen as the Hatches' company, but it was theirs only in terms of managerial responsibility, not ownership. Over at Seagram, by contrast, the families of Sam Bronfman's sons, Charles and Edgar, still held the commanding chunk of stock.

Investment dealers had begun to accumulate HW–GW stock and peddle the company as a potential "cash cow." Rumors began to spread that — horror of horrors — archrival Seagram might be planning an assault. Hatch was persuaded that the company should beat potential acquisitors to the punch. If HW-GW was a cash cow, it should milk itself. In 1979, Hatch began a strategy of defensive diversification. HW-GW merged with Toronto-based gas utility and oil explorer, Consumers' Gas Company. The amalgamated company became Hiram Walker Resources. The business rationale for the merger was that spirits would generate the cash and petroleum would provide the exciting opportunities. The first exciting opportunity was the purchase of Denver-based Davis Oil and Gas. It proved to be an opportunity to take a bath. In 1982, Hiram Walker Resources suffered a Can$177 million after-tax write-off on the deal.

Cliff Hatch, Sr., had become the first chairman of Hiram Walker Resources and had retired, as planned, in April 1981. When Davis hit the fan, Hatch was persuaded that he had to return. A little over two years later, Hatch retired for good, although he remained on the HWR board. His place at HWR was taken by the man who had succeeded him as head of Hiram Walker–Gooderham & Worts, Bud Downing, who was also revered in Walkerville. Downing's place in Walkerville was in turn taken by Cliff Hatch, Sr.'s son, Cliff Hatch, Jr.

In 1983, Hiram Walker, still concerned about its corporate vulnerability, entered into negotiations with another Toronto-based company, Interprovincial Pipe Line Limited (IPL), about a defensive share swap. IPL, as it happened, also had its offices in First Canadian Place.

Interprovincial was Canada's largest oil pipeline company, a chip off the old corporate block of its founder, Imperial Oil, the nation's highest-profile petroleum concern. IPL's 2,300-mile system was run by engineers who took pride in their level heads and their technical expertise. Interprovincial was a big, solid company, but, like Hiram Walker, it believed it had reached a level of maturity where it needed to diversify to grow. Hiram Walker and Interprovincial negotiated a share swap under which HWR would wind up with 34 percent of Interprovincial, and Interprovincial would hold 15.7 percent of HWR. Imperial would still hold 22 percent of Interprovincial.

The relationship between Hiram Walker and Interprovincial produced few benefits for either party. Meanwhile, the conglomerate structure that had been built around HW-GW via the merger with Consumers' Gas and the share swap with Interprovincial — far from protecting Hiram Walker Resources — in fact increased its attractiveness for acquisitors like the Reichmanns. The stock market tended to discount conglomerates, which had fallen from corporate fashion, giving them a value less than the sum of their parts. This made them attractive to acquire and dismantle. The absence of a controlling shareholder remained a critical vulnerability. Many believed it was just a matter of time before the Reichmanns made their move. The Reichmanns did not believe they were facing much in the way of opposition.

Bud Downing was a chemical engineer by training. He had spent his whole career with Hiram Walker's liquor business. He was the most solid of solid citizens, a pillar of both the corporate and local communities. Born in Mount Elgin, Ontario, he had interrupted his studies at the University of Toronto to serve with the Canadian Navy in World War II. Then he had returned to work his way through the management of HW-GW's worldwide liquor operations. Downing was not as financially sophisticated as Paul Reichmann, but his strength in the coming battle would be the corporate credo he had already outlined to Albert Reichmann: his concern was with getting the best price for his shareholders. It is uncertain if the Reichmanns appreciated the depth of that conviction. They were certainly surprised at the strategy to which the conviction would lead.

News of the Reichmanns' assault did not come as a complete surprise to Downing. He had been receiving reports for six months that the Reichmanns were talking to the Seagram Bronfmans. Word had also come via both Interprovincial and Imperial that the Reichmanns were planning a takeover. In February 1986, Gordon Capital's Jimmy Connacher, who had fallen out with the brothers, had told Imperial that the Reichmanns were coming. Bob Heule, Interprovincial's affable, slow-talking chairman, had passed on the information to Bud Downing, but Downing had been skeptical. The ink was barely dry on the Gulf Canada acquisition. The Reichmanns hardly seemed likely to go for another acquisition so quickly.

Nevertheless, a concerned Heule asked Downing, whom he greatly respected, if he thought he should approach Paul Reichmann to sound him out on his intentions. Downing said that was up to him, but he did not think it was a good idea. Downing also had a sneaking suspicion that Heule might have an eye on acquiring Hiram Walker itself.

Heule had quietly gone to see Paul Reichmann and tentatively suggested that they might act together to preserve the status quo at HWR. Interprovincial, as the largest shareholder in Hiram Walker, would accumulate no further shares as long as O&Y, as the second-largest shareholder, made a similar commitment. Heule wanted a standstill agreement. But Paul Reichmann had no desire to be part of a convoy at which everybody moved at the pace of the slowest thinker. Reichmann told Heule he would have to think about it.

Heule had indeed considered bidding for HWR himself, but his main concern now was that if the Reichmanns staged a successful assault on Hiram Walker, IPL might be left twisting in the wind, holding a minority stake. There was very little he could do but wait for the other shoe to drop.

Hiram Walker was another very big company. Its value was not far short of that of Gulf. By drawing a bead on it, Paul Reichmann was attempting what perhaps no private businessman had ever attempted before in global corporate history: to seize control of corporate assets worth close to Can$10 billion in less than a year. Gulf Canada ranked tenth by sales in the 1986 Financial Post 500 listing of the largest Canadian industrial companies. Hiram Walker ranked twenty-third. Combined, they would leap to fifth place, behind only General Motors of Canada, Canadian Pacific, Ford Motor Company of Canada, and Bell Canada Enterprises.

Hiram Walker's original attraction for the Reichmanns was

felt to lie in its resource assets, primarily Home Oil, a company with a long history in Alberta, and which had been acquired by Consumers before the Hiram Walker merger. But as the price of oil continued to drop in the early months of 1986, Home became a less desirable prize. Emphasis switched to the liquor business.

If the Reichmanns knew very little about oil and gas, they knew even less about liquor. That's why the Reichmanns had been talking to the Seagram Bronfmans in New York. The liquor business, HW-GW, was the heart of Hiram Walker. Liquor had contributed the largest element — just over 40 percent — of Hiram Walker's Can$665 million operating profit on sales of Can$3.8 billion in 1985. HW-GW's flagship product was still Canadian Club, but it also produced Ballantine's Scotch, Kahlúa, Tia Maria, Drambuie, and Courvoisier. As well as three major Canadian plants, it controlled both Corby and Meagher's distilleries in Canada and had plants from Mexico City to Dumbarton. Paul Reichmann initially appeared to have little idea what it was worth. But he had decided it would be his.

Astonishingly, given the complexity of the Gulf deal, O&Y had been looking at acquiring Hiram Walker throughout the Gulf takeover. Late in 1985, Paul Reichmann had "dusted off" the Walker files and decided to go for Hiram Walker. The instrument of acquisition would be Gulf.

Before its acquisition by the Reichmanns, there was about as much chance of Gulf Canada going after Hiram Walker as there was of John Stoik, Gulf's heavy-set former president and chief executive, flying around Gulf's downtown Toronto boardroom. Gulf Canada had long been restricted by its foreign ownership, but its management had never been renowned for qualities of lateral thinking. A Gulf under Reichmann control was a different matter. Gulf's uneasy and somewhat bewildered management, led by Stoik's successor Keith McWalter, suddenly felt less like reluctant actors under an unwelcome limelight than puppets with a strange — and unusually active — new set of hands suddenly working the strings. They were in the schizophrenic position of not knowing what they would do next.

The Reichmanns had always kept information and decisions within the smallest possible group, the main member of which had for a long time been Gil Newman, their roly-poly number-cruncher cum hard-nosed negotiator. However, a new member had been added to the group in October 1985, when the Reichmanns appointed former finance deputy minister Mickey Cohen head of Olympia & York Enterprises, the holding company for the Reichmanns' public interests. This inevitably created tensions.

Newman was absolutely devoted to the Reichmanns and was the embodiment of their hard-bargaining approach. "I'm a bastard," he once told a colleague, not without a little satisfaction. But now he saw his position as the number-one nonfamily henchman threatened. He had been disturbed when David Brown had been brought in from Burns Fry in 1984. But Brown had grown tired of being kept in the dark and left.

Issues of personal ego, and office politics, seemed to be either beyond the Reichmanns' comprehension or of no concern to them. Newman was obsessive about his access to Paul Reichmann. He had given his secretary instructions to inform him about visitors to his master's office, and when Mickey Cohen turned up for one of his first sessions with Paul Reichmann, Newman was hot on his heels. Cohen coolly told him he was not expected at the meeting, and the old retainer reportedly left in confusion. To complicate matters further, without consulting Cohen, Paul Reichmann appointed Newman to be Cohen's number-two man at O&Y Enterprises. Reichmann gave no indication of what their working relationship was to be. To Cohen, a man well versed in the nuances of power, Paul Reichmann's style and O&Y's organization, or rather lack of it, came as a profound shock. In Ottawa, he could assemble squadrons of economists and lawyers with a phone call. Moreover, financial decisions in Ottawa were made with the money of far-distant taxpayers. On the thirty-second floor of First Canadian Place, where it had taken several months for Cohen even to be allocated an office, there were no squadrons of high-priced staff. Moreover, those on whose behalf financial decisions were being made were down the hall.

Since Gulf was to bid for Hiram Walker, it seemed only appropriate, in the interests of etiquette as well as obeisance to Gulf's minority shareholders, to let Gulf know what was going on. Gulf's surprised top management were informed of their next move two days before the bid, on March 17. There was some concern that Gulf's outside directors might oppose the bid, since it would increase Gulf's already hefty debt burden. Not all the outside board members were present. Perhaps the most prominent, Alf Powis, was on a cruise ship off the coast of Uruguay, where Paul reached him to inform him of the proposed bid. However, neither Powis nor any of the other outside directors raised serious objections. Paul and Albert were eager to reassure the Gulf board that O&Y's financial strength would be behind the bid — even though they did not reveal the exact magnitude of that strength. Nevertheless, it was Gulf's corporate neck that was on the line.

The Reichmanns' rationale turned arguments about the weakness of the oil business on their head. Depressed oil markets meant that Gulf would not be spending so much money on exploration, so it should be directing its cash flow and its borrowing power elsewhere. Gulf was being told that because it was crippled, it had to move faster. On March 19, it broke into a trot.

When the Reichmanns had been calling Hiram Walker's directors on the morning of March 19, one of the questions they asked was what they thought the reaction of Interprovincial and Imperial Oil would be. At least one of the directors said that he thought they would be pretty upset. The men up at Imperial's headquarters on St. Clair Avenue would inevitably regard Gulf-Reichmann control as a challenge.

To get a more direct view of Interprovincial's attitude on March 19, Paul Reichmann called Bob Heule and said he would like to drop by. Heule had not heard the news. He wondered if this was the long-awaited response to his suggestion for a standstill agreement. Reichmann took the elevator up to IPL's corporate suite and was shown into Heule's office. He sat down and handed Bob Heule O&Y's press release. They were, he explained, going for control of Walker. Although Heule had been told the bid was coming, Reichmann's revelation was still a shock.

Reichmann wanted to size up Heule's reaction because he knew that IPL's 17 percent stake in Hiram Walker could be crucial. Reichmann knew that Interprovincial's main interest in HWR was Home Oil and realized that the oil and gas subsidiary could be used as a lever to gain Interprovincial's cooperation. He knew that he had another lever, which he had already applied simply by making a bid for less than all Hiram Walker's shares: IPL's fear of an impotent minority position in HWR. He told Heule that he would like his support, that he was aware of Interprovincial's interests, and that if Interprovincial gave its support, then he would try and accommodate those interests.

The details of the offer were announced to the Montreal and Toronto stock exchanges that morning and trading in Hiram Walker shares was temporarily suspended. Gulf's offer was Can$32 a share for 26 million Hiram Walker common shares and Can$28.62 for all the first series of the class D convertible preferreds. The offer, worth Can$1.2 billion, would be made through the Toronto and Montreal stock exchanges on April 4. When trading in Hiram Walker shares resumed around noon, they jumped three dollars to Can$31, while the class D preferred closed at Can$28.36, up $2.50. Gulf Canada dropped 25 cents to Can$16.62.

One newspaper reporter asked Paul Reichmann how he felt about working hard and long on such deals. Reichmann responded simply, "It's fun." But this particular deal would not prove fun for long. The Gulf acquisition had been a "friendly" affair. For Gulf Canada, no other attitude had been possible. Hiram Walker would turn out to be very different.

13

Saturday Night Specials and White Knights

AS SOON AS BUD DOWNING HAD PUT DOWN THE PHONE TO Albert Reichmann in California on March 19, his mind had to switch into a quite unaccustomed mode: combat. Downing had been caught both figuratively and literally with his pants down. Now he had to gird his loins for battle. He called the Toronto office and told Archibald McCallum, Hiram Walker Resources' chief financial officer, to start marshaling the troops for battle. Downing also called Hiram Walker's Toronto legal firm, McCarthy & McCarthy. Peter Beattie, the senior partner on the Hiram Walker account, was also on holiday, in Barbados, and it took him a couple of days to get back. Two other McCarthy lawyers who worked on Walker, Gary Girvan and Bob Forbes, soon gathered up their briefcases and hustled across King Street from their offices in the Toronto-Dominion Bank Tower to Hiram Walker's sixth-floor boardroom to begin the defensive brainstorming. The other key legal counsel called was George "Chip" Reid, an ace lawyer from the Washington, D.C., firm of Covington & Burling, which had represented Hiram Walker–Gooderham & Worts for thirty years.

Chief financial officer McCallum, meanwhile, called Walker's financial advisers at Toronto's Dominion Securities Pitfield (DSP) and New York's Morgan Guaranty Trust Co. Two of the investment firms' leading corporate strategists, Jimmy Pitblado for DSP and Roberto Mendoza for Morgan, took command.

Pitblado had a reputation for being tough and smart. He also had a sense of humor. The previous year he had helped mastermind the sale of more than Can$100 million of equity in the financially crippled Dome Petroleum. During the negotiations over the issue, Dome's chairman, Howard Macdonald, himself renowned for his wry wit, had spotted a fast-food truck that used to park near DSP's Commerce Court West offices. The truck bore the legend "Jimmy's Fine Foods on Wheels." Macdonald ribbed Pitblado about running the business on the side. At the closing of Dome's share issue in May 1985, Pitblado presented Macdonald with a framed photograph of himself standing with his foot on the fender of the truck. Beneath the picture was a little plaque with the words "It's Jimmy's for a Quick Meal and a Good Deal." Now Pitblado had to come up with not just a good deal for his clients at Hiram Walker Resources, he had to come up with a *better* deal. Morgan's Mendoza, too, was a lot more than just an éminence grise. A Cuban exile, he liked to get up and take on the opposition mano a mano.

By the time Downing returned from California later that day, the group had had its first meeting. HWR's management wanted to know how much time they had and what their best strategy would be. They asked the lawyers if they had to respond immediately, whether a press release should be issued and if so what it should say, and whether it would be appropriate to speak to the Reichmanns.

The lawyers told them that they did not have to respond at once, and that until the board had been gathered and the directors had been sounded out, they should not seek out the Reichmanns. However, they told Bud Downing that if Paul Reichmann attempted to make contact, then he should speak to him. Paul Reichmann made no contact. Downing, typically, did more listening than talking. His bottom line remained simple: he was not prepared to fight the bid for the sake of staying in power, but he was if the price was too low. The group quickly agreed that the price was unacceptably low.

The takeover game has its own rich terminology, filled with analogies from medieval history, the sporting world, and even pharmacology. But amid the white knights, lowballs, and poison pills, there is a well-known term from yet another arena: weaponry. A "Saturday Night Special" is a cheap handgun of the kind frequently used in the holdups of low-rent neighborhood liquor stores. In the takeover world, the term is applied to aggressive bids launched in the hope of grabbing control before a company's panicked management has had time to organize itself. Bud Downing and his advisers soon decided that the Reichmanns were trying to pull a Saturday Night Special. So, despite the mixed metaphor, they had to look for a white knight. Pitblado and Mendoza went forth as heralds. DSP was to concentrate its search in Canada, Morgan was to look elsewhere. A Canadian knight was preferable because of the potential for political problems with a foreign bidder.

Pitblado approached big Canadian companies like Bell Canada, Canadian Pacific, and Power Corporation. All expressed some interest, particularly Bell, but there was concern about whether they would be able to move quickly enough.

There was speculation about the Reichmanns' real objectives. Hiram Walker management and advisers thought that O&Y was really after Home Oil, and perhaps Consumers' Gas as well, and that it wanted to sell off the distilling business, but an article appeared in the *Financial Post* suggesting that was not the case. Paul Reichmann was quoted as saying: "A year ago oil would have been the attraction with Hiram Walker. This time the attraction is diversification. When we made our initial evaluation of Gulf, we never looked at this oil price. We considered U.S.$18 (per barrel) as a minimum. Now there is a good possibility that the price will settle below that for a number of years. If the price settles below U.S.$15, or at U.S.$15, the returns will be meager for a lengthy period . . . Gulf's cash flow will have to be invested to protect the company's reserve base. This is the reason for the bid: to bring other components into Gulf, where hopefully they will enable Gulf to be more patient in its investing."

The statement made little financial sense. The bottom line seemed to be that the initial rationale for taking over Hiram Walker had disappeared, so Paul Reichmann had to devise another one.

With an internal valuation of Can$40 a share in their hands, Hiram Walker's board was soon in a position to reject the Reichmann bid, which "significantly understates the value and does not reflect the prospects of Hiram Walker Resources. . . . The board considers the bid to be a coercive attempt to pressure shareholders into a hasty decision to sell their Hiram Walker shares."

There was frenzied trading in Hiram Walker shares. New York arbitrageurs, led by Ivan Boesky, betting on a bid-'em-up battle, were wading in. Boesky would wind up leading a group of speculators who spent U.S.$200 million on Hiram Walker shares. He would make a killing.

After ten days of press release shadow-boxing, going into the 1986 Easter weekend, the Reichmanns still refused to acknowledge they were in a fight. However, behind the scenes, both sides were preparing to unleash surprises. The Reichmanns, for once, would find themselves upstaged.

A few days after the Reichmanns' bid, Cliff Hatch, Jr., received a call in his Windsor office from Sir Derrick Holden-Brown, the head of a British company, Allied-Lyons, with which Walker had some joint liquor interests. Holden-Brown told Hatch that if Hiram Walker was interested in selling off its liquor operations, he would be a willing buyer.

Allied, which had sales of almost Can$7 billion in 1985, was a world-scale producer and distributor of food products and drinks. The company had been formed in 1978 from the amalgamation of Allied Breweries and J. Lyons & Co., of British teahouse fame. It operated 7,000 British pubs, 950 liquor stores, or "off licences" as they are called in Britain, and 46 hotels. Worldwide, the company had 71,000 employees. Its products included Tetley Tea, Baskin-Robbins Ice Cream, Harvey's Sherries, Double Diamond beer, and Lamb's Navy Rum.

Hatch and Holden-Brown knew each other well at both the corporate and personal level. Holden-Brown had known Cliff Hatch, Sr., for forty years. On the corporate level, Allied represented many of Hiram Walker's best-known brands in the U.K., and Walker and Allied also had small joint interests in Toronto. They considered themselves similar kinds of companies: old, established, decent. They understood each other. Sir Derrick had at one time even been a trainee with Hiram Walker. Like Cliff Hatch, Sr., he was a navy man and had served in the Canadian flotilla in the Mediterranean during the Second World War.

The Reichmanns' partial bid for Hiram Walker had been brought to the attention of John Clemes, Allied's gaunt and incisive finance director, by British merchant bank, Baring Brothers. Although Sir Derrick Holden-Brown strongly denied such assertions, a takeover of Hiram Walker's liquor operations might serve a purpose beyond corporate embellishment: it would make Allied more difficult to acquire. Allied, too, had recently come under the gaze of acquisitors, primarily the Australian company Elders IXL Limited, a brewing, agricultural, and consumer products conglomerate. Elders, although it was only one-quarter of Allied's size, had made a U.S.$3.7 billion offer for control of the British food and liquor giant.

The head of Elders and the man who had built the company, John Elliott, was a rough-talking, rugged-featured corporate brawler who was nevertheless well versed in the intricacies of convoluted, smoke-and-mirror financing. Nicknamed "the Thug" in Australian business circles, Elliott was not at all Sir Derrick's cup of Tetley's.

The previous October, Elliott had, as the *Financial Times* put it, "lumbered into the heart of the City to announce his plan to take over Allied-Lyons, pluck out the brewing plum, sell off most of the rump and — with relish — sack the . . . senior management."

Elliott had announced his intentions at the Barber-Surgeons' Hall in the City of London, with plasterwork death's-heads looking down, stylized bloodletting instruments called fleams glinting in the camera lights, and Holbein's portrait of Henry VIII scowling to his left. Glistening with sweat and sucking on a cigarette despite the No Smoking signs, Elliott had, according to the *Finan-*

cial Times, "served up a cocktail of mild slanders, leaden irony, lavatory jokes, a quote from Churchill — 'my mentor' — and the merest sprinkling of hard information on his scheme for a leveraged assault on one of the biggest companies in Britain."

Allied had valid reasons to be concerned about the Elders bid, quite apart from the distasteful prospect of uncouth antipodeans gaining control of yet another of Britain's leading companies (Elders' best-known international product was Foster's Lager. Foster's ads in Britain and North America all *rejoiced* in how uncouth the Aussies were). The Elders bid was to be financed with short-term borrowings. If it was successful, Allied feared that large chunks of the company would inevitably have to be sold off to pay down the debt.

The fight had turned nasty. Elders had waged what Allied considered a below-the-belt, personal press campaign against Sir Derrick and his management. Elliott's assault had made the British conglomerate aware of some of the shortcomings of its staunch emphasis on decentralization. For example, when letters were sent out under the chairman's name to Allied subsidiaries, a number were sent back by employees who had never heard of Allied-Lyons! Nevertheless, when Sir Derrick went out on the road to visit the troops, he found them overwhelmingly on his side. At the Ind Coope warehouse in Burton-on-Trent, one brewery worker declared, in terms typical of the hyperbole these battles generate: "Elliott's got a reputation in Australia as a right bastard of a gaffer. Tell him to piss off." Around the end of February 1986, Elders had sold his Allied stake at a profit. Nevertheless, Elliott claimed that he wanted to make another bid. Following considerable lobbying by Allied, the Elders bid had been referred to the British Monopolies and Mergers Commission, where it still sat when Holden-Brown made his transatlantic call.

Sir Derrick later claimed that he emerged from the public relations brawl with Elliott with a renewed conviction about the proper way to behave in such situations: "Never overreact." It was a lesson Paul Reichmann would learn the hard way.

When Holden-Brown called Cliff Hatch, Jr., expressing interest in Hiram Walker–Gooderham & Worts, Hatch told him to speak to Bud Downing in Toronto. When he did so, Downing thanked him for his interest and put him in touch with Morgan Guaranty's Mendoza. Hiram Walker's initial attitude toward Allied was that it was always good to have prospective buyers lined up, but that they did not want to split up the company.

One potential strategy suggested by Walker's U.S. advisers was a "self-tender" or "issuer bid" whereby Hiram Walker would play its own white knight, making an offer for its own shares superior to that of the Reichmanns. But there were potential tax problems. So the legal advisers suggested making the bid through a subsidiary. That, too, ran into problems because a subsidiary is not allowed to hold shares in its parent company. Then they came up with the idea of a friendly third party making the bid. In fact, why not *create* a friendly third party, in which HWR could own 48 percent, meaning that it would not be a legal subsidiary? The company they created, or rather revived, for the purpose, since it was a dormant subsidiary, was called Fingas.

The question was: where would Fingas find the money to make a bid for Hiram Walker? One alternative reluctantly considered was to sell part of the company. Hiram Walker management had never wanted to sell the company piecemeal, but the white knights were proving slow to saddle up. Bell Canada had expressed strong interest in acting via TransCanada PipeLines, the giant natural gas pipeline utility that it controlled, but TransCanada was interested primarily in Home Oil. It was not interested in the liquor.

Suddenly it all clicked into place: if Hiram Walker Resources could sell the liquor business, then the money could be earmarked to fund an alternative offer for Hiram Walker's own shares via Fingas. A sale agreement for the liquor subsidiary would also make Hiram Walker *more* attractive to a suitor like TransCanada, since the problem of disposing of the liquor interests would have been solved already. Meanwhile, if sale of the liquor business did not drive the Reichmanns away, the Fingas bid would force them to raise their bid.

Hiram Walker's management and advisers still thought, despite Paul Reichmann's statements, that he was after Home Oil. They believed the Reichmanns' strategy was based on the liquor assets being undervalued, and that he planned to acquire HWR cheaply, spin off the liquor for a hefty profit, perhaps also sell the stakes in Consumers' Gas and Interprovincial Pipe Line, and wind up with Home Oil for nothing. The liquor sale–Fingas strategy would prevent such a daylight robbery. All they needed now was a white knight to take the liquor business. Not only was such a figure waiting across the Atlantic. He was, to boot, a *real* knight.

Peter Rosewell, the jovial finance director of the wines and spirits division of Allied-Lyons, was in his office in Allied House in London on Wednesday, March 26, 1986, when he was given a portfolio of material on Hiram Walker's liquor division and told to come up with a rough valuation by five o'clock. The material had been sent across the Atlantic by Morgan Guaranty. Rosewell worked through the day, came up with a figure, and showed it to Allied's finance director, John Clemes. Clemes agreed with it and passed it on to Baring Brothers to confirm. Part of the ongoing activities of a large company like Allied is to keep a check on the values and market valuations of companies in similar businesses, so Rosewell, Clemes, and the merchant bankers were pretty sure of their estimates.

Morgan's Roberto Mendoza had been instructed to get a formal offer from Allied. Clemes spoke to Mendoza that night and affirmed Allied's interest in Hiram Walker's liquor business. He suggested that they might come over after the Easter weekend. Mendoza told him that if they were interested, they had better get over right away. The Reichmann time bomb was ticking away.

Peter Rosewell had to drive 125 miles to his home just outside the picturesque town of Yeovil, Somerset, to get his passport and a change of clothes, then dash back to Heathrow to catch the

Thursday morning flight to Toronto. With him were Clemes and Michael Jackaman, the wines and spirits division's chairman and chief executive. The jet-lagged Brits spent the next few days in a swirl of meetings. They hammered out a purchase price for the liquor business of Can$2.6 billion, a figure with which Hiram Walker was pleased. For Allied, the most unusual part of the deal was Fingas, the entity set up to make the offer to Hiram Walker shareholders. Allied agreed to be a shareholder in Fingas.

Allied and Hiram Walker lawyers spent the entire Easter weekend drafting the agreement, which was delivered by un-shaven McCarthy lawyer Gary Girvan to Hiram Walker's board at 9 A.M. on the Monday morning. Sir Derrick Holden-Brown, having jetted over from the U.K. via the Concorde to New York the previous day, attended the directors' meeting to present the case for Allied's acquisition of the liquor business. It was an emotional meeting for many of those present, who realized that the sale of the liquor operation was the sale of Hiram Walker's heart. It was particularly sad for Bud Downing. He believed that he was doing his duty to the shareholders, but Hiram Walker Resources would never be the same. The board duly approved the sale.

During the two nights of work over the Easter weekend, much of it in First Canadian Place, somebody joked that he hoped the Reichmanns would not turn the lights out. But the Reichmanns' lawyers had been doing a lot of work themselves. Ironically, all the key players in the battle were occupants of the same building. The thirty-second floor, where the Reichmanns had their tastefully postmodern executive offices, was seeking control of the sixth floor, where the more traditionally somber wood-paneling of Hiram Walker's head office was located. But going into the Easter weekend, the big question was what the thirty-seventh floor, Interprovincial headquarters, thought. One thing was for sure, the sixth floor was not talking to them.

When the Gulf bid had been announced, HWR management had cast Interprovincial as bad guys. The Walker men believed Interprovincial might even have *provoked* the bid by talking to the

Reichmanns. In fact, the Reichmanns had been coming anyway. Heule's visit to Paul Reichmann merely gave Reichmann an opportunity to size IPL up.

As for the Interprovincial management, they felt they now owed nothing to Hiram Walker. It was every man for himself. Their own shareholders came first. Of course, another irony was that the largest of the shareholders in Interprovincial was Hiram Walker.

Heule did not speak to Bud Downing for several days after the bid, which Hiram Walker took as further evidence that he had gone over to the Reichmann camp. In fact, IPL was considering whether to sell its shares into the Reichmann offer. This alternative was rejected and Heule again approached Downing. Downing told him that if he had any proposals he should speak to Hiram Walker's investment advisers.

For Heule, the worst position would be as part of neither camp. Time was running out. Heule went back to Downing again and explained that Interprovincial had made no commitments; they were available as allies. But Downing remained cool. Heule came away with the idea that HWR had no clear plan to defend Hiram Walker against the Reichmanns' assault. He seemed to have only one option. The ultimate irony was to be played out. The chairman of Interprovincial, one of the main bastions of Hiram Walker's corporate defense, because of a disastrous breakdown in communications, felt compelled to turn its guns on the company it was meant to defend. Downing's belief that Interprovincial might already be in bed with O&Y became a self-fulfilling prophecy: Bob Heule called Paul Reichmann and told him that he was prepared to work with him.

When Heule appeared in Reichmann's office, Reichmann asked him what he had in mind. Heule said he wanted Home Oil. Reichmann said they should talk, but that it would be difficult to give Interprovincial special treatment or make a deal on Home Oil. Securities authorities would not like that. Nevertheless, under an agreement reached on Easter Sunday between the Reichmanns and Interprovincial, Interprovincial would not tender its Hiram Walker shares into a new, marginally better, Gulf bid. In return, Gulf would extend its offer and make a follow-up to all the minority shareholders, including Interprovincial, so that all shareholders had the option of getting out for a mixture of cash and "paper," just as in the final Gulf deal. There would also be an option for Interprovincial to take control of Home Oil. If a higher bid came along from a third party, Interprovincial was free to tender into it.

Many observers subsequently asked why Interprovincial had jumped into bed with the Reichmanns before Hiram Walker's management had had a chance to respond to the Reichmann bid. Many believed that there had to be some other, secret quid pro quo that the Reichmanns had offered Interprovincial. But there was no secret quid pro quo. Interprovincial was simply scared. What chance did Hiram Walker stand against the Reichmanns, the mythical men with the bottomless pockets? The Reichmanns always got what they wanted, and now they wanted Hiram Walker.

During all these meetings and machinations, there was one other key player waiting in the wings. TransCanada PipeLines was Hiram Walker's ideal suitor — big and Canadian. But Trans-Canada was still deciding whether to strap on its armor and whether it should reach for the white or the black set. In the wake of Gulf's bid, TCPL chief executive Gerry Maier spoke both to Bud Downing and to Paul Reichmann.

Meanwhile, Paul Reichmann professed not to understand the apparent hostility of Hiram Walker's management. He had repeatedly claimed that he would never become involved in a hostile takeover. But it now appeared that there was a big assumption behind that stance: when Paul Reichmann decided to take you over, there was just no point in hostility. After all, you were bound to lose. Why fight it? Reichmann had clearly convinced Interprovincial of that.

After the Easter weekend, Paul Reichmann called several Hiram Walker directors, including Allen Lambert and Bill Wilder, to find out why Walker was not rolling over and accepting its fate. Reichmann told them he had thought that the whole thing would be more friendly. The message he received was that his offer was too low and that the responsibility of the board was to get the best price for shareholders. He told Allen Lambert that there was "a little change" possible in the Can$32 price. Anybody who knew Paul Reichmann's track record knew that he gave nothing away in business negotiations, so his stance was not out of character. Bill Wilder told Reichmann that he should sit down and talk with Bud Downing, Hiram Walker's chief executive. Astonishingly, this was not an alternative that Reichmann appeared to have considered before. Perhaps he expected that Bud Downing should by this time have approached him in order to negotiate a peaceful transition of control. Lambert came away from his telephone conversation with Reichmann with the impression that O&Y was not prepared to offer materially more for Hiram Walker.

The Reichmanns continued to suffer from a gap in their knowledge about the implications of having public shareholders, perhaps the result of operating so long as a private company. Public shareholders implied public accountability. But the Reichmanns still seemed to feel that their presence should be all the reassurance that minority shareholders needed. Perhaps, also, Paul Reichmann simply believed he had Walker in the bag.

The Reichmanns had always done their deals in private. Public display was painful to them. Business was something done with senior executives behind closed doors. The media are a nuisance, but they had their purpose, and Paul Reichmann had always used them brilliantly. Most often he used them to clarify what he regarded as public misperceptions. Back in 1982, when rumors had swirled about O&Y being in potential financial trouble, the man who had always declared O&Y's finances to be off limits had "allowed" that the business's net worth might be Can$5 billion. Despite the lack of any independent form of corroboration, the press had printed that figure.

Now, Reichmann told the *Financial Post* that it was really the liquor business that he was after in Hiram Walker rather than oil and gas. Astonishingly, he had not clarified his intentions to Hiram Walker up to this point.

On Easter Monday, both the Reichmanns and Hiram Walker had surprises for each other, and for TCPL's Gerry Maier. Gulf Canada made a new bid of Can$32 for all Hiram Walker's shares. It also announced that Interprovincial had joined the Reichmann camp. Hiram Walker then dropped its own bombshell: the sale of the liquor business to Allied-Lyons and the Fingas bid of Can$40 for half of Walker's shares.

Both announcements were a surprise to Maier. That the Reichmanns had made an agreement with Interprovincial was not good news, because Interprovincial wanted Home Oil. But the announcement of the Allied-Fingas deal was much more promising. TransCanada could make a bid for the whole company and then sell the liquor business to Allied.

Faced with the Hiram Walker announcement about the Allied deal, Gulf simply announced that it was postponing its bid, which had been due to close on April 4. Now O&Y and Interprovincial found themselves in the hot seat. And they were mad.

Paul Reichmann was intensely annoyed at Hiram Walker's unwillingness to meet its fate. The one thing O&Y and its advisers had never considered was that Hiram Walker would sell its liquor operations. They knew only too well that the defense of Walker's Windsor-based corporate heart had been the key element of corporate strategy since 1979. Hiram Walker's management was not playing its preassigned role at all. And if Hiram Walker was going to abandon the script, then the Reichmanns were going to have to abandon the role they had so carefully nurtured for themselves, too.

Paul Reichmann had declared that he would never engage in a hostile bid and had then pulled the Saturday Night Special on Hiram Walker. He had also claimed that he disliked using lawyers. A profile in the *Globe and Mail* in January 1984 had declared: "He shies away from putting lawyers in charge because he distrusts 'the teaching of the legal profession, where the adversarial role is prevalent, where the assumption is that what the other side wants is probably not right.' "

Now Paul Reichmann had already installed a lawyer, Mickey Cohen, as the head of O&Y's public interests. It became clear that if it was a choice between preserving his nonhostile, nonlitigious image and winning, Paul Reichmann would go for the win. If the win had to come through the courts, so be it. If that's the way Hiram Walker wanted it, then the gloves would have to come off.

No more Mr. Nice Guy.

14

"A Battle over Money"

ON TUESDAY, APRIL 1, 1986, WEIGHTY INJUNCTIONS STARTED arriving on the desks of Hiram Walker's directors. The Reichmanns, Gulf Canada, and Interprovincial all took part in the legal assault. The injunctions sought to prevent both the sale of the liquor business and the creation of Fingas. On Wednesday, April 2, at the Supreme Court of Ontario on Toronto's University Avenue, the battle commenced with a volley of affidavits.

The lawyers representing the Reichmann camp unleashed a two-pronged assault. On the one hand, they argued that the sale of the liquor assets could not be made without submission to Hiram Walker's shareholders; on the other, they claimed that the creation of Fingas was a sham whose main purpose was to entrench Hiram Walker management.

Walker's lawyers refuted these charges strongly. They responded that shareholder approval was necessary only if "all or substantially all" of a company's assets were put on the block. The liquor assets were less than half of Walker's total. To the second charge, they said that Fingas had been created, not to entrench management control, but to provide a better deal for shareholders.

Some of the tactics used by O&Y during the legal battle misfired. One that would continue to misfire like a defective firecracker for the remainder of the battle was a letter, appended to Mickey Cohen's affidavit, from Seagram's chairman Edgar Bronfman to Bud Downing. In it, Bronfman expressed Seagram's "strong interest" in buying the liquor business from Walker. The letter was intended to establish that Walker management was acting cosily with Allied-Lyons to pursue its own interests. But more intriguing was how the letter had come to be in Mickey

Cohen's hands. It could only have come from the Bronfmans. The Bronfman letter — and its implications of a Reichmann/ Bronfman link — would do far more damage to the Reichmanns than it would to Hiram Walker.

As the first week of the court battle came to a close, Walker management's strategy produced its first desired effect: on Friday, April 4, the Reichmanns increased their bid to Can$35 a share for all Walker shares. However, the amended offer would proceed only if the competing Fingas bid was blocked by the courts or withdrawn. This upped the stakes enormously. The Gulf/ Reichmann bid was now worth around Can$3 billion, plus the cost of taking out Interprovincial's stake.

Hiram Walker's shareholders looked on in confusion. The only bid officially on the table was still Gulf's revised offer for 40 million Hiram Walker shares at Can$32. The higher bid from Gulf and O&Y of Can$35 for all the shares was subject to the Fingas bid — Can$40 for half the shares — being blocked. The Fingas bid was in turn held up in court by O&Y's injunctions.

Meanwhile, in a filing with the Securities and Exchange Commission in Washington, O&Y said that preliminary discussions had taken place about the possible sale of some of Hiram Walker's non-Canadian liquor assets. Like the Bronfman letter, this revelation would prove troublesome to the Reichmanns.

On Wednesday, April 9, Mr. Justice Robert Montgomery brought down his findings. The injunctions sought by O&Y and Interprovincial were thrown out, and Montgomery delivered a devastating rejection of the claims of the Reichmann camp. He came down very hard on Cohen's suggestions of impropriety on the part of Hiram Walker's directors. "The directors of Walker," said the judge, "acted throughout . . . entirely for proper purposes and entirely in the best interests of Walker and for the purpose of maximizing the value to Walker shareholders of their investment."

Montgomery did not stop with defending the motives of Hiram Walker. He went on to attack those of the acquisitors. "This," he declared, "is a battle over money. Gulf and IPL want the company and its assets at the cheapest possible price. The [Hiram Walker] board wants the shareholders to get more . . . IPL feels prejudiced because IPL wants the bargain that is in sight and does not want the directors to keep it from IPL and provide it to all shareholders. The same may be said of Olympia & York."

The Reichmanns had always taken great care to appear scrupulously fair and upright in their dealings. Now they were being portrayed as corporate purse-snatchers. Montgomery had yet harder words. Referring to the legality of the creation of Fingas, he said, "When under attack the target does not have to sit idly by without defending itself. An earlier Goliath was dispatched with a slingshot. Fingas is neither a sham nor a puppet as suggested by the applicants."

That must have been the unkindest cut of all: Paul Reichmann compared with the giant Philistine of Gath, scourge of the Israelites.

Montgomery continued: "Neither Olympia & York nor IPL can represent [Hiram Walker] shareholders. They are antagonistic to and totally opposed to the interests of other shareholders. The applicants cannot identify with the acquisitor [Gulf] and at the same time purport to represent the shareholders it seeks to vanquish." His conclusion was that the sale to Allied and the Fingas deal could go ahead.

Ill feelings continued to simmer between the two sides. Interprovincial's annual meeting happened to be on the same day as Montgomery's decision. Hiram Walker investment banker Roberto Mendoza, the Cuban exile with a sharp mind and an equally sharp tongue, turned up at the meeting with one objective: to make a monkey out of Bob Heule.

The meeting at first followed the usual course of prearranged nominations and elections. Then Heule, turning to Hiram Walker, said that Interprovincial would consider both any Trans-Canada bid and that from Gulf/O&Y. However, he was unequivocal in rejecting Hiram Walker's alternative bid through Fingas. He reiterated that the attraction of the Reichmann bid was that it would give Interprovincial an option to exchange its

Walker shares for an equity position in Home Oil. But he made the mistake of suggesting that Interprovincial had done a deal on the basis of an offer from the Reichmanns of Can$35 a share when the deal was done with the offer at Can$32.

Mendoza rose from the audience and proceeded verbally to slice Heule into little pieces. Heule had no idea who Mendoza was, but the New York banker peppered the slow-talking engineer with questions about his actions. Heule became tongue-tied and had to call up lawyer Fred Huycke for help. The Interprovincial directors present thought it was "dirty pool." But whoever had sent Mendoza obviously thought it was what the IPL chairman deserved.

Heule, however, made one prescient statement. "It isn't over yet," he said. "If there's a higher bid on the table . . . we clearly can take advantage of the higher bid. We have complete flexibility."

And sure enough, that very same day, TransCanada PipeLines, armor glinting in the sun, finally rode onto the scene, offering to buy all Hiram Walker's common and preferred shares at Can$36.50 in cash. The bid, worth Can$4.1 billion, was the biggest in Canadian history. TransCanada also declared that the sale of the distilling interests to Allied would go ahead as planned.

Reichmann's legal challenge had been crushed. He had been cast by the Ontario Supreme Court as a predator, while Hiram Walker's management and board were portrayed as models of responsibility to shareholders. And now TransCanada PipeLines had finally galloped up, willing not only to top Gulf's last bid, but also to honor the sale of the liquor business to Allied. To tender O&Y's 11 percent of Walker into TransCanada's Can$36.50 a share offer would mean a tidy profit for the Reichmanns. But this was not simply about profit. Business decisions are always about far more than economics and bottom lines. Corporate life is driven to a greater extent by ego and personal likes and dislikes than executives will ever admit. There was now more at stake in the Hiram Walker affair than mere money.

On Friday, April 11, there appeared an extraordinary interview with Paul Reichmann in the *Globe and Mail*. In it, Reichmann did what, for senior executives, was almost unheard of: he admitted that he had made a mistake: "My brother and I goofed somewhere along the line. A misunderstanding developed . . . Had we known it would be unfriendly, we would not have gone near it. It's not our style."

Reichmann claimed that the problem had arisen because of a misunderstanding about O&Y's intentions for Walker. "They [Walker] thought we were going to dismember the company. Our purpose was the opposite. We wanted to diversify. . . . We goofed because we didn't get the message across clearly enough until they were too deep into another route. . . . It's the first time in thirty years we have gone to court. It's not the kind of thing we do."

Reichmann seemed to be bending over backward to put the Walker directors in a good light: "I personally think that Walker directors thought what they did was in the best interests of their shareholders." "On March 31 [Easter Monday]," went the story, "O&Y told Walker that it was planning to improve its offer and expected Walker to sit down and negotiate a price. Instead, Walker executives telephoned O&Y to say they had other plans.

" 'They should have listened to us,' Mr. Reichmann said. 'They could have negotiated with us and got the same result as with TransCanada without too much ado.' "

According to Hiram Walker board members, including Bud Downing and Allen Lambert, this account was a fabrication. Hiram Walker's alleged failure to sit down with Paul Reichmann was based on its management's belief, which was in turn based on Paul Reichmann's own statements, that Paul Reichmann was not prepared to make any material advance in his partial, Can$32 a share, bid. Paul Reichmann had thought he had them in the bag and could dictate terms. He'd been outsmarted. But that did not mean he was prepared to lose. His interview in the *Globe and Mail* was not an attempt at a graceful exit from an ugly situation. It was not a *mea culpa*. It was part of the groundwork for the *coup de grâce*. The day on which the interview appeared, Gulf upped its bid for all

Hiram Walker shares to Can$38. TransCanada, after discussing it for several days, decided not to bid higher.

On Friday, April 18, Walker shares were yet again the most active on the Toronto Stock Exchange, but now they were on the way down. The stock dropped $1.25 to Can$37.12. The market knew the battle was over. Or at least the battle to acquire Hiram Walker. The question was: exactly what had Paul Reichmann acquired?

Hiram Walker's distilling interests, the very asset the Reichmanns claimed they most desired, had been sold, and the Ontario Supreme Court's Mr. Justice Robert Montgomery had dismissed the injunctions of both the Reichmanns and Interprovincial Pipe Line to halt the sale.

Paul Reichmann appeared to have made a quite uncharacteristic move. Had his actions been inspired by emotion rather than economics? If the sale to Allied went through — as it now appeared that it would — then instead of diversifying, all the Reichmanns would acquire was more oil and gas assets and a gas distribution system, a small prize for such a complex and acrimonious battle.

There were good, though unannounced, financial reasons for the Reichmanns to fight the sale to Allied. The most compelling was that, if the sale went through, they would be lumbered with an estimated Can$300 million tax bill. But there was more to be saved than cash. There was also face. There may even have been an eye for an eye and a tooth for a tooth. Olympia & York Enterprises went back to court to challenge Judge Montgomery's decision.

Another unusual interview with Paul Reichmann appeared in the *Globe.* He appeared to admit that he had made another gaffe: "Had we been advised that the spirits business was irretrievably sold, we still would have made an offer, but we would have pursued it less aggressively." Then he admitted that if the distillery was sold, "the purpose of our offer will be defeated."

Was it really possible that Reichmann had made his Can$3.3 billion bid without checking whether the distillery was "irretrievably sold"? Did he think that the Allied sale was a mere delaying tactic? If so, he was terribly wrong. Allied-Lyons wanted Hiram Walker–Gooderham & Worts and believed they had a binding contract to buy it.

Paul Reichmann would now pull out all the stops to prevent that sale. His actions would have nothing to do with a vague concept like fairness. They would be predicated on a relentless desire to win, seemingly at all costs. At the same time, there appeared to be a psychological struggle going on within Reichmann himself, a struggle that caused him to mount a confused campaign to establish that his intentions had been misunderstood, even though he did not appear himself to understand what his intentions had been.

On the morning of Sunday, April 20, Bill Shields, the business editor of the *Windsor Star*, received one of those phone calls of which newsmen dream. The caller announced that Paul Reichmann wished to give an exclusive interview to the *Star*. He wanted specifically to give it to Brian Bannon, the young business reporter who had been covering the Hiram Walker story. When did Mr. Reichmann have in mind? asked Shields. Today, Sunday, came the reply. Well, hold on now, said Shields, it was not that easy to get to Toronto on a Sunday. No matter, said the O&Y representative. Paul Reichmann would send down the jet.

Shields could not contact Bannon until that night. Bannon called O&Y and told them he could come down the next morning. At first, Paul Reichmann said that would not be possible; the Abitibi-Price annual meeting was to take place that day. However, he then decided that it was so important that his side of the story be told that he reshuffled his schedule.

Reichmann was mightily upset because of a letter brought to his attention the previous Friday. Under the name of Hiram Walker liquor executive Dennis Stoakes, it had been sent to one of the distillery's customers. It asked for the customer's support in gaining political approval for the sale to Allied-Lyons and in rebuffing the legal roadblocks of the Reichmanns. Not only did it point to the enormous layoffs at Gulf Canada in the wake of its acquisition by O&Y and the sale of the downstream to Petro-Canada, but it also suggested that the Reichmanns were in league with the Seagram Bronfmans and planned to split up the Hiram Walker liquor business. These allegations, in Reichmann's mind, were all "lies, falsehoods, or misconceptions."

The Stoakes letter was part of a larger campaign. As soon as Allied-Lyons had made its bid for the liquor business, with the initial support of Hiram Walker management, the Windsor head-quarters had organized a campaign of letters to local businesses and organizations — from the Chamber of Commerce to the Art Gallery of Windsor — asking them to write to Investment Canada in support of Allied's bid. The local community had responded quickly and positively. There was widespread fear in Windsor that Reichmann control would mean the splitting up and selling off of the liquor division. Local unions feared rationalization and job losses.

Paul Reichmann was now claiming through his press conduits that he had never intended to split up Walker and that he had always wanted the liquor business. Why were people not believing him? Why were they doubting his word? The simple answer was that Gulf had admitted talking to third parties about sales of parts of the liquor business, while Reichmann himself had admitted talking to Edgar Bronfman and half a dozen other prospective purchasers of the liquor assets.

Irrelevant, said Paul Reichmann. Everybody should now just forget those details. In the rarefied atmosphere of Paul Reichmann's business world, his word was simply to be believed. That people were refusing to do so, although he appeared to be speaking in riddles, perhaps even economizing with the truth, was intensely annoying to him.

The contentious sale of the liquor business to Allied was now a matter of government approval and legality, but Reichmann — while his staff lobbied away in Ottawa and his phalanxes of lawyers dreamed up obstructions to the sale — appeared to want something else: he wanted Windsor to want him.

On Monday morning, April 21, Bannon turned up at the reception area of O&Y in First Canadian Place. It was not every day that you got to interview Paul Reichmann. Come to think of it, nobody *ever* got to interview him unless he had a message to broadcast or a misapprehension to correct. He did not give interviews simply for the purpose of general enlightenment. Still, Bannon did not have Paul Reichmann's skillful manipulation of the press uppermost in his mind as he was ushered into the O&Y executive vice-president's sedate office.

Reichmann kept him for an hour, during which, in Bannon's own words, he "spoke like a school teacher." The reporter noted that he could "narrow his deep-set, sad eyes when something annoyed him and then, a minute later, chuckle over the foibles of big business."

Paul Reichmann's eyes were particularly sad over "misunderstandings" about his intentions. He noted that he had called Ontario Premier David Peterson to inform him of the offer for Hiram Walker Resources and to assure him that there would be no negative impact from the takeover, but then he admitted that he should have followed this up "with calls to Windsor and so on, but, in time, circumstances came about–what is referred to as the takeover battle–which then made us attach our focus to other aspects and we were remiss in not communicating this properly."

But, as with his earlier attempts to set the record straight over Hiram Walker, this *mea culpa* was a prelude to something else. That something else was the "lies, falsehoods and misconceptions" of the Stoakes letter. Reichmann admitted that he had spoken to Edgar Bronfman, but claimed that he had called him in Europe before the opening bid for Walker in order "to tell him that the bid is for the purpose of diversification and it's not to buy Home Oil to make Gulf stronger in oil and gas, just so there is no misunderstanding. Unfortunately we were not aware some people were going by that rumor and we failed to communicate."

How people were expected to know about Reichmann's private conversation was not laid out.

Bannon brought up the issue of how Edgar Bronfman's letter to Bud Downing had found its way into the hands of the Reichmanns. Reichmann did not explain. Then Bannon asked the central question: "So the idea of selling the spirits business in whole, or selling off a number of brands was never a part of the plan?"

Reichmann said no.

But earlier in the interview, Paul Reichmann had said, "[Gulf] does not intend to dispose of the parts of the *Canadian* business of Hiram Walker Resources, with the exception of Home Oil." (Author's italics.)

If Reichmann had never considered selling off foreign parts of the business, why had he specifically said "Canadian"? He went on to say, "Gulf, and myself as the controlling shareholder of Gulf, are making statements that the operations of Hiram Walker will not be affected *in the Windsor area, nor will they be in British Columbia.*" (Author's italics.)

Reichmann's statements also indicated ignorance about Hiram Walker's structure. He did not appear to realize that a substantial part of the Windsor head office's employment related to the legal, financial, and management functions of the international organization. If overseas assets were sold off, how could their Windsor head office functions be maintained?

Then Reichmann went on the attack. He claimed there could be adverse implications if Elders' attack on Allied-Lyons was successful: ". . . it may look like the British company will take Hiram Walker and everything will be fine from here on after. But the facts are that Allied-Lyons and Hiram Walker will be too large and if the Australians are successful, the first thing they will do is dump Hiram Walker, and who will get it is anyone's guess. You could say if they dump it to another foreign company, it means Investment Canada can take a second look at it, but what if they dump it to a Canadian company like Seagrams or anybody else."

For a man who had always been reported to take the high road, these statements seemed very close to scare tactics.

There was another issue that Paul Reichmann was very keen to address in the press: that of the proposed plan of arrangement by which Hiram Walker shareholders could take "paper," or some mixture of cash and paper, at a later date instead of tendering for Can$38 in cash immediately. Reichmann wanted to sell the plan because if everybody tendered for cash, the total cost to Gulf and O&Y would be Can$3.3 billion. The first Can$2.1 billion would come from Gulf, the remainder from O&Y. The more paper that shareholders could be persuaded to take, the less O&Y would have to fork out.

Reichmann had already done some selling of this still vague plan through the press. He had told the *Financial Post*: "We are giving an all-cash offer. But we are also saying, 'Have a look at the plan of arrangement.' In our view, the great majority of shareholders would prefer to stay with the company, and therefore become shareholders in a larger and stronger company . . . That is part of our strategy; to widen the shareholder base of Gulf. O&Y could end up with 50% to 60% of Gulf."

However, Reichmann's view of what the "majority of shareholders would prefer" was transparently self-interested wishful thinking. The proposed plan of arrangement was fuzzy, but Can$38 in hard cash was very clear. The New York "arbs" were rumored to have now accumulated up to 30 percent of Hiram Walker's shares. They certainly were not interested in any plan of arrangement. They wanted to cash out.

Meanwhile, although Paul Reichmann may have satisfied himself that he had set the record straight, his answers were less than satisfactory from Windsor's point of view. He had spoken of "lies and misconceptions" about a possible sale to Seagram, and yet he had admitted speaking to Edgar Bronfman. Moreover, he had given no explanation of how Bronfman's letter to Downing had found its way into the hands of O&Y's lawyers. He had denied that selling off either all of Hiram Walker or any of its brands was ever part of his plans, and yet he had emphasized the safety of the Canadian part of the business rather than the business as a whole.

The day the Reichmann interview appeared, April 22, also saw Gulf Canada's annual meeting, where Gulf chief executive Keith McWalter further confused the issue of the Reichmanns' intentions. McWalter gave the appearance of a man up to his hip-wallet in alligators. He had to put a brave corporate face on a series of events outside Gulf's control.

Once assets sales were stripped out, Gulf's financial results were a disaster. Earnings for the first quarter of 1986 were Can$9 million, down from Can$52 million the previous year. Oil revenues had been hit by the price collapse, but the main reason for the precipitous decline was the increase in Gulf's interest expenses, the result of debt piled on by the Reichmanns. Moreover, if Hiram Walker shareholders accepted Gulf's cash offer, its debt was going to climb further. McWalter, not surprisingly, made an enthusiastic pitch to Hiram Walker shareholders to hang on and wait for the paper. As support, he noted how well those who had held onto Gulf shares had done. In fact, they'd done about as well as those who had opted for cash.

That Gulf shares had held up was indeed remarkable. The Gulf plan of arrangement had been hatched when the oil price was more than U.S.$30 a barrel, but had been put into effect as OPEC's collapse was sending it tumbling below U.S.$18. Looked at in those terms, it was amazing that anybody had been persuaded to switch into the equity of the "new" Gulf at all. Just as surprising was the fact that, although the oil price had subsequently slumped below U.S.$10 and as McWalter spoke was trading below U.S.$15, the share price was still holding up. It looked like more than a remarkable act of faith in the Reichmanns' ability to wave their magic wand over a slumping oil business and somehow make it attractive. It looked like somebody, or perhaps several entities, were engaged in that old practice of "stabilizing the market," which, when it is done by any lesser entity than a major investment house, is known as stock manipulation.

McWalter had been under pressure from Hiram Walker's union, which had assumed that the chief executive of the company in the process of taking them over might know what was going on. A letter under McWalter's name had been sent to United Auto Workers Local 2027, whose 500 members were employed at the Walkerville plant. The letter claimed: "It is unfortunate there have been recent rumors misrepresenting our intentions and creating undue concern among Hiram Walker's employees. Let me assure you and your client that if we are the eventual owner of Hiram Walker's distilled spirits business it would be our intention to retain the operations affecting your client." But the Gulf-O&Y camp had done it again. By qualifying the word "operations" with the phrase "affecting your client," McWalter had once more raised the specter of a sale of foreign assets. What he, like Reichmann, apparently failed to appreciate was that the sale of *any* of the liquor assets affected the employment prospects in Windsor.

At the meeting, McWalter increased the confusion by telling the audience: "If, ultimately, Gulf is the owner of the Hiram Walker distilled spirits business, it would be our intention to retain the *Canadian* operations." (Author's italics.)

After the meeting, he flatly contradicted Reichmann's *Star* interview. When asked directly about Gulf-O&Y's intentions for the foreign liquor operations, he said that the options were "open."

On stock exchanges, ahead of the closing, Hiram Walker trading increased to unprecedented volumes. But now the trading was not frantic; it consisted of the systematic liquidation of the arbs' huge blocks. On the TSE alone, 5.8 million shares were traded, including the largest-ever block trade, when McLeod Young Weir crossed 5.2 million shares at $37.75.

On Wednesday, April 23, at 8:30 A.M., on the floors of the Toronto and Montreal stock exchanges, Hiram Walker shareholders gave their response to Reichmann's and McWalter's appeal to hang onto their shares. The industry's traders went to the men from Merrill Lynch and McLeod Young Weir who were responsible for taking in Hiram Walker shares, and quietly placed their sell orders. When it was all over, the answer was unequivocal: just over 90 percent of the minority shares were tendered for cash. The Walker shareholders were voting with their feet. In droves.

Gulf-O&Y was now another Can$3 billion in the hole.

15

Unhappy Union

ON JULY 12, 1812, BRIGADIER-GENERAL WILLIAM HULL, Commander of the North Western Army of the United States, crossed the Detroit River and landed with 2,000 men on the site of what is today the Hiram Walker distillery in Windsor. Like Paul Reichmann, General Hull considered himself a man of good intention, convinced that he had come to "liberate Canada from oppression." But British-controlled Canada, rather like Hiram Walker–Gooderham & Worts, did not want liberating. In less than three weeks, after British General Isaac Brock had appeared with reinforcements, Hull and his men were forced to take to their boats and retreat across the river.

When Sir Derrick Holden-Brown arrived in Windsor on the afternoon of Wednesday, April 30, 1986, he received a welcome similar to that of his fellow countryman Brock 174 years before. He was seen as a saviour.

Some thought that Windsor might be able to save Sir Derrick, too. They believed that events in the international arena had made Allied's enthusiasm for the Hiram Walker acquisition even greater. Even though Elders' first bid was still stalled in front of the British Monopolies and Mergers Commission, and the Australian company had disposed of its initial Allied holding in the market at a profit, Elders' John Elliott had not given up. In late February, he had set up a battle headquarters in London.

John Elliott, hoping that the Reichmanns' court challenge would be successful, said that the Allied-Walker deal "has been put together in altogether indecent haste, and contributes nothing to either company."

Sir Derrick Holden-Brown begged to differ.

On Wednesday, April 30, before heading for Windsor, Sir Derrick brought his case to Toronto. At 11 A.M. he appeared at a press conference at the Westin Hotel as part of a strategy to acquaint Canadians with his company. Full-page Allied-Lyons ads had appeared in the media that morning, emphasizing the wide range of the company's products.

Sir Derrick, who had flown into New York via the Concorde the previous evening, sported a Canadian Maple Leaf tie given him by the man who had been his commanding officer during the war, Tommy Ladner, a well-known Vancouver lawyer.

He told those assembled, in his well-modulated tones, that Hiram Walker would form a major part of a new, larger Allied-Lyons. He pointed out that any notion that the wedding with Walker was part of an Allied defensive strategy against the unwelcome advances of the Elders IXL group was quite erroneous. "I can state," he said, "that our company is under no serious threat of a takeover by either Elders IXL of Australia, or anyone else." He ended his presentation with a subtle dig at the O&Y group, obviously intended to stir fears that the Reichmanns might be corporate vampires, interested only in sucking off the financial lifeblood of the liquor business. "There will be no draining off of the cash flow or net earnings of Hiram Walker to finance adventures in other industries, be it aerospace, energy, or anything else."

Aerospace was just thrown in. He meant energy.

Sir Derrick's resolve, in his deferentially British way, seemed total. "Gulf . . . has indicated that they are not interested in the whole of Hiram Walker," he said. "I have indicated that I'm not interested in part of it."

That afternoon he flew to Windsor to receive his saviour's welcome.

At a press conference at Windsor's riverfront Hilton Hotel, he delivered a message similar to that he had given that morning in Toronto: Hiram Walker–Gooderham & Worts under Allied-Lyons control would remain a "Canadian-directed" business under its current management. Although Holden-Brown acknowledged that the local executives were in a "very difficult and delicate position," they made no effort to restrain their enthusiasm for him. When he went to the distillery the next day, his brief presentation to management was greeted with a standing ovation.

Holden-Brown seemed almost embarrassed by the level of local support. Even the Windsor City Council had sent a letter on Allied's behalf to Investment Canada. Local politicians of all stripes showered good wishes upon the gratified British executive.

Holden-Brown's blue blood might have seemed a little out of place in Windsor, but the Hiram Walker workers could identify with his example of corporate paternalism. His emphasis on tradition was not out of place in Hiram Walker's headquarters. When Sir Derrick stepped into those headquarters on May 1, he felt very much at home. With their wood trimmings and their glass office partitions, they looked very much like a British merchant bank. Indeed, at one time the ground floor had been taken up by a bank.

Holden-Brown departed Walkerville in no doubt that the community was behind his bid. From Windsor airport, he headed with his entourage for Ottawa to meet with Industry Minister Sinclair Stevens and officials from Investment Canada, which had been inundated with letters supporting the Allied bid.

That weekend, Sir Derrick flew home. He hoped to spend the following Monday, a British bank holiday, on his sloop moored at Lymington, Hampshire. He needed a brief period of relaxation, for he was facing a hectic three-week period leading up to the extraordinary shareholders' meeting in London on May 27 at which his bid for Hiram Walker–Gooderham & Worts was to be put to shareholders.

While Sir Derrick was making what was almost a royal tour, back in Toronto the Reichmanns were moving in on Hiram Walker. Mickey Cohen called Bud Downing and told him that he wanted all capital expenditures halted; he also wanted the resignations of all board members except for Downing and the heads of the three operating subsidiaries.

On Friday, May 2, there was a brief meeting of the board at

Hiram Walker's First Canadian Place head office. The outside directors handed in their resignations and were replaced by the Reichmanns' nominees, most of whom were directors of Gulf. The new directors, since they were there to serve the interests of the shareholders, had little real part to play. Paul Reichmann controlled the majority of Walker shares, and he had never felt that his interests needed looking after by a board of directors. Nevertheless, one new board subcommittee was set up to study potential loopholes in the contract under which the liquor business had been sold to Allied-Lyons. It consisted of Cohen, Newman, McWalter, and Powis.

Paul Reichmann had claimed that he had never wanted a battle. Now he had a corporate civil war on his hands. He continued to claim he found it all very hard to understand.

The day after the Gulf annual meeting, on Wednesday, April 23, Paul and Albert met for eighty minutes with Howard McCurdy, the New Democrat MP for Windsor-Walkerville. Said McCurdy after his audience, "They certainly did seem anxious to reassure the people of Windsor that their acquisition does not spell out a threat to employment levels."

Nevertheless, McCurdy would later refute a story in the *Windsor Star*, which he claimed suggested that he might support the Gulf bid. After all, McCurdy was a socialist and had to keep an eye on union opinion. Union opinion was firmly behind Allied-Lyons. Once again, that support had increased because the union could not get a straight answer out of Gulf-O&Y.

Local 2027 of the UAW was headed by Ron Dickson, a feisty, witty, and articulate union man whose accent still bore a strong Scottish brogue. Hiram Walker–Gooderham & Worts got on well with its union. The company had been plagued by strikes in the early 1970s, but the last two wage agreements had been signed almost a year ahead of schedule.

At first, Dickson was inclined to follow the lead of management in supporting Allied-Lyons, but then decided it would be prudent to gain outside help. Ironically, Dickson would, much to Paul Reichmann's frustration, become Allied-Lyons' greatest supporter, while most of the management he had originally followed would change sides and throw their support behind the Reichmanns.

Paul Reichmann had said in his *Windsor Star* interview: "We did communicate to a number of people but not well enough for the people directly affected to be informed." Dickson represented the people "directly affected." Thus he felt it not unreasonable that if Paul Reichmann could give exclusive interviews to the *Windsor Star*, then somebody senior from Gulf-O&Y should speak to him too. Between April 22 and May 4, the union's lawyer, Leon Paroian, had three conversations with Gulf head Keith McWalter. In the last, McWalter had said that he wanted to meet with union representatives and would be calling back within a day or so to confirm the time and place. Ten days later, they had heard nothing. McWalter was now dancing to the Reichmanns' tune. The difficulty was in getting Paul Reichmann to play for him. The unions, meanwhile, found Sir Derrick's melody much more beguiling.

The week of Reichmann's *Windsor Star* interview and the Gulf annual meeting, Dickson and two colleagues had crossed the Atlantic to meet with Allied's unions and management and visit the company's facilities in London, Bristol, and Shepton Mallet. The representatives of the British Transport & General Workers' Union, the TGWU, spoke in glowing terms about Allied and were enthusiastic for a link with Walker, which they thought would increase the markets for British products. Dickson met briefly with Sir Derrick Holden-Brown and Allied's board. He subsequently joked that when he had been growing up in Scotland, anybody with a double-barrelled name was either the landlord or the local Tory candidate, which gave him a negative bias. But he was impressed by Holden-Brown's sincerity, and he came away from Britain even more enthusiastic for the Allied alternative.

As a result of Paroian's lack of success in tying down Mc-Walter, the union decided to draw some attention to itself. On May 14, Dickson held a press conference at Toronto's Sheraton Centre, at which he delivered an impassioned attack on the Reichmann bid. The union leader pointed out that he had sought, and was in the process of obtaining, written undertakings from Allied-Lyons about the future of all of HW-GW's Canadian operations and its workers, not just the members of the UAW. Allied was being cooperative; Gulf and the Reichmanns were not.

Dickson outlined his union's problems in obtaining a response from the Reichmanns and made a devastating attack on their way of doing business. He scorned their apparent lack of concern for the workers of Gulf Canada. He castigated them for their ignorance about HW-GW, noting that any sale of the company's foreign assets would mean job losses in Walkerville. His bottom line was that the union believed that the Reichmann group had "a hidden agenda which is not in the best interests of the employees, or the community." As evidence, he pointed yet again to the smoking guns of the Reichmanns' possession of the Bronfman letter and to Gulf's admission of third party talks about the disposal of Hiram Walker assets.

Dickson's remarks certainly got O&Y's attention, but O&Y was still hoping to win through escalating the legal battle and increasing political pressure. Gulf also announced a proposed reorganization under which the Hiram Walker spirits business would become one of three "legs" of the Gulf organization, alongside forest products and oil and gas. The release declared that the restructuring plan would "establish within Gulf Canada Corporation a diversified business and earnings base, which will strengthen the basic businesses and enable them to expand and compete more effectively in Canadian and international business markets."

But how was tying Hiram Walker's spirits division to a deeply indebted Gulf Canada going to help it? Indeed, how could Gulf Canada be "strengthened" unless it was drawing financial support from Hiram Walker and Abitibi?

This constant questioning was now growing too much for Paul Reichmann. He decided that the "lies and misconceptions" had gone far enough. It was time for him to take his message to a wider audience. It was time to meet the press and people of Windsor.

Tuesday, May 27, dawned damp and gray in Windsor. From his suite in the Windsor Hilton, Paul Reichmann could look across at the black towers of Detroit's giant Renaissance Center, which rose almost menacingly above the mists of the Detroit River. Today would be an unusual day in his life. The man who claimed never to have courted publicity was calling his first press conference. He was also scheduled to meet with both the management and the unions at the Hiram Walker–Gooderham & Worts head office. Reichmann did not relish the task ahead, but he felt that misconceptions continued to abound. He had come to make another attempt at putting them straight.

He had not been pleased with his "exclusive" *Windsor Star* interview, even though it had quoted him verbatim. Perhaps it was because the story had also quoted union leader Ron Dickson's skepticism about Reichmann's intentions and his honesty. Reichmann had agreed to give another interview to Brian Bannon, but this time he insisted that a third party be present with a tape recorder. But if Reichmann thought that the presence of a tape recorder was going to get him the media coverage he desired, he misunderstood both the media and himself. What he really objected to in the press was that they failed to catch the purity of his *intentions*. Those did not show up on magnetic tape. Perhaps a polygraph would have been more appropriate.

As Paul Reichmann prepared himself for the greatest public exposure of his life, 4,000 miles away, at noon London time, Sir Derrick Holden-Brown, the chairman of Allied-Lyons, was submitting his proposed acquisition of Hiram Walker's spirits business to his shareholders. At the meeting, which was held in the ancient Plaisterers' Hall in the heart of the City, support for the Walker deal was overwhelming.

Yet again, the solidity of Holden-Brown's support contrasted sharply with the situation in the Reichmann camp. O&Y's new legal attack on the Allied deal had infuriated Walker's old management. The previous week, Bud Downing had stepped down from his position as president of Hiram Walker Resources and been replaced by Mickey Cohen. Bill Fatt, Walker's vice-president and treasurer, had resigned. Meanwhile, Reichmann's persistent denials of a sale of all or part of Hiram Walker's liquor business to Seagram seemed even less credible after Edgar Bronfman declared at the Seagram annual meeting in Montreal that he was still interested in Hiram Walker. If Paul Reichmann had unequivocally told Bronfman that he was not going to sell any of the liquor business, then how could Bronfman still claim to be interested?

At 9:30 A.M. Mickey Cohen stood chatting in the driveway of the Windsor Hilton with the chauffeur of Paul Reichmann's limousine. A couple of minutes later, the tall, looming figure of Paul Reichmann appeared from the elevator and walked his slow, deliberate walk out to the car. The limo pulled off up Riverside Drive for the short trip to the Hiram Walker plant.

At 10 A.M. Reichmann and Cohen met with Ron Dickson and union representatives. Reichmann had almost certainly failed initially to understand how important appeasing the union, which meant Dickson, was to his political efforts to have the sale of HW-GW quashed. What spooked Dickson about the Reichmann bid was the persistent Bronfman rumors. When he was finally introduced to Paul Reichmann that morning by Cliff Hatch, Jr., Dickson found Reichmann a formidable presence. Nevertheless, the union leader had decided to start the meeting on a positive note. He pulled a bottle of Canadian Club Classic, a 12-year-old version of the famous brand, from his briefcase and presented it to Reichmann as a gift from the employees of Walkerville. Reichmann and Cohen smiled. The tension was eased. But when they were seated around the table, with Cliff Hatch, Jr., at its head and Paul Reichmann across from Dickson, Dickson noticed that Reichmann gave him a long, hard look. Dickson returned the look with equal intensity. He was not a man to blink.

Paul Reichmann then began to read from a prepared statement. Noting that the meeting was overdue, Reichmann talked about inevitable uncertainties and misunderstandings, but pointed to an "exciting" future as part of a new Gulf conglomerate. Then he came to the heart of his problem: the sale to Allied-Lyons. "I would like to make clear the position regarding ownership of Hiram Walker–Gooderham & Worts. With the purchase of 69 percent of the shares of its parent company, Hiram Walker Resources, Gulf Canada is now the owner of this important distilling business. The purported agreement to sell the distilling business to Allied-Lyons PLC was prompted by the mistaken belief that if Gulf Canada acquired control, it would sell the distilled spirits and wines business to The Seagram Company. The notion that we intend to sell the liquor business to Seagram's has plagued this entire matter and is patently untrue."

Reichmann went on to warn that legal proceedings with Allied might be protracted. (That morning, Allied's finance director John Clemes had admitted at the extraordinary general meeting in London that Allied was being hampered because the new owners were refusing access to information about Hiram Walker. As soon as their acquisition was official, the Reichmanns had "pulled down the shutters.") Nevertheless, Reichmann went on to give what looked like a very solid reassurance to the workers about the future of the company. "As owner, Gulf Canada will work with your management and with you to ensure that all operations continue as before, under the same terms and conditions regarding employment, with the same employees and management, and that management's plans for the profitability and growth of the business will be supported and implemented. It is key to this plan that this business be developed and expanded both inside and outside Canada."

Reichmann said being part of the new Gulf conglomerate would help HW-GW, whose management had told him, he said, that being part of HWR had kept them short of money. Ron Dickson was surprised when he heard these remarks. He began to get the sneaking suspicion that Reichmann had managed to coopt Walkerville's management. Occasionally, Reichmann would look up from his brief and stare at Dickson as if to gauge his reaction. Dickson would stare straight back.

Paul Reichmann then attempted to clarify the point about the sale of the non-Canadian parts of the business. "I also would like to emphasize that we have absolutely no intention of selling any segment of the spirits business to others. The international spirits operations will not be sold because, as you know yourselves, its operations and its revenues are essential to Canadian activities."

His audience certainly knew that. But as recently as a few weeks before, neither the Reichmanns nor Gulf's Keith Mc-Walter had appeared to know it.

Reichmann expressed concern about the declining portion of HW-GW's domestic Canadian profits. "As Canadians running a Canadian-controlled business," he said, "we recognize the urgent need for such a reversal and we will encourage the development of new Canadian-distilled products that will find acceptance at home and abroad and return Canadian operations to their prominence of past years."

Later that day, when the liquor company's middle management heard those statements, they almost burst out laughing. Their business was 130 years old. Most of them had worked in it all their lives, and now a family of Toronto real estate developers with an ex-bureaucrat as their main hired help was going to tell them what new products they should be producing. That did not sound very convincing.

Reichmann claimed that Abitibi had done well under Reichmann control. He also pointed to the family's excellent record in developing Canadian jobs as a result of its international activities, in particular construction in the United States. He finished by saying, "This is a fine company that has raised the Canadian profile around the world. It has become a truly great Canadian multinational built and managed right here in Windsor. When Cliff Hatch, Sr., joined this company . . . the gross assets were about Can$63 million and annual sales were about Can$64 million. Currently both assets and sales have increased about twenty-four times from those 1937 levels. With the help of Cliff Hatch, Jr., and your exceptionally well-qualified management team, and with the vital help of all of you, I have no doubt that this pattern of growth can continue."

Dickson was unimpressed. He considered Reichmann's

"plans" for HW-GW vague and ill-informed. At one point in the lengthy delivery, Dickson had interrupted Reichmann, concerned that there might be no time for questions. He said he was encouraged by Reichmann's words, but had still heard nothing that might cause him to shift his allegiance from Allied-Lyons. Allied, after all, was in the same business; they could introduce new products — and thus hopefully jobs — into Walkerville's brand line-up. Allied could also distribute HW-GW products in Britain.

Reichmann patiently but firmly said it would be naive to believe that the profits from HW-GW, under Allied's control, would remain in Canada. O&Y's mastermind also tried a little of the Reichmann charm on Dickson. His researchers had told him that Dickson had arrived in Canada in 1955. He pointed out to the union leader that he, too, had arrived in 1955. "Yes," said Dickson, "and we've both done well."

At the end of the meeting, Ron Dickson said he wanted Paul Reichmann's commitments in writing. In the labor movement, there was an old saying: "A verbal agreement is only as good as the paper it's written on." Dickson also asked about future contacts. Paul Reichmann motioned to Mickey Cohen to take care of it. Then it was time to meet the press.

Shortly after 11 A.M., Reichmann entered Hiram Walker's "Canadian Club" room, resplendent with 1960s art that, twenty years later, was all too clearly not timeless. As the shutters clicked and the television cameras rolled, he read his prepared statement again.

There followed a brief question-and-answer period. Reichmann was asked about recent trips by Mickey Cohen to the U.K. Were the Reichmanns trying to make a deal with Allied? "We have agreed to listen to suggestions they might have," said Reichmann, "and they have agreed to listen to suggestions that we may have."

Soon, Mickey Cohen, who was sitting at the back of the room, began to make signals to Hiram Walker public relations officer Al Milne to draw the conference to a close. Reichmann was still answering questions, but Cohen knew he wanted to get out of there. He motioned again: close it down. Milne brought the conference to an end.

Photographers continued to thrust cameras into Reichmann's face as he walked out the side door of the building into the beautiful Hiram Walker garden, whose honey locusts, hawthorns, junipers, and yews stood drinking up the rain. Reichmann and Mickey Cohen walked across to the main building and disappeared up its steps to have lunch with Cliff Hatch, Jr., and his executives.

After lunch, Reichmann returned to the "Canadian Club" room to give his same speech to Walker's management. He was politely received but did not get the standing ovation that Sir Derrick Holden-Brown had received three weeks earlier. Later in the afternoon, he met with Windsor's mayor, David Burr, who tried to sell him on supporting the plan for a local water park and wave pool. Reichmann escaped as soon as possible. He also gave another exclusive interview to the *Windsor Star*'s Brian Bannon, this time with his own tape recorder present. And then, with relief, he drove to the airport. He was due to fly to New York to meet with Edgar Bronfman, to ask him to stop talking about buying Hiram Walker.

At a meeting with senior management the next day, union leader Ron Dickson had his suspicions about their switching to the Reichmann side confirmed. When he declared that he was still supporting Allied-Lyons, his remarks were greeted by an ominous silence. When Cliff Hatch asked the group what they thought their public position should be, Ian Wilson-Smith, the English-born and Cambridge-educated head of the company's administrative group, declared: "We have a duty to support our largest shareholder, which happens to be the Reichmanns." Public relations officer Al Milne expressed concern about how switching sides would look in the local community. Dickson reaffirmed that the union favored Allied-Lyons. He left the meeting convinced that most of the senior management had changed sides, although he still was not sure about Cliff Hatch, Jr.

A key part of the public relations fight between the Reichmanns and Allied over custody of HW–GW in the summer of 1986 — attempting to sway Investment Canada's assessment of the deal — turned on the commitments made by the competitors to the future of Walkerville. The irony was that, as the acquisition was taking place, HW–GW's own middle management was declaring that they strongly disliked Walkerville and the centralized style for which it stood. Much of that discontent inevitably focused on Cliff Hatch, Jr.

Following a Harvard MBA, Cliff Hatch, Jr., had spent virtually his whole working life at Hiram Walker. Slim and sensitive, with boyish looks, he was not outgoing like his father. People often took this reserve and diffidence for aloofness. He was constantly aware of the silver spoon whispers, of the digs that he had been "born on third base." Hatch, Jr.'s position was summed up by a question he himself posed while later conducting a seminar on HW–GW at the University of Western Ontario: "What about the family situation?" he asked the class. "Have I earned my job or am I a member of the lucky sperm club?" The question had raised a laugh, but it had not raised an answer.

From the time he had first come to Walkerville, some within the company had played up to him because of his name, hoping to ride on his coattails; others had almost automatically challenged whatever he said or did as a means of asserting their independence. The regard in which his father was held was both an advantage and a problem. Cliff Hatch, Sr., had not become head of Hiram Walker–Gooderham & Worts until eighteen years after his father had died. Cliff, Jr., found himself bustled into the top job at HW–GW while his father was still very much around. Not everyone was convinced that Cliff, Jr., was ready.

Following Bud Downing's appointment as chief executive of Hiram Walker Resources in Toronto, Hatch, Jr., had found himself, at barely forty years of age, the chief executive of the company his grandfather had put together. But it was a troubled company in 1984, operating in a no-growth liquor market.

While Bud Downing had still been in charge at Walkerville, in

1982, a strategic planning process had been started to examine how to stimulate corporate growth. Three years later, after Downing had been called to Toronto to head Hiram Walker Resources, the process had lost momentum. In 1985, Hatch, Jr., faced with increasing discontent, decided to examine change more actively. A survey of middle management revealed an almost universal discontent with Walkerville. Senior management was not considered aggressive enough. They weren't going after acquisitions within the industry; they weren't developing new products. Headquarters demanded too much useless data; it took too long to get answers from management; the company was too centralized and bureaucratic.

As a result of these and similar findings, two middle management task forces were set up to examine "organizational issues." They went about their work with a will. At the beginning of April 1986, as the Reichmann-Allied battle was in full swing, they had delivered a withering criticism of the cumbersome way the company was run.

For Cliff Hatch, Jr., and his senior managers, these were the toughest of times. The disputed sale of their company created a bizarre situation. Since the sale had not been finalized, the Reichmanns held control of the head office, while Allied-Lyons management was not allowed near the premises. HW–GW senior management now almost literally had the Reichmanns' lieutenants breathing down their necks. Meanwhile, they were faced with calls for an internal reorganization which threatened their status within the company. What the hell, some of Hatch's senior managers asked him, were they doing talking about reorganization in the middle of being taken over?

Senior Walkerville management was concerned because they had found out that — unlike HW-GW — Allied-Lyons was a very decentralized company. Just like the management of Gulf Canada before them, HW-GW's senior managers felt they would be more likely to be left in charge of the company under the Reichmanns than under Allied-Lyons. Ron Dickson discovered that the senior managers had met with the Reichmanns in Toronto on May 20. He believed that meeting had been crucial. They must have been persuaded that the Reichmanns were going to win the battle for Walkerville.

In his prepared statement, Reichmann had warned that the legal battle could go on for "years." This was designed perhaps not only to frighten off Allied but to spook the men at HW–GW. Certainly, the legal fight with Allied was being escalated by all means possible. The latest move was the unannounced withdrawal by the now Reichmann-controlled Hiram Walker of a submission required in the United States under the Hart-Scott-Rodino Anti-trust Improvements Act, seeking approval of the Allied takeover. When Allied found out about the maneuver, its executives were incensed. If the Reichmanns wanted to play tough, they would play tough too.

The week after Reichmann's Windsor press conference, Sir Derrick came steaming back across the Atlantic like Margaret Thatcher heading for the Falklands. He felt that he had the force of justice on his side. The Reichmanns had to be taught a lesson. On Monday, June 2, he appeared at a press conference in Toronto to announce that Allied-Lyons was taking a little legal action of its own. It was suing the Reichmanns for Can$9 billion. Since Pennzoil had been awarded more than U.S.$12 billion in a similar suit against Texaco in the United States the preceding year, the action was not to be taken lightly. In addition to the damages, Allied was seeking an injunction to restrain all defendants from "interfering" with the shares or assets of the liquor business.

Sir Derrick told the news conference that "while it is not in keeping with Allied's philosophy to conduct its business by litigation, it is wholly unreasonable to expect us to stand idly by while hostile attempts are made to frustrate our binding agreement to acquire the spirits and wine division of Hiram Walker."

He pointed out that the agreement between Allied and Hiram Walker Resources clearly stated that both sides should use their "best efforts" to satisfy the precompletion conditions, but that the Reichmanns were "totally ignoring both the spirit and the word-

ing of the agreement in a blatant attempt to prevent completion."
Sir Derrick cited Hiram Walker Resources' withdrawal of the
Hart-Scott-Rodino antitrust filing as a "glaring example" of the
breach.

When Sir Derrick addressed the Toronto Society of Financial
Analysts two days later, the very model of British probity, he was a
big hit with the crowd. His performance was in sharp contrast to
the much less polished presentation of Paul Reichmann in Windsor the week before. His public relations battle with Elliott the
previous year had been a valuable piece of preparation. But, at the
end of the day, the Allied-Reichmann affair was not a beauty
contest; it was a legal and political battle.

O&Y's Mickey Cohen was spending a great deal of time
working his old bureaucratic and political network in Ottawa.
Although Cohen, because of his close connections with the Trudeau Liberals, was non grata with the Tory government, many of
the public servants who had worked for him were still in power.
Paul Reichmann was also making the rounds of ministers to put
the O&Y case. But there was a feeling that the Reichmanns had
used up all their "credits," and more, in the Gulf Canada
acquisition.

Olympia & York may at last have realized how important Ron
Dickson and the union were to its efforts. Cohen got wind of a
meeting, scheduled for June 19, between Dickson and representatives of Investment Canada. He called Dickson and asked
whether Dickson would like to meet with Paul Reichmann again.
Dickson agreed. It would turn out to be an extraordinarily revealing meeting.

16

Losing It

ON THE MORNING OF JUNE 19, 1986, WHEN RON DICKSON turned up with union lawyer Leon Paroian at Paul Reichmann's room in Ottawa's Four Seasons Hotel, they were not only surprised to find Reichmann in shirt sleeves, they were surprised to find him apparently alone. Reichmann greeted them with a smile and said: "You're seven minutes late."

Reichmann quickly got down to business, handing Dickson a list of assurances similar to those Dickson had already received from Allied's Mike Jackaman. Then, to the astonishment of Dickson and Paroian, Reichmann began to berate the Jackaman assurances as worthless. If Allied won, he said, Walkerville would be orphaned, would inevitably deteriorate. He told Dickson he owed it to his membership to support Gulf.

When Paroian suggested that Investment Canada may have already decided in favor of Allied, Reichmann denied the claim vigorously. He said he had been meeting with members of the Mulroney cabinet. He was due to meet that day with Energy Minister Pat Carney.

Dickson heard Reichmann out but then said he still supported Allied-Lyons. Nevertheless, he told Reichmann that he would give "proper weight" to his assurances when he met with Investment Canada.

Then, wanting to make clear to Paul Reichmann exactly where he stood, Dickson pulled out a copy of a letter he had written to the *Windsor Star*. The letter was not designed to please Reichmann. Although it described him as a "man of immense, understated charm which he uses to his great advantage," it went on to declare ". . . one is almost tempted to say the emperor has no clothes when one considers how inept Mr. Reichmann and his colleagues have been throughout the Walker deal. Moreover," it continued, "despite Mr. Reichmann's many attributes as a successful businessman and decent human being, and his devotion to duty, family and religion, he still has something to learn even from a Scottish working man of the old school. That is, to be a part of humankind, one must be a participant in the affairs of humankind and not an aloof observer. Additionally, in the real world of less celebrated men, that part of the planet where most of us dwell, a man's word is not enough unfortunately. That is why, being the unredemptive realists that we are, we at local 2027 prefer Allied-Lyons as our new employer. Anything they say they sign. We invite Mr. Reichmann to do the same. . . ."

When he had read the letter, Reichmann got up and began to stride around the room, delivering an angry denunciation of those who were trying to thwart him in the takeover. He called Justice Robert Montgomery, the man who had thrown out O&Y's injunctions against the Allied sale, a "traffic court judge" who knew nothing of corporate law. "If Montgomery knew the facts," he told Dickson and Paroian, "he'd support the position of O&Y."

Reichmann acknowledged that mistakes had been made, but when Dickson again brought up Seagram, and reminded Reichmann that it had been the threat of a sell-off to Seagram that had been crucial in the union's support for Allied-Lyons, Reichmann became more and more agitated. He vigorously denied any sale to Seagram, but then declared that even if Seagram did acquire Hiram Walker they would not close down Walkerville's operations. "No," said Dickson, "but they sure as hell will close down most of Seagram's operations."

Again, Reichmann had misread the situation and Dickson's motivations. As a good union man, Dickson was not just concerned about Walkerville, he was concerned about liquor industry jobs in general. Reichmann brushed his comment aside. "In any event," he said, "Seagram would be a better owner of Hiram Walker than Allied-Lyons."

Then Reichmann turned on the Fingas proposal. Damning the

deal as a "charade," Reichmann asked, "Do you know how much [Hiram Walker director] Martin Goldfarb invested [to be a partner in Fingas]? Eleven dollars!" Fingas was a sham and a fraud, said Reichmann, who then delivered a tirade against Bud Downing, Allen Lambert, and Bill Fatt (a senior HWR executive who had managed to escape with his golden parachute despite Reichmann attempts to block the money). "Even today," said Reichmann petulantly, "I refuse to speak to Allen Lambert." Then he added, "I could have taken this further, but. . . ."

Dickson and Paroian sat transfixed as Reichmann continued his denunciation of all those who had opposed him in the Walker deal. Then, to Ron Dickson's astonishment, he said to the union leader: "The Englishmen are laughing at you behind your back."

Then, as if to deliver a final blow to the union's support for Allied-Lyons, Reichmann went to his briefcase and produced a letter, which he threw across the table to Dickson. Although the letter was not signed, it carried the names of four senior HW-GW executives. Its message was that those named were withdrawing their support for Allied-Lyons and transferring it to Gulf. Reichmann claimed that Cliff Hatch, Jr., had written the letter, but had not signed it because of a conflict of interest. The letter confirmed Dickson's suspicions that management had switched sides.

Toward the end of the meeting, Dickson, now plainly needling his opponent, reminded Paul Reichmann of his reputation for a deal being a deal. Hadn't Allied made a deal with Hiram Walker? Reichmann replied, condescendingly in Dickson's view, that it was Dickson's job to get the best deal possible for the people he represented. He said he was surprised that Dickson would support a foreign takeover. Then, around noon, Reichmann looked at his watch and apologized that he was already late for his meeting with Pat Carney. They all shook hands and Reichmann said to Dickson: "Well, whoever becomes the new owners of Hiram Walker, I hope we can still be friends."

The suggestion seemed more than incongruous, it seemed ridiculous.

Descending in the elevator, Leon Paroian said to Ron Dickson: "That man is incapable of listening to anybody." They both found Reichmann's performance disconcerting. His self-interest was transparent. But one of the most disturbing aspects of the meeting was Reichmann's tossing across the table the letter to Investment Canada bearing the names of the Hiram Walker executives. It was not so much the letter itself that was a shock, it was that Paul Reichmann would have shown it to them, thus revealing that the HW-GW managers had switched sides. The last person the managers would have wanted that letter shown to was Ron Dickson. The action of showing the letter could be interpreted as less than honorable. It was the action of a man determined to win at all costs.

At a meeting with Cliff Hatch, Jr., the next day, Dickson told HW-GW's chief executive about the confrontation with Paul Reichmann. Hatch was surprised that Reichmann had shown him the letter. He asked Dickson not to mention it to the executives involved. Hatch told Dickson his greater concern was that he had just been looking through the half-inch-thick Gulf plan of arrangement. Gulf was up to its neck in debt. When Dickson asked Hatch where he stood between the Reichmanns and Allied-Lyons, Hatch avoided the question. Cliff Hatch, Jr., still felt himself part of a proud family tradition. He felt it important to do the right thing for Walkerville. But he still wasn't quite sure what that was.

On July 9, the Ontario Supreme Court brought down its decision: the Reichmanns' appeal was rejected and the validity of the sale to Allied was upheld. The following day, Paul Reichmann gave an interview to the *Toronto Star*'s Diane Francis. Again he brought up the Seagram straw man. Pointing to the brothers' successful relationship with Abitibi-Price, he observed: "We were sure that would have happened with Hiram Walker, and it would have, without that silly rumor from Seagram. That's what poisoned the whole thing."

Reichmann said that Dickson's UAW workers were "naive," and claimed that the union represented only 460 workers out of a work force of 1,680. "Dickson and his workers are at no risk, whoever ends up owning it. But the other huge number of head office employees will stand a great risk if Allied-Lyons takes over."

It was uncertain where Reichmann thought he was going to win friends by such statements. He was insulting the union and hardly likely to put himself on a better footing with nonunionized employees because of that.

Speaking of Allied's purchase, he said: "That is not to say Allied did anything wrong. In sum total, it did what a good businessman does: trouble brewing creates an opportunity and a bargain."

That statement raised questions about his own motivations and methods.

With an eye to the Investment Canada decision, Reichmann commented: "It's quite, quite clear the sale would be a big net detriment . . . [T]here are statements by Allied it will introduce in Canada pear juice, cider or whatever. But that's an irrelevant kind of matter. . . ."

Francis's probing interview continued with a question about Allied's pledges being in writing. She was obviously unaware that Reichmann had given written pledges to Dickson. Nevertheless, Reichmann then made the astonishing statement: "It means nothing to put it in writing. The government knows that whatever they want from us they can have."

This was not the interview of a man who was in charge of events.

On July 11, the day Reichmann's "rare and candid" interview appeared in the *Star*, Investment Canada brought down its decision: the sale to Allied was declared to be of net benefit to Canada and could go ahead. Paul Reichmann, it appeared, had been beaten on every front.

The influential CBC radio program *As It Happens* contacted O&Y for comment on the decision. Paul Reichmann's secretary called back and said that Reichmann himself would comment. She gave a number in New York at which he could be reached. When one of the program's producers, Harry Schachter, called the number, Paul Reichmann answered. Reichmann said he was prepared to speak but he was in a hotel room with some other people. They would be leaving soon and he would call back in half an hour.

Schachter typed out a line of questions for the program's host, Dennis Trudeau, and waited. Reichmann called back just as the item was due to be aired. Reichmann listened on the telephone to his introduction: "The wealthy Reichmann family of Toronto has enjoyed spectacular business success for years. Today, they suffered a rare setback. Investment Canada has given the go-ahead to a British company, Allied-Lyons, to take over the Hiram Walker distillery. The Reichmanns, through Gulf Canada Corporation, recently bought Hiram Walker Resources and they badly wanted the Windsor-based liquor business as part of the package. Paul Reichmann is vice-chairman of Olympia & York Enterprises."

Trudeau opened by asking: "Mr. Reichmann, you've been fighting very hard to keep the distiller part of Hiram Walker in your company, Hiram Walker Resources. How big a blow to your plans is this Investment Canada decision?"

Paul Reichmann began a convoluted rebuttal. "OK," he said, "first I want to react to the introductory comments about the setback. First of all the basic issues are legal. Investment Canada was just one of the conditions that would be required if there were a legally binding agreement. Fundamental issues have to do with the questions: is there a legally binding agreement? If there is one, is there a provision in the agreement whereby by some payment the agreement can be cancelled. Furthermore, is there a requirement on a group that was not party to the agreement to facilitate actions which are conditions that have to be fulfilled . . ."

Trudeau interrupted: "You're talking there to me about the contract that Hiram Walker Resources made to sell the distiller to Allied-Lyons before you took over Hiram Walker. You're contesting that in court. . . . You've lost at Investment Canada. You've lost another decision about whether they had to consult the shareholders to sell the distiller. Why are you fighting so hard over this? Why do you want the distiller so badly?"

"First of all," Reichmann responded, "it's very important for Gulf Canada in its present circumstances of the world prices of oil to have a diversification in a stable product and assure its ability in the future to continue its exploration and development of oil reserves. But that is not the principal question at this point in time. Sometimes one might look at this as if it were a soccer game, let's say, where scoring is what counts. That is not the situation. There are five important legal issues before the court. In the first one, the court of appeal this week when they dismissed our appeal stated that part of the agreement had a contravention to the Canada Corporation Act and that the er . . . I do not have the document in front of me. . . ."

Paul Reichmann had become lost in his own legal web.

Trudeau moved in to help him out. "I understand," he said, "there are very fine legal points being debated here, but it remains, Mr. Reichmann, that you have taken a high profile and you've taken quite many steps to hold onto the distillers. Why is that income so important to you? Why do you think it is even important to Canada? Why do you oppose the Investment Canada decision?"

The response was once again tangential. ". . . As a matter of principle. As an individual. As a Canadian citizen, I believe that Canada should have an open-door policy and all kinds of investment should be welcome whether it's of benefit or not, because I think that for a nation, the importance of benefit is to the economy as a whole in the long run, not every single action as such . . ."

Trudeau interrupted: "Surely, though, you would have liked to have another decision from Investment Canada?"

Reichmann continued: "All that we have been saying is that as long as there is a statute in our books that says that investment criteria is net benefit to Canada, we are convinced that if Allied-Lyons were successful, this would be of substantial detriment to Canada."

When Trudeau asked him why, his answer was so complicated that the host had to cut him off.

It had been a less than sparkling performance by Paul

Reichmann. Despite the defeats he had suffered, Reichmann seemed determined to fight on. Both sides had declared that they wanted a summary judgment so that Hiram Walker's liquor business could continue without the shadow of contested ownership. Allied wanted a decision enforcing its contract. The Reichmanns wanted the contract thrown out. Then there was the Can$9 billion lawsuit. At least one piece of the deal fell into place to the Reichmanns' advantage. Interprovincial agreed, in a typically convoluted deal, to pay Can$1.1 billion for Home Oil. The Reichmanns, through Hiram Walker and Gulf, still held 40 percent of Interprovincial, so Home remained significantly under their control.

Faced with personal exposure in court in support of what almost everybody now agreed was a lost cause, Paul Reichmann's lieutenants would have one last go at snatching victory from the jaws of defeat.

In August 1986, while the various court cases between the Reichmanns and Allied-Lyons proceeded toward trial in Toronto, the Reichmann brothers traveled to London with Mickey Cohen. They had come, they claimed, to ask for peace. Allied realized that the Reichmanns could, as Paul Reichmann had threatened, hold them up in court "for years." Nevertheless, Sir Derrick Holden-Brown was resolute. He was prepared to make an arrangement that would help the Reichmanns save face, but he was determined to take control of HW-GW. When the team from O&Y sat down with him, he had his minimum demands ready: 51 percent of HW-GW and control of the board and management. The meeting appeared to go well. They shook hands on an agreement.

Problems became apparent two or three weeks later, when Allied's lawyers and management were in Toronto and discovered that the Reichmanns' negotiators had a very different understanding as to what had been agreed between Paul and Sir Derrick. In the words of an Allied executive: "Their second-line managers were all falling over themselves to be smart boys." Allied's Toronto lawyers, Fasken and Calvin, were getting uptight, and Allied's financial people were getting frustrated. Meanwhile, the

Hart-Scott-Rodino filing — which was a requirement for the takeover — had not been made by O&Y, despite a commitment to do so. Allied executives became concerned that they were being led into a trap. The Reichmanns were pleading tax complications and also the complexities of the Hiram Walker/Gulf corporate reorganization.

For Allied, the focus of frustration was Gil Newman. Every time they felt they were close to a deal, he would try to cut off another slice for the Reichmanns. It could have been that he was trying to prove his worth to his bosses — as part of his ongoing competition with Mickey Cohen — but it seems unlikely that he would have been acting without the knowledge of the Reichmanns. Rather, this was another example of the Reichmann technique of winning through a process of negotiation to the point of exhaustion.

According to an Allied lawyer: "They have a different style of negotiating and they tried it on Sir Derrick. He just didn't buy it. They don't start at issue one and go to issue twenty. They deliberately obfuscate the issues. I'm used to clients taking it out on their lawyers. But this is different. It is the principals who make deals. If they meet and think they have a deal and then don't choose to bring in lawyers and clarify things immediately to get out the wrinkles, if later the lawyers can't figure out what they meant, then they only have themselves to blame. That's a principal's problem, not a lawyer's problem. Their style of negotiating is one that is very hard to cope with. You can never get an issue settled. They keep chopping away at you, and you find that at the end of the day you have more issues than those with which you started."

In the end, Sir Derrick, who was in Toronto to help finalize the details, called Paul Reichmann and told him in no uncertain terms that his team was being met by frustration at every twist and turn. What had happened to the London agreement? Why was it being changed? Reichmann took the heat from Sir Derrick and apologized, saying that there must have been a series of "misunderstandings." It was a Friday. Reichmann explained that he could not work on the Sabbath, but he asked Sir Derrick to remain behind until the Sunday. The team from Allied, frustrated primarily with Gil Newman, left. On the Sunday morning, Reichmann went to the King Edward Hotel, where Sir Derrick was staying, and, within the space of an hour or so, the original agreement was resurrected.

Sir Derrick subsequently claimed: "I said all along that I felt that Paul and Albert would act in a totally honorable manner and that we must respect the problems that they were having. And in the end of course they did file Hart-Scott-Rodino and it did come through."

On September 5, 1986, agreement was reached under which Allied would control 51 percent of Hiram Walker, and the Reichmanns, 49 percent. The crucial part of the shareholders' agreement was a "put and call" arrangement under which Allied could buy Gulf's stake. Everybody believed this was a face-saving maneuver, allowing the Reichmanns to bow out of HW-GW after a decent period had elapsed. Finally, all litigation was ended, with each party bearing its own costs.

The conclusion of the Hiram Walker affair would mark the end of a remarkable period for the Reichmanns. They had been responsible, within a year, for the two largest acquisitions in Canadian history. Within a decade, Paul Reichmann had increased by twentyfold the assets under the family's control and built an empire that matched in size those of Canada's largest publicly owned companies, Bell Canada and Canadian Pacific. Half the growth had come in the previous year. But it was a troubled empire, exposed to the glare of political controversy and apparently deeply in debt.

The Gulf Canada acquisition had not merely been disastrously timed. It had stirred controversy about the use of taxpayers' funds to facilitate the growth of private empires. In Hiram Walker, Paul Reichmann had proved himself not only less than omniscient but also indecisive. He had underestimated the resolve of Hiram Walker's management and carried through with a hostile takeover, which he had claimed he would never do. He had called forth legions of lawyers to assert the right to Hiram Walker's liquor assets, again something he had previously claimed was not his "style." The acquisitions had also weakened the empire's financial position, although nobody knew how much. Significantly, however, most of the debt load had fallen on the companies the Reichmanns had acquired, principally Gulf.

The now even more fascinated press wrote stories in the summer of 1986 suggesting that a change had come over the Reichmanns; they were somehow acting — in particular in the Hiram Walker/Allied battle — "out of character." But the Reichmanns had not acted out of character; it was just that few people understood Paul Reichmann's apparently relentlessly acquisitive, driven, business persona.

The Reichmanns' compulsive secrecy had also created problems. Their unexplained actions had inevitably and repeatedly caused what Paul Reichmann euphemistically called "misunderstandings" because ultimately the Reichmanns did not *want* others to understand what they were doing. The communications breakdown in the case of Hiram Walker was far from unique.

Paul Reichmann claimed to understand people, but what he understood best was the sometimes ruthless art of dealmaking. Paul Reichmann's skill was in making money with money.

There also appeared a peculiarly Canadian — and peculiarly dangerous — element to the Reichmann story. The Reichmanns had been encouraged by a financial and political system that loved size and that indulged Canadians with talent and chutzpah to the point of folly. It was the Canadian corporate equivalent of the Peter Principle. It might even be called the "Paul Principle." As corporate executives tended to be promoted to the level of their incompetence, so Canadian companies in a prevailing climate of mega-loans and economic nationalism tended to expand to the point of self-destruction. Dome Petroleum, the company that had already given Canada a world-scale basket case, was the classic example.

The Reichmanns were very different from Dome's corporate odd couple, Jack Gallagher and Bill Richards, but the Dome executives, too, had been perceived as having "the golden touch," and had wound up Can$8 billion in the hole. Like Dome, the Reichmanns had been encouraged by the government to expand with the help of public money, and, like Dome in its halcyon days, they had found banks and financial institutions only too glad to open their vaults. Would they, like Dome, eventually choke themselves on the bankers' largesse? Where would Paul Reichmann's restless ambition take him next?

The first formal meeting of the new Hiram Walker–Gooderham & Worts board was held on March 12, 1987, the same day on which Sir Derrick spoke to the Empire Club in Toronto. Sir Derrick was a little apprehensive about what to expect, and took the trouble the day before the meeting to go through the agenda with Paul and Albert. The meeting proved to be a great success.

Afterwards, Sir Derrick took the Reichmanns to one side and asked if the presentations were to their liking. They expressed themselves well pleased. They decided that they liked Allied; they liked Sir Derrick. Paul asked Sir Derrick if he would do him a favor: could he send over any information he had on a development in London's docklands called Canary Wharf?

17

Canary Wharf:
Cheaper by the Dozen

IN THE LATE 1970S, WHEN THEY TOOK CONTROL OF ENGLISH Property, the Reichmanns had become involved in the construction of a three-story office building in London's fashionable Knightsbridge. Such were the frustrations of obtaining approvals and permits, and the delays in construction, that the project took the same time to complete as the seventy-two-story First Canadian Place. The brothers decided that Britain was not for them. Two leading members of their development team, Keith Roberts and John Norris, both British, felt the same way. Roberts and Norris had flourished in Canada, where development was not hampered by traditional rigidities and echoes of class rivalries. In Canada, they found, nothing was put off to tomorrow if it could be done today. In Britain, they would talk about it next week. The Reichmanns decided they wanted no part of the "British disease."

Less than ten years later, there appeared to have been a revolution in British attitudes. The person who had achieved this astonishing transformation was Prime Minister Margaret Thatcher. Her thundering 100-seat majority in the June 1987 general election — her third consecutive victory — made her the most successful British prime minister of the century. Reversing the slide into disaster that had led to the IMF bailing out the British Labour Government in 1976, Thatcher had revitalized the economy. She had broken the hammerlock of trade union power. She had reversed the intrusive role of the state. She had promoted "people's capitalism" via her extensive privatizations, and increased the base of her support through sales of state-owned "council houses." Perhaps most important, she had significantly changed British attitudes toward business, installing an "Enterprise Culture," where individual effort was allowed to reap its own rewards. She had also shown in the Falklands that Britain was prepared to assert its beliefs by force if necessary.

Paul Reichmann noted all this and found it to his liking. He told the British magazine, *Business*, "Things have dramatically changed. There is a different attitude that cuts through from top management to labour. There is little in common with the old system."

The new environment meant new opportunities. The "Big Bang" of financial deregulation in October 1986 produced a boom in the Square Mile, London's ancient financial heart. But the heart was showing signs of arteriosclerosis. With Japanese and American bankers clamoring for space and its narrow streets clogged with Porsches, the City appeared on the point of system overload.

London's problems had antedated the Big Bang. Its buildings were antiquated. They lacked the capacity to accommodate the sophisticated computers and telecommunications that were essential to the global financial revolution. Moreover, property seemed to be controlled by a tight cartel and strict development restrictions. Americans found this particularly frustrating.

In February 1985, Michael Von Clemm, Eurodollar virtuoso and chairman of Credit Suisse First Boston, an aggressive financial institution with Swiss/American parentage, visited the Isle of Dogs, a derelict area set within a loop of the Thames, two-and-a-half miles east of the City, the financial center of London, and just upstream from the magnificent architecture of Royal Greenwich. Von Clemm was looking for a packaging plant for a client. This derelict area, once the home of the West India Docks, a bustling symbol of Britain's trading empire, had been declared an "Enterprise Zone" by the Thatcher government; developers were offered free land and tax breaks, a somewhat un-Thatcherite approach, but one felt necessary to rejuvenate a national eyesore.

In 1981, Margaret Thatcher had created the London Docklands Development Corporation (LDDC) to buy land and control development in the Docklands. The Thatcher government's vision had not been grandiose. Sir Nigel Broackes, first chairman of the LDDC, thought in terms of new housing and light industry. It was with those limited objectives in mind that CS First Boston's Von Clemm made his trip down the Thames in early 1985.

While eating lunch on a barge, Von Clemm spotted a disused banana warehouse on a site known as Canary Wharf, named for its trade with the Canary Islands. He began to toy with the idea of converting it into a "back office" for his own company. After paying several more visits to the site, Von Clemm consulted with G. Ware Travelstead, a beefy, six-foot-six American developer and real estate consultant from Kentucky. Travelstead was already an adviser to First Boston Corp., one of Von Clemm's corporate parents. After looking over the site, Travelstead — who was nicknamed "Gee Whizz" by the British — took Von Clemm's light bulb and transformed it into a conceptual chandelier.

Travelstead knew that Von Clemm's financial institution had been searching for several years for a new head office location. Why not make Canary Wharf the front office instead of the back office? Indeed, why not turn this part of London into a "Wall Street on the water," a new location for financial institutions that would give them breathing space from the claustrophobic conditions of the Square Mile?

The concept was audacious but appealing to Von Clemm, who had come up against London's cliquey property establishment when he tried to promote a new City development at Bishopsgate. Von Clemm knew others felt as he did. Whenever a likely building came on the market, Von Clemm found himself in line with the same group of Wall Street expatriates. "Every time I went to see some place," he told the *Sunday Times*'s Ivan Fallon, "I saw Morgan Stanley or Salomon Brothers or Goldman Sachs either emerging as I was going in or going in as I was coming out."

No self-respecting starch-collared London agent would have dreamed of showing Von Clemm anything for his own use further down the river than the Tower of London. The East End of London, within which the Docklands sat, was the capital's least fashionable area, a warren of seedy sweatshops and tight-knit working-class communities in bleak terraced houses and drab public housing. Nevertheless, one thing the Docklands offered was lots of space.

Creating a completely new business location had a European precedent in La Defense, a huge turnkey development that had been built outside the center of Paris. Travelstead's plan also bore some similarities to the development of the World Financial Center in New York, although that project was still only a walk from Wall Street. Nevertheless, Von Clemm had noted that it took less than ten minutes to drive from Threadneedle Street, home of the Bank of England, to Canary Wharf.

Travelstead persuaded Credit Suisse First Boston and Morgan Stanley, which had been considering back office capacity at Canary Wharf, to expand the scope of the project on a massive scale, to build a series of eighty-five-story Manhattan-style towers with 10 million square feet of space.

The project had first been brought to Paul Reichmann's attention by Chuck Young, the former president of Citibank Canada, whose office had been two floors from Reichmann's in First Canadian Place. Young had gotten to know Reichmann when Reichmann had briefly served on Citibank Canada's board. In 1986, Young was transferred to London by Citibank, heard of the Canary Wharf plans, and mentioned them several times to Paul Reichmann. When Reichmann was in London in September 1986 making peace with Allied-Lyons, he called on Young. Young wanted to take him to the Docklands, but Reichmann begged off. He was a busy man.

Then, toward the end of 1986, Travelstead called O&Y's Michael Dennis, looking for partners. Dennis presented the scheme again to Paul Reichmann, who now looked at it and was attracted and intrigued by its scope. The World Financial Center was now all but sewn up, and Paul Reichmann was looking for a new project. Inevitably it had to be a big one.

Dennis entered negotiations with Travelstead and his partners, now not merely CS First Boston but also CSFB's parent, Credit Suisse, and Morgan Stanley. On several occasions, they thought they were close to a deal, but negotiations fell apart, claimed Dennis, over a "clash of cultures." One of the main problems was that the Reichmanns insisted on control. They also planned to make Travelstead's already ambitious scheme even more grandiose. According to Dennis, they told Travelstead's group: " 'If you want to come along as partners, that's fine. But understand we might want to spend a lot of money in nontraditional ways.' And they became concerned they could get spent into the ground. At the end of the day, although Travelstead wanted to go on, the time frame for real estate investment is very different from the time frame that investment banks, who are traders, look at. They are not used to tying up money and waiting five years or longer for substantial return." In any case, Paul Reichmann quietly told associates, Travelstead really was not the kind of partner that he liked to deal with.

The two sides parted in February 1987, and O&Y heard no more from the American group. Then, in the latter half of June, Dennis bumped into an executive with First Boston who told him that the British government had set a deadline of July 17 for an agreement on the development, and that, according to Dennis, "the only way anything would happen was if we were involved." There was a perception that the scheme would disintegrate because Travelstead's partners were not willing to make the kind of commitments the British government wanted, including contributions to the transportation infrastructure in return for the free land and tax breaks.

Dennis mentioned this to Paul Reichmann, who called former Ontario premier, Bill Davis, who was on the board of First Boston and who had known the Reichmanns since they had leapt to prominence in Toronto. Davis spoke to the head of First Boston, Peter Buchanan, then called Paul back and announced there was a deal to be made. The following day, Michael Dennis and Davies Ward & Beck lawyer Derek Watchorn were on a plane headed for London. Within days, Paul flew over and a handshake deal was made. In the following ten days of early July 1987, the immense documentation was completed and, by the deadline, a new agreement had been signed. The Reichmanns reportedly bought out Travelstead and his group for U.S.$112 million.

Said Dennis, "Paul stood up and took all our breath away by saying 'Yes, I will build ten million feet in seven years, by 1996.'" The project was forecast to cost between £3 billion and £4 billion.

Paul Reichmann saw an opportunity to build a monument that would change the face of London. He saw Canary Wharf by analogy to other developments, principally Manhattan's Rockefeller Center, which had played a dramatic role in shifting Big Apple business to mid-town. He realized that Canary Wharf, however spectacular, could not rival the prestige of a City or West End address. Nevertheless, he believed that clients could be attracted by a combination of high-tech space in manicured surroundings and rents at little more than half then prevailing City levels of over £50 a square foot. He believed that the financial advantages would be sufficient for the project to overcome initial image problems. Then, when he had created another "new address," he would be able to hoist rents, eventually to 90 percent of City levels.

His initial cost advantage would be based on the fact that he was effectively getting the land for free, although he had made commitments to help fund infrastructure, in particular transportation. But even when these costs were included, he calculated his land costs would only be £50 a square foot versus up to £500 in the City. The other cost advantage would lie in the tax breaks attached to the Docklands. He developed a plan under which he would pass on these tax breaks to his financial backers in return for a lower rate of interest.

There were a number of flaws in Paul Reichmann's theories that are much easier to see in hindsight. The first was the unwillingness of Britons to move to a new location; the second was the unlikelihood that the Docklands' chronic transportation infrastructure problems would be solved in time; the third related to Paul Reichmann's views on property cycles. He had explained to

Travelstead during earlier negotiations that one of the reasons O&Y had moved into New York was because the property cycles were different from Toronto. Similarly, he told Travelstead, London would be different again, thus providing a countercyclical balancing out. But the whole point about global deregulation was that it would not merely create global financial markets, it would make property markets global too. Reichmann also did not foresee the startling developments that would occur behind the Iron Curtain toward the end of the 1980s, events that promised fundamentally to change Europe's center of gravity. This denting of the theory of London's European centrality was further affected, ironically, by Thatcher's opposition to closer European integration.

In addition, there was already evidence that the City would not take Canary Wharf lying down. In fact, the City of London had changed the planning rules more than a year before the Reichmanns agreed to undertake the Canary Wharf project. In May 1986, the Corporation of London had announced that the plot ratio would change from a varied formula of between 3 to 1 and 5 to 1 to a blanket 5 to 1. In other words, developers would henceforth be able to build five square feet up for every one square foot at ground level. Although this change did not lead to any single project as spectacular as Canary Wharf, it did contribute toward an unprecedented surge of building in the City. Indeed, the development rush was already under way when the Reichmanns began planning their massive venture.

In 1986, Maggie Thatcher, clad in Tory blue and crowned with a hard hat, had taken the controls of a crane and swung the final chunk of granite into place at the Broadgate office complex on the edge of the financial district. At the time, it was the largest project undertaken in London since the Great Fire of 1666. By mid-1987, some were already saying that the impact of the Big Bang might have been greatly exaggerated. The Jeremiahs seemed to be corroborated by the New York stock market crash of October 1987 and its global aftershocks. But in fact, insofar as financial authorities responded to the crash by lowering interest rates and pumping up the money supply, the banks wound up pouring even more cash into bricks and mortar. Just weeks after the crash, a single pile driver broke symbolic ground at the Canary Wharf site.

The project remained controversial. Part of the disagreement between Travelstead and the Reichmanns had been over the form of the development. Although the Reichmanns took over the master plan that had been created for Travelstead by New York–based Skidmore Owings & Merrill, they set about redesigning the buildings and their relationship to the river. Travelstead had wanted to pile multilevel parking lots above the site of the Docklands Light Railway. But this meant that the buildings themselves moved well above the waterline. The Reichmanns opted for underground parking and brought the project back down to the water. They also abandoned the idea of three gigantic towers, and instead decided to have one major tower, designed by the World Financial Center's master architect, Cesar Pelli. This great fifty-story block topped by a pyramidal "hat" was very much a cousin of Pelli's WFC buildings — it was pure Manhattan. Pelli knew that it would not appeal to British traditionalists, and in particular to the most prominent British architectural traditionalist of them all.

When Pelli unveiled the design at a presentation early in 1988, he said, with prescience and attempted diplomacy: "I think what Prince Charles has done in architecture has been wonderful, and I just hope I am not going to be at the end of one of his salvoes." Prince Charles's reaction to the tower?: "I personally would go mad if I had to work in a building like that." When Paul Reichmann presented a model of the tower to a top government official, the official reportedly declared: "Mr. Reichmann, I have been alive now for sixty years, and we are sitting on the sixteenth floor and I think that's about as high as any human being ought to be." Chuck Young, who had now left Citibank and joined the Reichmanns, looked at the official and asked himself: "Is this 1987 or 1887?"

Another inevitable source of flak was the Docklands community, which reacted strongly to this potential alien incursion.

Nevertheless, the Reichmanns were sensitive in their consultations and committed to providing local jobs. In line with their old technique of coopting opposition, they hired Peter Wade, the chairman of the Association of Island Communities, an umbrella body representing more than sixty Isle of Dogs organizations, as community relations officer. The noise and dust from the site would cause much understandable grumbling. The greatest outcry emerged when it was discovered that the tower interfered with local television reception.

Across the river, the borough of Greenwich strongly objected to the project's impact on the vista from the hill in Greenwich Park, on which sat the Royal Observatory. Michael Dennis made the trek to the hill, to stand beside the statue of General Wolfe, the British general who had earned a central place in Canadian history through his defeat of the French on the Plains of Abraham. Dennis pronounced: "The Isle of Dogs is no great wonder to look at from Greenwich today."

Dennis was right, but he was missing the subtle point; like the top government official, the borough of Greenwich was really objecting to the notion of foreign invasion and affront to tradition. Like Wolfe, the British had been used to doing the conquering. They did not like the idea of foreigners seizing local territory, even if it was desolate. The ghosts of the Astronomers Royal would spin in their graves. Still, Greenwich had already challenged the project in the High Court and lost. So Wolfe would now look on impassively as the greatest private development in British history took form across the river.

Far from being daunted by the 1987 stock market crash, Paul Reichmann claimed that the project was now even better than he had first imagined. In March 1988, he made one of his reverse *mea culpas*: "We took the wrong approach with Canary Wharf," he told the Toronto *Globe and Mail*. "It won't work as a satellite." Then came the kicker: Canary Wharf would become the center of a whole new "third business district" for London.

"We have realized that our success is not dependent on one area of the economy, financial services, but rather all of the U.K.

economy because of the revolution that is taking place in British business and British businessmen."

Reichmann pronounced himself a convert to the powers of the Thatcher revolution. "Each time I go to London, the more enthusiastic I become as I meet the younger people. Their attitude is quite different from that of their parents.

"In 1979, when we acquired English Property Corp., the business environment was stale. The young people I interviewed for jobs were bureaucratic. They had goals, but their goals were just to live, to carry on.

"Today, that is totally changed. Young graduates want to be entrepreneurs, to go into business where they can be creative."

Then he stared the god of hubris in the face and declared: "This is not a risky project. Doing one building there would be risky; doing a dozen is not. On a scale of one to ten, if you say the risk with the World Financial Center was nine, here it would be one."

He continued: "When we built the World Financial Center, I thought there'd be no repeat of that. Then the San Francisco redevelopment came along. But something like this . . . I can't imagine anything like Canary Wharf coming up again. It's exciting, lots of fun."

The last time he had mentioned business as being "fun" was at the beginning of the Hiram Walker affair. Canary Wharf would prove even more problematic.

The immediate problem facing O&Y was the construction of a project of unprecedented size and scope within a time frame that astonished the British construction industry. Travelstead had lined up five of the U.K.'s largest contractors for his project, but O&Y relegated them to the building of Westferry Circus — the traffic roundabout at the western edge of the development — and replaced them with Lehrer-McGovern International, the U.S. project manager owned by British building giant Bovis. LMI integrated its operation with O&Y's initially slim London construction organization, led by senior vice-presidents Richard Griffiths and George Iacobescu. Canada's second largest contrac-

tor, Ellis-Don, was paired with British management contractor Sir
Robert McAlpine to build the two tallest buildings on the wharf,
the principal of which was the tower.

By the end of 1988, there were 1,200 staff and workers on the
site, which was being fed by up to ten bargeloads of construction
material a day, brought from a transshipment point downriver at
Tilbury Docks. Soon there were three dozen tower cranes operating at Canary Wharf. The site threw up a wall of sound, a
cacophony of heaving and whining machinery, clanking metal,
and workers' shouts, against the background of the dull thud of the
pile drivers. Within the site's trailers, meanwhile, there was the
quieter dissonance of cultures clashing.

Richard Griffiths, the man in charge of construction, was a
slim, chain-smoking architect who had followed Michael Dennis
to O&Y from the City of Toronto's planning department.
Griffiths was a Canadian but he had been educated partly in
London. He had become involved with Canary Wharf from New
York. Dennis asked him to work on the the construction, and he
and George Iacobescu — with whom Griffiths had worked for
five years on the World Financial Center — had wound up
running the show, "by default" claimed Griffiths.

Said Griffiths: "We had a huge project on our hands; we knew
we had to start building it very fast; and we knew that we didn't
have internally, nor could we import from North America, all the
talent, all the resources needed. So our theory, my theory, was to
draw on as much management as we could. So we took on board
Lehrer-McGovern International, which at that time was 50 percent owned by Bovis. We thought there we were getting the best
of both worlds in terms of American energy, greater willingness to
change and look at things in new ways, plus an understanding of
the British marketplace.

"O&Y/LMI would be the great common denominator, the
project manager, the strategists. They would bring the common
elements to the job, everything from logistical planning and
organizing common facilities to dealing with statutory outside
agencies and local authorities. But at the building construction

level we felt we needed to bring in local talent. That's why we hired management contractors."

Griffiths soon found problems with control. The stratified British system, with its long chain of command, meant that messages got lost in translation. Griffiths would speak to the management contractor, the management contractor would speak to the manager of the subcontractors, the manager of the subcontractors would speak to the work force, who were broken up into different groupings. It was like the classic Second World War joke about passing a message down the military line by word of mouth: "Send us reinforcements, we're going to advance" became "Send us three and fourpence, we're going to a dance."

Griffiths wanted to get out in the mud and speak directly with the men on the site, but this was not the British way. There was a pecking order and territorial defensiveness that had to be observed. O&Y found the British construction industry to be as stratified as the British class system. The architects and engineers were the aristocracy. On their right hand sat the quantity surveyor, with a very clear area of control. On the other hand sat the electrical engineers. Then came the contractors, who were considered little more than ciphers. In North America, contractors had higher status and were used to creative input. In Britain, they concentrated on "building the drawing."

Problems were partly laid at the door of the notorious British unions, who were, in the words of Philip Reichmann, "more gentlemanly but much less susceptible to innovation. Innovation is welcome in New York. With the British unions, it's more: 'We just want to do it the way we've always done it.' "

The notion of being constantly ready to think of a "better way," to keep that light bulb at the ready, was not only alien, it was considered a "pain in the arse." Griffiths found that spreading the Reichmann construction gospel was an uphill struggle. "To us," he told the suspicious subcontractors, "the man who builds it is just as important as the man who designs. He should be heard from and listened to on a constant basis." But the British were quite happy in their niches. The man on the site knew that the route into the trailer or office was not likely paved with originality, but with conformity. In North America, the site superintendents would feel free to call senior development management. In Britain, that was unthinkable. Construction people knew their place and believed it inappropriate to go through other than "proper channels."

In the summer of 1989, although the project was moving at breakneck speed by British standards, it was hit by an eight-week unofficial strike by steel erectors, followed by a work-to-rule. The slowdown hit Canary Wharf's most prominent element — the tower — hardest, leaving it at only twelve stories at the end of the year. In March 1990, with the tower up to the twenty-first floor but behind schedule, O&Y fired Ellis-Don McAlpine and took over the contracting position itself.

This was partly due to the fall behind schedule, but also to a desire by O&Y, in Griffiths's words, "to take over our own destiny, and control things in a more direct manner than we were able to with Ellis-Don. We wanted to get our hands on the people who were dealing with the individual pieces of the work. The same was true for all the management contractors, but the tower happened to be the largest and most significant piece of the project."

In the meantime, a whole different set of battles was being quietly and cheerfully fought by O&Y's procurement wizard, George Iacobescu, part of O&Y's "Romanian Mafia." Many British suppliers had rubbed their hands at the prospect of taking O&Y to the cleaners in a tight construction market, but Iacobescu thwarted them with the global supply intelligence he had built up while working with his Romanian colleague Otto Blau in New York. He placed contracts all over the world. Still, he too was frustrated by the British lack of flexibility and originality.

In North America, Iacobescu was used to getting input from contractors. He would send them drawings and ask: "Does this make sense? How can we do this more efficiently, cheaper?" But the British management contractors just wanted to build the drawing. To them, the architects and the engineers were the "White Gods." The architects and engineers had done nothing to dispel this impression, as was shown in Iacobescu's problems with the centerpiece fountain in Cabot Square. For once, Iacobescu had managed to coax some originality out of the manufacturer when he'd asked: "How can we do this better, cheaper?" The manufacturer had suggested improvements in the pumping system. But Skidmore, Owings & Merrill had balked at violating the sanctity of their design. If O&Y wanted to change it, they declared, then SOM would not be able to supply a performance guarantee. Iacobescu sacrificed the performance guarantee, but made savings of twice that amount on the costs. For Iacobescu, the fountain was one of a hundred problems to be solved all over the site, while his team plotted the movement of supplies from around the world. The marble, stone, and slate alone came from a United Nations of suppliers in Brazil, Guatemala, Finland, Bulgaria, Italy, Germany, England, and India. The Bulgarian marble for the job had reputedly been polished by the Bulgarian army.

At least Iacobescu found that the unions were prepared to permit more prefabrication than would have been allowed in Manhattan. For example, washrooms came in modules, complete with marble floors, paneled walls, and fittings. This modular approach also made pilfering less easy, although of course it still took place.

Part of Iacobescu's procurement was almost a thousand mature trees that would be planted around the project in an attempt to bestow an instant past upon it. Iacobescu had to go to a German nursery to find trees in the quantity and of the size the project demanded. His competitor for instant history, perhaps appropriately, was another even greater master of illusion, the Walt Disney organization, which also needed trees for its Euro Disney project in Paris. Both Paul Reichmann and the late Walt Disney were essentially in the same business: that of making dreams come true.

From time to time, Paul Reichmann would appear without warning on the site, a stooped, attentive figure, listening as Iacobescu or Griffiths briefed him on details. Of course, there was no reason for Paul Reichmann to appear at Canary Wharf at all, but it was a symbol of his pride in power and ownership. He was the man who was making all this happen. He wanted to experience it up close. His presence was also symptomatic of his constant attention to detail. Workers would see him peering closely at the quality of the marble, or standing at the platform of the Docklands Light Railway, cocking an ear to see if the noise levels had been reduced enough.

Showing a visitor round the site in the summer of 1990, George Iacobescu spoke with a combination of admiration and affection for his boss, but also a little tongue in cheek. He acknowledged that Paul often changed his mind, but nobody ever doubted that the new direction was the right one. Said Iacobescu, with a pointed reference to his godlike status: "We propose, Paul disposes." Iacobescu said that Paul had told him: "I never mind doing a U-turn, if I can find something better." Little changes here and there were justified by the scope of what they were doing — making a project that would be there long after they had all gone.

Said Iacobescu: "People think we're crazy: the quality of materials we're putting into this job; the care we're taking." But people still thought they were crazy for other reasons too. By the beginning of 1990, the doubting Thomases were having a field day. The London property market was all but on the point of collapse. And people were still concerned that you just would not be able to to get there from here, or from virtually anywhere.

The Reichmanns had swept into Canary Wharf and developed the scheme on a scale and at a speed quite beyond the original intentions of the British government for Docklands. When he had taken the project over, Paul Reichmann had perhaps concentrated too much on the free land and tax breaks, and not enough on access. As others, too, developed Docklands projects, the existing arteries to the city became even more clogged. The main city link, the East India Dock Road, became a river of carbon monoxide. New roads were planned, but they took time. The Docklands Light Railway was swamped and was prone to breakdowns. It was derisively dubbed the "Toytown Railway." The development critical for success was the construction of an extension to the Jubilee subway line. The Reichmanns had committed £400 million toward the proposed cost of this line (a high profile and much-quoted figure whose present value, since the money would be paid out over many years, was much lower). But approval for the line was taking much longer than expected. At the earliest, the new line would not be in before 1996, leaving the project with a three-year twilight zone when access could prove a nightmare.

Other problems that could have been foreseen earlier, in particular the spate of new developments in the City, were also becoming painfully obvious. At the beginning of 1990, Godfrey Bradman, whose Rosehaugh had been one of the joint developers of the Broadgate complex, sent tremors through the British stock market when he went to his shareholders for £125 million. But then Paul Reichmann, who had already taken a third share in Bradman's Broadgate partner, Stuart Lipton's Stanhope, also bought 8 percent of Rosehaugh. He seemed to be making yet another countercyclical vote of confidence in London.

At its Great George Street offices, just off Parliament Square, O&Y had set up a no-expenses-spared presentation suite, where prospective tenants and dignitaries — including Prime Minister Thatcher — were wooed with scale models both of Canary Wharf and some of the Reichmanns' other developments.

In the first room were models of the Reichmanns' jewels, First Canadian Place and the World Financial Center. There was also a model of the Queen's Quay development in Toronto, displayed as an example of the success of mixed-used development such as that planned at Canary Wharf. In fact, Queen's Quay had not been a great commercial success.

In the next room was a huge model of London, stretching from the City airport in the east to beyond the West End. This model, which contained every major building in the London area, was intended to demonstrate that Canary Wharf was no farther from the City than was the West End. Canary Wharf was subtly highlighted by a small spotlight, making it appear as if a shaft of divine approval was falling upon it from above.

O&Y demonstrators would press buttons and dotted lights of various colors appeared, tracing the courses of the planned expansions of old and new transportation routes linking the City and Canary Wharf. On one wall was an aerial photograph of The Mall, stretching from Buckingham Palace to Admiralty Arch. Upon it was superimposed an outline of Canary Wharf, intended to give some indication of the size of the project. But the notion of plonking down this development behemoth in the Queen's — not to mention Prince Charles's — backyard hinted at sacrilege.

Next came a larger presentation of the whole project, then an even larger scale model of the main tower, Cabot Square, and its other flanking buildings. All around were displayed sections of the marble and other materials that would be used in the project, including a slab of the stainless steel plating that would cover the tower. There was even a mock-up of a corner office, where you could sample the views from the tower's four corners.

Finally came an even larger scale model of the retail section, which would sit on either side of the main station of the Docklands Light Railway. At the west end of the building was to be a livery hall, the location, the leasing agents told visitors, for banquets and cocktail parties and concerts and company meetings, perhaps even proxy fights.

Floundering companies might one day hold press conferences there.

Prospective clients would be taken down to the pier at Westminster for the launch trip down the river and the tour of the site. Then they would return to Great George Street by limo. One visitor noticed that the O&Y man very pointedly looked at his watch as they arrived back and said, "Twenty-two minutes." The visitor asked if he always timed the trip. "Oh yes," said the man. The traveling time was very important.

Michael Dennis, sitting upstairs at Great George Street, with Big Ben chiming in the background, noted wryly that development was always a business of frustrations. He held his hands out in front of him, like a fisherman demonstrating the size of the one that got away. "What a developer does," he said, "is that he has a string this long, and it's full of knots. He just goes down the string untying knots, and somebody comes along knotting the string after him. It's no different anywhere."

But Dennis also acknowledged that no development was scientific. It was a subtle blend of building and marketing. It was also a gigantic psychological game. Blue-chip tenants would not even consider moving to a new "address" unless they knew they would have other blue-chip tenants as their neighbors. Luring in such tenants had not been easy.

It was not simply a matter of the need for more tenants. Under the complex, secret agreements that Paul Reichmann had negotiated with G. Ware Travelstead's original partners — Morgan Stanley and Credit Suisse First Boston (who would own their own buildings at Canary Wharf) — they could both sublease if other major financial institutions did not sign up for significant chunks of space. That could prove disastrous for the project's status as a banking center.

Following round-the-clock negotiations in June 1990, Manufacturers Hanover and American Express signed up, effectively putting the project over that leasing hump. Other major tenants by then included oil giant Texaco, advertising company Ogilvy & Mather, and Conrad Black's *Daily Telegraph*. Anchor tenants for the project's retailing component included the doyen of British retailing, Marks and Spencer.

But luring tenants was growing more expensive. The collapse in rents and the continuing doubts over transport meant that greater incentives had to be offered: rent-free periods, buying up old leases. This meant a drastic hauling down in projected cash flows from the development, which in turn dramatically pulled down its present value. Its present value determined its finance-ability. Behind the open battles on the construction site and the more subtle negotiations over leasing, the greatest challenge was the project's financing. That was proving the most difficult juggling trick of all.

The Reichmann myth had always been an essential feature in the financing of O&Y. But early in 1990, that myth had taken a severe knock when Paul Reichmann had found himself up to his neck in one of the greatest financial debacles of the decade: the collapse of the huge but hastily ill-assembled empire of Canadian developer, Robert Campeau. Once again, that involvement was based in Paul Reichmann's acquisitiveness rather than his desire to build.

18

Strange Bedfellows

PAUL REICHMANN HAD FIRST SPOKEN TO ROBERT CAMPEAU during the Royal Trust affair, calling to explain that he had not bought Royal Trust's shares in order to thwart Campeau, but as an investment. "That," he later said, "was my first mistake."

The distinction he made with his call was a fine one. As a Campeau adviser — embittered by subsequent events — noted: "Paul Reichmann may have called, but it was like him saying, 'Bob, I've stuck a knife in your back, but I haven't done it for the Toronto Establishment, I've done it for myself.' "

Nevertheless, Campeau appreciated the call. He felt it created a bond between Paul Reichmann and himself. It was most unlikely that Paul Reichmann shared the feeling. Apart from the fact that they were both successful developers, two more dissimilar personalities with completely different backgrounds could hardly be imagined.

Bob Campeau was as high-strung, gregarious, and vain as Paul Reichmann was low-key, retiring, and superficially modest. Campeau was a staunch Roman Catholic who often seemed haunted by his religion, particularly when it came to his complex marital arrangements. He had had children with his current wife, Ilse, before he had separated from his first wife, Clauda, who had subsequently died of cancer. Paul Reichmann's Orthodox Judaism, by contrast, seemed to be a source of strength. No Ilses or Marla Mapleses or Leona Helmsleys for Paul. Bob liked to party; Paul liked to walk and relax with the Talmud. Both were risk takers, but Paul Reichmann's risks reputedly came after the most intensive analysis; they were seemingly exercises in pure logic. Bob Campeau's risks were ambitious fliers that became entangled with his insecurities. Paul Reichmann was not displeased with the suspicion that he had a crystal ball. Bob Campeau was more concerned simply with proving he had balls.

Nevertheless, beneath the surface, the men had a good deal in common. Paul Reichmann's ego was at least as large as that of Bob Campeau. Moreover, in the Hiram Walker affair, he had shown that he could become emotionally involved, perhaps to the detriment of his business judgment. Both men were possessed by consuming business ambition. Both managed like owners. The most important activity in their respective organizations went on inside their own heads. Neither felt any need to keep management or advisers informed. Both were relentless negotiators. Both were outsiders. Both possessed that peculiar entrepreneurial solipsism called vision that is at the root of capitalism's greatest achievements, and greatest disasters. Certainly, no organization would be big enough for both of them.

Robert Campeau had been born to a poor French-Canadian family in Chelmsford, near the stark moonscape of Sudbury, Ontario. As a child, he could imagine no greater luxury than indoor plumbing. Fiercely competitive, he had early on decided he wanted to work for himself. Like Paul Reichmann and his warehouse, Campeau had found his avocation when he built a house. He moved to larger and larger housing ventures, where his commitment to quality became legendary, and then to commercial developments, primarily in and around Ottawa. He undertook many developments for the government, exploiting both French-Canadian connections and loose bureaucratic control of costs. Thence he turned to pioneering development of the Toronto waterfront, including the Harbour Castle Hotel.

Despite his business success, much of what he regarded as the Establishment never took him seriously. He was just terminally *nouveau*. They nodded sagely about stories of volatile behavior, nervous breakdowns, and lawsuits with his children; they tittered about rumors of toupees, hair transplants, and facelifts.

Undaunted, he turned to his most ambitious development. His financial opponents could hardly ignore Scotia Plaza, the sixty-eight-story granite-clad monolith he erected in the heart of downtown Toronto's financial district. In 1984, during the building's construction, Campeau moved into a 25,000-square-foot imitation-Norman chateau on Toronto's exclusive Bridle Path. But despite a huge house-warming where the guests included former Canadian prime minister Pierre Trudeau, Emmett Cardinal Carter, and the Ontario premier, William Davis, and where Paul Anka crooned a special adaptation of "My Way," Campeau had still arrived only in terms of location. What he craved — acceptance — was still being withheld. It was perhaps this continued position as an outsider that led to a severe bout of depression in 1984 and 1985, when, according to colleagues, Campeau "disappeared." But then he bounced back. If they would not accept him in Canada, he would go to the United States, where people were ranked by their merits and achievements rather than their backgrounds and connections.

In 1986, having assembled a band of adventurous Wall Street advisers, Campeau drew a bead on Manhattan-based Allied Stores Corp., which controlled close to 700 department and specialty stores, including the Brooks Brothers and Ann Taylor chains. Allied's market value was ten times that of Campeau. It looked like an attempt by a beaver to swallow a buffalo. But these were the glory days of the leveraged buyout, when high-interest junk-bond financing was available to anyone with a target, and the bigger the better. The business rationale was that the Allied chains remaining after disposals to pay down debt could be used to anchor shopping mall developments.

The mastermind behind Campeau's assault on Allied was Bruce Wasserstein, a First Boston Corp. investment banker who had a "dare to be great" speech that he trotted out whenever his clients looked like flinching in the face of potentially crippling obligations. The speech proved particularly inspiring for Robert Campeau, to whom Wasserstein referred as "the real estate guy."

Instead of going the more standard, tender-offer route, Campeau bought control of Allied in the market, via a Wasserstein-inspired "Street Sweep," for a total of U.S.$3.6 billion. In the process, he ran up a tab of more than U.S.$3 billion with syndicates led by Citibank (despite the fact that Campeau's in-house nickname at the bank was "Mad Bomber") and First Boston, who broke new investment-banking ground by putting its own money behind the deal. First Boston's chief executive, Peter Buchanan (who had played an intermediary role in helping the Reichmanns into Canary Wharf), would later call Campeau "a living water torture." Thomas Macioce, Allied's strait-laced chief executive, subsequently claimed that he'd been "blindsided by a trainload of clowns."

Nevertheless, apart from the backing of some of Wall Street's biggest names, Campeau could also claim the backing of one of America's richest and shrewdest developers, Edward DeBartolo. DeBartolo, based in Youngstown, Ohio, was regarded as the king of U.S. shopping malls, controlling around one-tenth of the country's retail mall space. He also controlled the franchises of the National Hockey League's Pittsburgh Penguins and the National Football League's San Francisco 49ers. The stone-faced developer reportedly worked thirteen hours a day and took neither vacations nor prisoners. He had originally been a prospective "white knight" for Allied, but having failed to rescue it, he had — to the surprise of many — done a deal with Campeau, lending him money and buying some of Allied's assets.

Once the deal was done and the money had been lent, a slight problem appeared: Robert Campeau could not come up with the U.S.$300 million in equity he had promised as a down payment. If he had been negotiating a mortgage on a house and had not come through, he would have been kicked out of the realtor's office, but since there were hundreds of millions in fees attached to the deal, his financial associates scrambled around to help him find the money. Half the money came, bizarrely, from a Can$150 million loan from the Citibank office in Toronto — a strange form of "equity." To find the other half, Campeau's First Boston advisers put together a list of prospective investors, including Ivan Boesky, who had not yet been caught, Donald Trump, who had not yet glitzed himself to the point of bankruptcy, and the

Reichmanns. Boesky and Trump had never heard of Campeau and said no. That left the Reichmanns.

Kim Fennebresque, a colleague of Wasserstein at First Boston, arranged a meeting in Toronto between Paul Reichmann and Campeau. The merchant banker, according to John Rothchild's entertaining *Going for Broke*, "observed that Campeau, who he knew could be gruff and short-tempered, acted solicitously, almost fawningly, towards the . . . billionaire with the rabbinical beard." But Paul Reichmann politely but firmly turned down the offer to put up Campeau's equity. He said he did not invest in things he knew nothing about, and he did not know retailing.

On the flight back to New York, Fennebresque wondered if he was not doing business with the wrong Canadian developer. "The Reichmanns were obviously much richer than Campeau," he recalled, "but the gulf between them was not just financial. Compared to Paul Reichmann, Campeau was a supplicant, a lightweight, a parvenu."

Campeau was reckoned to admire Reichmann, not only for his immense corporate achievements, but for his reputation as a scholarly and tasteful person. Also, according to one former insider, "There is no doubt that Bob's deference appealed to an aspect of Paul Reichmann's ego. Bob clearly set great store by the advice that Paul gave him. Paul Reichmann didn't aspire to be any role model for Robert Campeau, but I think he felt flattered by the attentions of a clearly talented and very successful man. Anyone would."

There was also claimed to be a certain attraction of opposites. "Paul Reichmann, for all his great talents," said the same observer, "is not a particularly gregarious person. He's a rather shy man, and he liked and respected in Bob Campeau certain qualities that he did not himself possess. There is nothing unhealthy in that. Campeau is a very charming, gregarious character."

Nevertheless, Paul Reichmann was not known as a man who would allow business decisions to be clouded by personal considerations. Any deal he did with Campeau would be purely for his own advantage, and Campeau did have something that Paul Reichmann coveted: Scotia Plaza.

Although he was not interested in the Allied deal, Paul Reichmann agreed to buy half of Scotia Plaza, thus providing Campeau with the rest of the equity needed to complete Allied. The Reichmanns negotiated very attractive terms. They also bought further shares and some convertible debentures in Campeau Corporation.

Despite a revolving door in Allied's executive suite, due to Campeau's inability to let managers manage, Campeau and his surviving lieutenants were able to sell assets and pay down a lot of Allied debt, thus surprising many critics. But once he had proved the pundits wrong on Allied, Bob Campeau could not stop. Moreover, he was associated with a Wall Street gang that had no desire for him to stop.

As one former Campeau director said: "I think you had a bunch of megalomaniacs playing together. When a susceptible ego like Bob starts to think of grandiose designs — and he is a man who has successfully executed some grandiose and ambitious plans — when you get a person with a history like that, the conventional wisdom is that he will go a bridge too far. In that situation, a man needs advisers who are some sort of brake on his natural tendencies. One of Bob's weaknesses happens to be his predilection for wildly ambitious ideas. Somebody should have been saying: 'You've struggled for forty years to get to this position. Don't bet the ranch on a long shot.' As far as I know, there was not one single voice of caution in that whole deal." In fact, following the Allied closing, the financiers and lenders had a party at which they were all given cowboy hats emblazoned with the legend: "We Bet the Ranch."

While the attentions of the Wall Street crowd catered to Campeau's considerable ego needs, he did not realize that many of them looked at him as a fall guy. Campeau was like the taboo-bound primitive tribal "stranger kings" described by Freud. In some cases, Freud noted, the demands and constraints of primitive regency were so great that tribes could persuade only strangers to take the top job. Bob Campeau thought he had been accepted at last, and not by the minor league Toronto Establishment, but by Wall Street's "big swinging dicks," the free enterprise masters of the universe. But he was really just the stranger king, the smiling rube ascending the throne with no idea of the price he would have to pay for his elevation. The Wall Street tribe was delighted that somebody was prepared to take on the job. Following the Allied deal, Campeau had a celebratory party at the Metropolitan Museum of Art, where the tables were packed with happy tribesmen who had raked in some U.S.$210 million in fees. "Go on, King Bob," they cheered. "Do it again." King Bob was glad to oblige.

Encouraged by the October 1987 plummet in stock prices, and "so full of himself, he was breaking out of his skin," Campeau began looking for a bigger target. His advisers came up with Cincinnati-based Federated Department Stores, an organization a whole magnitude bigger than Allied. Federated sold more merchandise than any other department store retailer except for Sears and K mart. Its flagship chain was the Manhattan-based institution, Bloomingdale's. It had annual sales of U.S.$10.5 billion, assets of U.S.$6.2 billion, 22 divisions, 650 stores, and 134,000 employees.

Cheered onwards by hungry bankers, lawyers, and other advisers thrilled by the prospect of further enormous fees, Campeau turned once more to DeBartolo and Paul Reichmann. On February 2, 1988, Campeau held meetings at New York's Waldorf Astoria with both Reichmann and DeBartolo. Significantly, Reichmann and DeBartolo did not meet. A week or so later, he had deals with both men. DeBartolo would lend him U.S.$480 million and form a partnership to develop U.S. real estate. Paul Reichmann agreed to buy U.S.$260 million of convertible debentures in Campeau Corporation. These debentures were backed by Campeau's Canadian real estate, which through a process of corporate pyramiding Reichmann believed would be isolated from the American business if things went wrong. If things went well, the debentures' convertibility into Campeau common shares gave them additional value.

What Bob Campeau did not tell Paul Reichmann was that DeBartolo's loan would be not only secured by U.S. assets but also guaranteed by Campeau Corporation, and might — in a financial collapse — rank in front of Paul Reichmann's debentures. This put Reichmann and DeBartolo on a collision course.

As a condition for his investment in the debentures, Paul Reichmann insisted that Bob Campeau get rid of Campeau Corp.'s special class of preference shares, which had ten votes to the one vote held by common and other preference shares. All these "super-voting" shares were held by Campeau himself. If the Reichmanns were to invest, said Paul Reichmann, all shares had to have the same voting power. Bob Campeau agreed, but became concerned about losing control of his company. Not only was he giving up some control by canceling his own super-voting shares, there was also the possibility of a large increase in the Reichmanns' equity if they converted the debentures.

Although Reichmann assured him they had no intention of acquiring his company, Bob Campeau was still concerned. Almost twenty years before, he had suffered a great bout of depression following an intricate swap arrangement with fellow French-Canadian Paul Desmarais, under which Campeau had acquired the rich real estate assets of Desmarais's Power Corp. in return for ceding control to Desmarais.

Desmarais, significantly, was the other great Canadian entrepreneur with whom Campeau had sought a close relationship, although it was reckoned to be based on an intense rivalry, at least on Campeau's part. Like Campeau, Desmarais came from Northern Ontario, but had a relatively well-heeled background. His father was a prosperous Sudbury lawyer. But Campeau may have imagined he had more in common with Desmarais than Desmarais thought he had in common with him. Campeau was never invited on the board of Power Corp., and once he realized he had lost control of what he had built, he was described as "close to being a vegetable."

Campeau regained control of his company, but Desmarais undoubtedly remained as a reference point for him. One insider reckoned that, as well as showing the Canadian Establishment he didn't need them, his American sorties were also intended "to put him into a higher league than Paul Desmarais." Desmarais and he were supposedly friends, but he was thought to harbor bitter resentments against the head of Power Corp.

Campeau's relationship with Paul Reichmann was quite different. They came from different worlds, and rivalry did not enter into it. Campeau deferred to Reichmann as to an elder brother. Still, as much as he admired Reichmann, he did not want to lose control of his company to him. So, just to buttress his position and assure more than 50 percent control, Campeau bought another hefty bunch of Campeau stock — with borrowed money, most of it from the National Bank of Canada.

To lend Can$150 million to someone to buy shares represents major exposure, especially given that the collateral for the loan was the shares themselves, equity in a company that was taking some big risks. But then the National could take comfort from the fact that Bob had the Reichmanns backing him. The Reichmanns did not make mistakes.

The battle for Federated turned out to be nasty and ego-driven. Another department store giant, Macy's, was brought in as a potential white knight by Federated. After a drawn-out, and some-times vicious, battle, Campeau won, winding up – as with Allied and DeBartolo – doing a deal with Macy's. Albert Reichmann, who had gone on the Campeau board, had raised concerns that the bidding was getting out of hand, but the Reichmanns were now on the merry-go-round.

Paul Reichmann saw little cause for concern. Indeed, he may even have regarded Campeau's self-destruction as inevitable and put himself in a position to take advantage of it. That view seemed to be borne out by an article that appeared in the *Wall Street Journal* on April 4, 1988. Headlined "Betting the Store" and written by Bryan Burrough (who would go on to co-author *Barbarians at the Gate*) and Jacquie McNish, the story read: "Toronto's Reichmann family also gained increasing leverage over Mr. Campeau, agreeing to buy $260 million of Campeau Corp. debentures in an accord that forces Mr. Campeau to lower his stake in the company to about 50 percent from 86 percent. The Reichmanns will raise theirs to 22 percent from 8 percent." Then came the shocker: "A Reichmann official makes clear that Mr. Campeau can't afford to stumble. 'We're like the Allied powers in World War II,' the executive says. 'When the war is over we'll be moving in to scoop up as many of the pieces as we can.' "

If the "Reichmann official" wasn't Paul Reichmann, then it was presumably someone who knew Paul Reichmann's thinking. When Campeau saw the article, he was outraged. He demanded a meeting with the *Journal*'s editors and threatened McNish with a lawsuit. But neither the meeting nor the lawsuit took place.

Following the completion of the U.S.$6.6 billion Federated deal, the Wall Street crowd held another party with more cowboy hats. This time the message said: "We Bet the Ranch. Again!"

This proved to be one time too many.

From the day Bob Campeau won control of Federated, his retailing empire was fighting for its corporate life. The fine line dividing debt as a concentrator of corporate minds from debt as an unbearable and morale-sapping burden had been crossed. And then some. As with all leveraged buyouts, Federated was now burdened with the cost of its own acquisition. Part of those costs would have to be met by selling divisions. Remaining divisions would be saddled with interest payments made all the heavier by junk-bond financings. Part of the cost of buying Federated was provided from the proceeds of selling Allied assets, thus weakening Allied and enraging its junk-bond holders and other lenders. The incubus of debt quickly began to drain the life from both Allied and Federated. Employees were thrown out of work in the name of cost savings; store renovations had to be postponed because the lenders came first; finally, the operations were bled of cash with which to buy merchandise, threatening the nightmare of empty shelves. Debt stalked the aisles and hung over counters like an invisible army of shoplifters.

By April 1989, the U.S. operations were in such desperate

straits that documents were prepared to seek Chapter 11 protection from creditors. Campeau went to Reichmann and said he needed U.S.$150 million of working capital immediately. The stores had payrolls to meet and merchandise to buy. Reichmann said he would look at the proposal. Campeau said there was no time; he needed the money right now. Reichmann subsequently claimed that Campeau pressured him and that he "reluctantly" agreed to forward U.S.$75 million, but Paul Reichmann demanded a price. The U.S.$75 million was backed by a second mortgage on Campeau's half of Scotia Plaza. That was the prize Paul Reichmann was after.

In August 1989, a desperate Campeau was back again. He visited Reichmann in Switzerland, where Reichmann holidays with his family. Campeau said Allied-Federated needed U.S.$250 million of working capital to buy stock to tide them over the all-important Christmas season. Reichmann — who had set financial investigators to work on the Allied-Federated situation and discovered it looked hopeless — said he thought Campeau should put the U.S. retailing operations into Chapter 11. Campeau countered that no major retailing chain had ever made it out of Chapter 11. After intensive negotiations in Zurich and London, Paul Reichmann agreed to make the U.S.$250 million available to stock the Christmas shelves. The loan would be backed by essentially all Campeau Corporation's unpledged real estate assets — a raft of office and mixed-use developments, shopping centers, and business parks, primarily in Ontario and Quebec. Once again, Paul Reichmann was positioning himself to "pick up the pieces" in the wake of a Campeau default, but he was concerned that he might be perceived as taking advantage of Campeau. He had been annoyed and embarrassed by the 1988 *Wall Street Journal* story.

The risks of the investment Bob Campeau was begging Paul Reichmann to make were much greater for Bob Campeau himself, since all his wealth, and his considerable personal borrowings, were attached to his shares in Campeau Corporation. But Bob Campeau was desperate, prepared to lay his personal fortune on the line. Paul Reichmann was his only hope.

Paul Reichmann made an extraordinary request of Campeau.

He told him: "Bob, you are optimistic by nature. You are aggressive. If you make a mistake, there is no way back. If this is done and it doesn't work, and you go into Chapter 11 after the moneys have been spent in the U.S., then it's too late for you. For me it's a question of degree of security of the loan. I will not discuss it further until you have cleared it with your wife and children."

To imagine that Bob Campeau would be swayed in a business decision by his family seems the height of naiveté, unless you regarded the request more as a salve on the conscience of the man who knew he was on the point of taking Bob Campeau's empire away from him.

Part of the deal hammered out with Campeau in London early in September 1989 was that the Reichmanns would purchase additional warrants which, when exercised and included with the other convertible financial instruments the Reichmanns held, would give them 38.6 percent of Campeau's equity, versus the 38.8 percent controlled by Bob Campeau.

Then Paul Reichmann had a nasty shock: he found out about the DeBartolo U.S.$480 million guarantee. Suddenly, instead of being in a position to pick up the pieces, he found himself up to his neck in Campeau's financial morass. Instead of him taking Campeau, Campeau had taken him. Reichmann now had to become involved in a potential restructuring of the whole Campeau-Allied-Federated empire in order to salvage his investment. The most bizarre media interpretation of what happened next was that Paul Reichmann was helping out an old friend.

Olympia & York made an agreement with Campeau under which the Reichmanns would appoint three directors to the Campeau board. One of the O&Y directors, Lionel Dodd, the former Gulf executive who was now O&Y's low-key high priest of added value, would be chairman of a four-man restructuring committee. The restructuring committee would also be responsible for appointing new senior executives to Campeau's U.S. holding company. These executives would report directly to Dodd's committee. A separate board committee was set up to make restructuring decisions on U.S. affairs. Bob Campeau would not be one of its members.

With the announcement of the U.S.$250 million loan facility and the restructuring agreement on September 12, 1989, Paul Reichmann had placed himself front and center of the Campeau situation. Campeau's bankers raised hallelujahs. The Campeau share price rebounded. But the fact was that Paul Reichmann was no more on top of the situation than Robert Campeau. His mythical image was about to receive another jolt.

If the value of the Reichmann investment was to be maintained, the U.S. Campeau empire could not be allowed to go down, because then DeBartolo would come over the border looking for his money. The U.S. survival plan hammered out by Campeau and Reichmann had two key requirements: that Bloomingdale's be sold, and that the holders of over U.S.$2 billion of Federated junk bonds be bought out at a deep discount. Neither part of the survival strategy proved workable.

Campeau had persuaded Reichmann that Bloomingdale's would fetch at least U.S.$1.8 billion. Reichmann was encouraged because of the premium price Campeau had obtained for Brooks Brothers from British retailing giant Marks and Spencer. A number of potential buyers were identified, in particular certain Japanese groups, but they began to catch the acrid whiff of disaster in Campeau's heavy-handed salesmanship. The Reichmanns came to believe that Campeau was deliberately asking too much for Bloomingdale's because he did not really want to sell it. After all, it was the retailing empire's crown jewel. But a potentially hefty tax liability was also found attached to a sale, along with further adverse tax implications from the junk-bond buyback. Indeed, the survival package as originally hatched by Campeau and Reichmann could have *damaged* cash flow. In any case, the bondholders did not like the idea of being bought out for cents on the dollar just so that Bob Campeau's personal fortune could be saved.

In the meantime, the Reichmann team found that the financial position of Allied-Federated was much worse than they had been led to believe. Not only had they been shown overly optimistic sales forecasts, but expense projections had been understated. The situation was like trying to fill a bath with the plug out. In fact, Chapter 11 would not be pulling the plug, it would be putting it in. That now seemed the only option.

Campeau's bankers begged the mastermind of O&Y not to put in the plug — and thus cut off their flows of interest. But by the turn of the year, the O&Y team had decided the position was unsalvageable. It became clear that Paul Reichmann had taken on more than even his legendary powers of lateral financial thinking could handle. Both Allied and Federated were put into Chapter 11.

Campeau already felt that Reichmann had been ignoring him, which indeed he had. Reichmann had discovered, like Campeau's U.S. financiers, that Campeau's badgering could be intolerable. Where Campeau had once flattered and cajoled Reichmann, now he accused him of bad faith. Reichmann, Campeau claimed to anybody who would listen, had promised to come up with a restructuring proposal and had not done so. Furthermore, only U.S.$175 million of the promised U.S.$250 million had been forwarded by the Reichmanns to the U.S. operations, and U.S.$25 million of that had already been paid back.

Campeau also blamed Paul Reichmann for his personal financial problems. In Campeau's eyes, if Paul Reichmann had not insisted that the class of super-voting shares held by Campeau be cancelled when O&Y bought convertible debentures back in 1988, then he would not have had to borrow all that money to buy more shares and bolster his control position. Moreover, now that the U.S.$175 million had failed to save Federated-Allied, Campeau saw that loan not only as futile, but also, since it was secured against the assets of the Campeau Corporation, as having robbed his own shares of their value.

Not only Campeau associates but miffed bankers fed stories to the press that the Reichmanns' commitment to rescuing the company had been only half-hearted. But the truth of the matter was that commercial bankers had, as with the Third World debt crisis, experienced a collective loss of sanity in the Campeau affair. Any bank that was annoyed with Paul Reichmann was annoyed not because he had walked away from Campeau — anybody in their right mind would have done that — but because he had failed to work magic.

For his part, Paul Reichmann thought he had plenty to be annoyed about. He had devoted a great deal of time to trying to save Campeau Corporation, whatever his initial motives, even if he was in the end concerned only with saving his own investment. Reichmann had discovered that he had been fed numbers by Campeau management that stretched the definition of optimism. Reichmann regarded Campeau's claims that O&Y was responsible for his personal situation as derisory. There had been no need for Campeau to borrow all that money back in 1988 to buy more shares. Also, claims that Reichmann had somehow reneged on his commitment by forwarding only U.S.$175 million to Allied-Federated were ludicrous. The loan had been for *up to* U.S.$250 million to buy stock, and U.S.$175 million had been all that was needed.

But Paul Reichmann had to bear the blame for his embarrassing position. Campeau's unpredictability and volatility were no secret. Getting involved with Campeau had been a lapse of judgment motivated by the desire to grab Campeau's "trophy" building, Scotia Plaza. His further involvements were based on gaining control of Campeau's whole portfolio. Paul Reichmann's chief motivation had been greed.

Robert Campeau had always wanted to become a big name in the United States. In 1990 he got his wish. He made the cover of *Fortune* magazine. The title of the story was "The Biggest Looniest Deal Ever." The *Wall Street Journal*, meanwhile, wrote of the controversial Canadian real estate developer: "It took the special genius of Robert Campeau to figure out how to bankrupt more than 250 profitable department stores." Campeau could never have done it alone.

By the beginning of 1990, Reichmann ranked close to the top of Campeau's personal demonology, but what concerned Reichmann most was that his faltering attempts to salvage the Campeau situation might make it appear that he had lost his magic touch. Paul Reichmann did not relish the conclusion that he might at last have reached the limits of his powers. Or that he might be losing it. Also, this was a very bad time to upset the banking community, because the Reichmanns happened to be the greatest private borrowers on the face of the earth. And their need for money had never been greater.

One of the big problems, in Paul Reichmann's mind, was the press.

19

Bad Press

IN THE SUMMER OF 1990, PAUL REICHMANN CALLED A journalist to whom he had given two lengthy interviews. The interviews had been granted on a "background" basis, but with the agreement that selected quotations would be permitted after consultation. Reichmann struggled painfully through some small talk, like a man who did not like children suddenly presented with a baby to admire. He quickly put down the conversational infant and got down to business. He was calling, he said in an apologetic tone, because he had decided not to be quoted. In the face of a round of adverse publicity, he had decided he wanted to "stay away from the press" for a while.

A story had appeared that morning in the Toronto *Globe and Mail* suggesting that if developers Donald Trump and Robert Campeau were in trouble, the Reichmanns might not be far behind. The story quoted a money manager who was recommending shorting the bonds of Olympia & York. Paul Reichmann told the journalist, with scarcely disguised frustration, that there were no such financial instruments, only nonrecourse bonds backed by certain of the family's buildings. The story also quoted James Grant of the New York publication, *Grant's Interest Rate Observer*, who had speculated that if "the world is taking a deflationary turn, the evidence is bound to show up in even the Reichmanns' finances." In making his assessment, Grant had counted empty office floors in some of the Reichmanns' New York buildings. There might be vacant floors, said Reichmann, but the rent was still being paid.

The litany of complaint continued. Paul Reichmann had just returned from London, where he had given a briefing on Canary

Wharf to the leading British newspapers. Not only had the resulting reports continued to imply that the development would be either a white elephant or a North American ghetto, some had misinterpreted his remarks to suggest that O&Y needed money. The *idea*.

But as with Robert Campeau, there were perhaps more similarities between Paul Reichmann and Donald Trump than met the eye.

Trump, himself the son of a property developer, had become almost a symbol of the 1980s. He had built an empire of real estate, casinos, and an airline on borrowed money and the assumption that New York real estate would rise in value for ever. Trump's life was a media event. His landmark development was the Trump Tower, a condominium next to Tiffany's on Manhattan's Fifth Avenue that held enormous appeal for discreet investors like "Baby Doc" Duvalier and other assorted Third World Kleptocrats and First World nouveaus riches. The fifty-eight-story structure (which Trump had turned into an apparent sixty-eight-story structure by jumping ten floors in the middle), with its golden entrance, 80-foot waterfall, and rose-peach-and-orange-coloured marble, became the symbol of Trump glamour. But perhaps Trump's most significant contribution to the building's design was to intercept the shop drawings and double the height of his own name at the entrance.

He made Trump a trademark for glitz. This was not merely ego; it also turned out to be exceptionally good business. As *Fortune* noted in November 1988 in an article entitled "Will Donald Trump Own the World?": "The enormous success of Trump Tower enabled Trump to introduce a brand name to a class of products that previously had no brands, a textbook marketing strategy." In fact, the Reichmanns perfectly understood Trump's approach. Just as he had very deliberately built a high-profile image as part of his business franchise, they had cultivated a low-profile one as part of the creation of a very deliberate "mystique." As Trump had once said: "The name sells. It's all a game really."

In the Reichmanns' case, the name of the game was "integrity." But the Reichmanns' "integrity" never represented any kind of contradiction or business sacrifice. Despite the frequent horrors reported in the business pages, integrity was not exceptional for businessmen. For the Reichmanns, it was part of their franchise. It made business smoother and brought business back. Albert's son Philip has admitted: "This emphasis on the Reichmann ethics is something that's perplexed me for the longest time. There are hundreds of thousands of quite ethical business people out there. I can't figure out why everybody is so impressed. We're just doing what any other good business person would do. We value our reputation. We understand the value of our reputation. We have to maintain our credibility. But every businessman does that."

By mid-1990, Donald Trump was losing his. Following a spectacular divorce case with his almost equally high-profile wife, Ivana, Trump was in trouble with his bankers. Benjamin Schore, an authority on the real estate market who teaches at Columbia University's business school, noted: "People tend to be mesmerized by his personality and his attitude and his record. Sure, bankers are affected by it. They're human."

In one of his self-promoting books, *The Art of the Deal*, Trump had written: "The worst thing you can possibly do in a deal is seem desperate to make it. That makes the other guy smell blood, and then you're dead." What both Trump and Reichmann knew was that a superhuman image was critical to the banks. Both had set about creating such an image, albeit that one was under neon lights and the other sat behind a discreet veil.

But perhaps the biggest difference between the two men was that when it came to both gambling and borrowing, Donald Trump was nowhere in the same class. He did not know what debt was. And he had never attempted anything approaching the scale and financial requirements of Canary Wharf. At this stage, it was critical that the Reichmanns' bankers on that project not "smell blood."

Paul Reichmann betrayed increasing frustration with a media he had for years so skillfully courted, and which had enjoyed being courted. There was no doubt that Paul Reichmann was a fascinating character. As the proprietor of the London *Daily Telegraph*, Conrad Black, said: "He is so comprehensively and relentlessly an assault on the stereotype of the billionaire. It's his inscrutability and his rabbinical central European inaccessibility. He's just so different."

The media often filled gaps in knowledge with attitudes that betrayed their own hang-ups, leading to assessments ranging from the so-dull-they're-interesting, through philosopher-king-amid-business-midgets, to mysterious-inheritor-and-guardian-of-dark-family-secrets. In one way or another, all these assessments were rooted in reactions to the single most obvious — but unvoiced — feature of Paul and his brothers: their Jewishness. Along with a strain of reverse anti-Semitism, a certain amount of anti-business sentiment may have figured in the Reichmanns' glowing coverage; the brothers were a stick with which to beat the rest of the supposedly fear- and greed-driven capitalist hordes; they were so upright and moral, they were so *different*.

But being put on a pedestal inevitably attracted both skeptics and iconoclasts. The issue had exploded in November 1987, when *Toronto Life* magazine devoted a whole issue to an article by Elaine Dewar entitled "The Mysterious Reichmanns: The Untold Story." It purported to tell: "How Toronto's ultra-Orthodox business geniuses escaped the Holocaust, made a fortune in wartime Tangier, and founded one of the world's preeminent financial dynasties."

The story was filled with bizarre, untrue or false allegations, among them: that Samuel Reichmann and his wife Renee, who was in fact a renowned philanthropist and a wartime heroine in her efforts on behalf of Jews in the concentration camps, had engaged in illegal currency transactions, money laundering, and smuggling; that they had traded with the Nazis; and that Renee Reichmann's philanthropic efforts had been used to enrich the family, which had used the great postwar boom "as a cover for their new wealth." Dewar further claimed that this allegedly devious way of doing business had been inherited by the sons at O&Y. The Reichmanns brought a Can$95 million lawsuit against Dewar and *Toronto Life*.

In response to the Reichmann lawyers' catalogue of errors, misquotes, and illogical inferences, *Toronto Life*'s defense claimed not that Dewar's allegations were true, but that, when read in its entirety, the article had portrayed Renee Reichmann as "a heroine and the best representative of her civilization": a kind of praise by faint damnation. The magazine's lawyers also claimed Dewar had made negative speculations, but said nice things too: that there had been as many band-aids as cuts. Moreover, claimed the lawyers, just because Dewar had posed questions of the "When did they stop beating their wives?" variety, it did not mean she believed them to be true.

But the Reichmanns' legal action had a downside. At the Canadian National Magazine Award ceremonies early in 1988, Elaine Dewar was presented with two prizes and a standing ovation. Placardeers from the Writers Union of Canada appeared outside First Canadian Place, chanting "Reichmann. Ralph, Albert, and Paul. Don't put writers to the wall."

Many who had not read the story or the court documents inferred that the Reichmanns were indeed warning people off. In March 1988, the Reichmanns brought a Can$2.6 million suit against the *Globe and Mail* for an article alleging that the *Toronto Life* suit had been intended to send the message "Stay out of our past." They also sued the *Toronto Sun* columnist Diane Francis for a piece congratulating Elaine Dewar on her efforts and repeating the allegations that Samuel engaged in "questionable currency exchange transactions."

The *Globe and Mail* story had quoted a Canadian writer named Leo Heaps, who claimed, "What they've done to *Toronto Life* is a warning." It went on to repeat allegations in an earlier *Globe* story that a book Heaps had written about the Reichmanns had been suppressed by his Toronto publisher, McClelland & Stewart, because of the Reichmann family's wealth and power.

In fact, there was a lot more to the Heaps story than appeared in the *Globe and Mail.* Heaps had first approached the Reichmanns in 1985 about writing an authorized biography. When they refused, he told them he had discovered certain "disturbing information" about their father and "strongly" suggested they meet with him. When they again refused, he wrote, warning, "No one . . . can be free from the antagonism of the society in which they live." Paul and Albert met with Heaps and told him that his "disturbing" information was demonstrably false. Nevertheless, Heaps threatened that, unless the Reichmanns authorized him to write a complimentary biography, he would proceed with the book containing the information. In a statement of claim for libel against the *Globe and Mail*, the Reichmanns alleged that Heaps proposed that they either authorize him to write a "favorable" biography, pay him Can$250,000 to write an official history, or — astonishingly — pay him a million dollars. Failing any of these, he said he would publish the damaging allegations. Heaps had already suggested to Avie Bennett, the head of McClelland & Stewart, that he be paid Can$1 million for abandoning his project. Bennett, who was appalled, says, "I dismissed the suggestion out of hand." The Reichmanns also refused. Bennett concluded Heaps's manuscript was "unpublishable."

Heaps managed to stir media interest in his cause. He even convinced powerful members of the Ontario provincial New Democratic Party, of which his father had been a prominent member, to intervene on his behalf. He also interested another Toronto publishing house, Fitzhenry & Whiteside, in buying his manuscript from McClelland. Robert Fitzhenry briefly mounted the white charger of editorial freedom, but when he discovered the whole story, he, like the politicians, quietly withdrew.

Ironically, the Reichmanns seemed to suffer more from the *Toronto Life* libel suit than from the story itself, which was so long and convoluted as to be almost impregnable. The size of the damages sought produced a perception that, instead of justice, the Reichmanns were seeking revenge in a settlement that would put *Toronto Life* out of business. In fact, what the Reichmanns wanted was a judgment that, point by point, refuted *Toronto Life*'s malicious defamations. In the end, the case was settled out of court, with *Toronto Life* giving an unspecified sum to charity and, in March 1991, issuing an abject and sincere retraction. It declared: "An exhaustive review, since the action started, of thousands of archival documents from various countries as well as the pre-trial testimony by members of the Reichmann family and others and a review of the family's own papers have confirmed that none of the allegations and insinuations should ever have been raised.

"We made serious mistakes in the writing, editing and presentation of the article . . . [A]ll negative insinuations and allegations in the article about the Reichmann family and Olympia & York are totally false.

"The Reichmann family has earned an enviable reputation over the years, not only since coming to Canada but also prior to that in Tangier, Vienna and Hungary, as a family of great integrity and charity and adhering to strict ethical principles in all of its activities."

The problem with the *Toronto Life* retraction was that it had taken the Reichmanns back from the ridiculous to the sublime, sticking them back up on a pedestal. The irony was that by the time the retraction appeared, the pedestal was crumbling.

Paul Reichmann was not an egotistical man, but he realized that image had its uses. He was also only human. In the end, he grew attached to the superhuman aura that much of the press bestowed upon him. He also proved intensely sensitive when the image was attacked or his judgment questioned. But when Paul Reichmann spoke to the media, he was not interested in the promotion of some abstract version of absolute truth: he was using the media for his business ends. To that extent, he revealed the information that suited him. In an interview with *Time* magazine in April 1990, he had mentioned the example of his father as a source of ethical guidance. Paul said: "His dedication to the truth was such that uttering anything not totally true was for him synonymous with a most hideous crime." But was it "totally true" to disseminate selective information, and to maintain that things were going well when they were not? This all entered the murky area of "vision" and "truth in advertising."

Nevertheless, his employees genuinely appeared to believe that their masters subscribed to higher standards than other corporate executives. Said O&Y Enterprises chief operating officer Lionel Dodd: "I think what you have is the dilemma of a private company, with its desires to retain all the benefits of a private company, yet having moved in a public sphere, whether it's through a public company, or Canary Wharf. You have the continual tugs of wanting to be private, but being part of a bigger world. He gets very bothered by any kind of negative comment, particularly if it's totally inaccurate. It's just an affront. So he tries to deal with it. Paul has an immaculate image and reputation, which I think is a true reflection of the man. He doesn't want to be public, but he does want to perform in a public spirit. He does want to own public companies. He does want to succeed at Canary Wharf."

Dodd noted that Reichmann's sensitivity was wrapped up with identification with, and ownership of, his empire. "When you come from a public company environment, you're probably too much the other way. You shrug it off. When I was at Ford, I went through the rusty car period [when poor quality control led to early rusting of Ford cars and a spate of consumer complaints]. You do become rather blasé, to the detriment of the company . . . I think coming up through the public company background, you're more inclined to shrug it off and say, 'Well what does that reporter know about anything anyway? What does one article matter?' During the rusty car period at Ford, it really wasn't *us* that was rusting. Whereas when criticisms are made of O&Y, it's personal, so there is a difference."

But Paul Reichmann wanted to eat his cake and have it too. His predilection for background media briefings might have been partly due to his fear of being misquoted, but it was perhaps a fear of being accurately quoted too. He disliked "ill-informed" criticism, but was reluctant publicly to give the information that would

allay it, unless it suited his purposes. He not only seemed to expect
the media to make deductive leaps on the basis of limited information, he expected them to see through his actions to what he
regarded as his own good intentions — not to question what he
did, just trust him. But that was not the media's business. Still, Paul
Reichmann continued to have an almost mesmerizing effect on
members of the fourth estate.

When he had taken over Canary Wharf, he had been greeted
with an extraordinary display of media adulation. The *Sunday
Telegraph* had reported: "Softly spoken and politely reticent about
the family company's overall worth, he is nevertheless very articulate, immensely sharp, pleasantly charming and unexpectedly
witty, the latter quality demonstrated by his response to a press
conference question as to what had changed since February when
the originator of the scheme, G. Ware Travelstead, first approached O&Y to rescue his ailing Docklands dream — an approach which then came to nothing. 'Not much with us,' came the
chuckled reply."

Clearly the writer was not expecting too much in the wit
department. Meanwhile, another British Sunday paper gushed:
"Paul Reichmann is blessed with humility and humour in almost
equal proportions." But over the subsequent three years, skepticism had inevitably mounted, and Paul Reichmann had displayed
increasing frustration that the British media in particular were
refusing to share his dream, although they were doing nothing
more than reflecting the sharp deterioration in the real estate
environment and the continued problems with transportation
infrastructure.

What raised his ire in the summer of 1990 was that he had
decided, along with a round of "background" briefings, to go
public with selected details about leasing progress and funding
intentions. The previous April, an O&Y spokesman told the
Financial Post that "the arrangements we make with our tenants
are completely private." Once again, Paul was changing his mind
to suit the circumstances.

Paul Reichmann told the media that no tenants had been

offered "meaningful rent-free periods" and that O&Y was not taking on tenants' existing space, although it was working with them to dispose of leases. He also announced that O&Y had started talks with several banks about refinancing the first phase of the project. He said the intention was to transfer the debt to a project loan secured by the development with no recourse to O&Y.

But instead of calming speculation, the press briefing merely increased it. Analysts were reported to be skeptical about the details. The *Independent* interpreted the refinancing plan as a "warning sign" that Canary Wharf was going wrong. According to both Reichmann and his London lieutenant, Michael Dennis, it was the fault of the press that the leasings were going so slowly. Dennis fingered the anti-Thatcher *Independent* and *Guardian* in particular, along with "innate British conservatism." Said Dennis: "They seem to have lost touch with how growth happens, how cities grow, because there's been no real growth in London since the Second World War. I have this plan of London in the 1860s, with no Kensington, no Earl's Court, no west side of Chelsea, no Wimbledon, none of that. No railways. The railways go in and thirty or forty years later it's all changed. Anybody who's lived through what's happened in the States or Canada — put in an expressway, put in a subway, and whoosh. It's an iron law, providing the city's not dying because of total failure of the economy. Growth follows the transportation corridors. Why will Canary Wharf succeed? Because it's an iron law."

The problem with Canary Wharf was that they'd done it back-to-front. O&Y had put up the buildings in advance of the transportation corridors.

"A lot of our problem here," continued Dennis, "Paul being depressed or frustrated by the reaction, is the fact that, to us, no development is scientific. So much of a sense of how a city is going to grow is half research and half learning from what's happened in other places. This city and its commentators and critics are truly insular.

"There are some comparisons between the U.K. and Japan.

There are tremendous similarities: small islands, not much resource base, different dialects by district, a history of warring
clans. The one tremendous difference is that the Japanese will
imitate anybody. The British are very sure that their way is the
right way.

"Neither Paul nor I fully realized how much about development in North America we take for granted. But we know it will
work. The business leaders all understand the quality of what
we're talking about. The presidents or chairmen of half the major
companies have had stints of working in North America. They
know the kinds of quality we're talking about. But then you get the
reaction, will it work? They somehow forget about their three or
four years in Lower Manhattan. It evaporates. Those worries will
all be gone in a year."

Paul Reichmann endlessly reminded journalists to whom he
gave his myriad off-the-record briefings that the project's trump
card was Maggie Thatcher. He would produce letters from the
great lady, indicating her wholehearted support. One such letter
said: "The objective we share is that Docklands should succeed as
the third business centre of London." Paul Reichmann noted that
Maggie had "put herself on the line."

Reichmann's firm belief was that, once the development had
gone up and the tower's pyramidal hat had been bolted on, people
would be able to get a sense of the place, of its scale and quality, see
that it was only half the distance from uptown to downtown New
York (as if insular Londoners thought that way). But the media
doggedly refused to share his vision. Every time he saw a report
that it sometimes took an hour to get from the City to Canary
Wharf, it was like a personal insult. He commissioned Peat
Marwick to do a study of traveling times from various parts of
London. According to Reichmann, the study said that the journey
from the Bank of England to Canary Wharf was eleven minutes in
peak traffic. But part of the problem was that even if that was the
average time, it could sometimes take twice as long. Moreover,
crawling along the East India Dock Road could be the ugliest and
most frustrating eleven minutes you could ever imagine.

Paul Reichmann seemed to believe that all that was needed to make the traffic go away was an act of will. "There is no traffic issue really," he said, "but the press makes it so." The new roads were coming; the Docklands Light Railway was being improved and extended; the subway was on its way (not that they really needed it anyway).

One phrase in particular increasingly came to annoy Paul Reichmann: "white elephant." His response to all such potentially disastrous allegations were that they were "childish," "idiotic," or simply "rubbish." "This," he continued to claim, "will be the greatest real estate development success of all time."

Despite his public confidence, 1990 had been a terrible year for him. In January, the Campeau debacle had hit the headlines. In February, his mother had died with the *Toronto Life* suit still hanging over the family. Throughout the spring and summer he had trekked back and forth to London to meet with prospective lessees, delivering them the low-temperature sales pitch that had proved so effective in Toronto and New York. Indeed, as one of the people who had bought it, Ogilvy & Mather chairman Michael Walsh, said: "It was not a sales pitch at all, but simply reassurance." Paul Reichmann came in as the "closer" of the deal and convinced Walsh that he was building a new business center for London. But although Amex and Manufacturers Hanover had signed up in mid-year, the project was losing momentum in a dismal market.

At the beginning of August, Saddam Hussein invaded Kuwait. By the end of the year, with Iraqi Scud missiles threatening Jerusalem, CNN was one more thing Paul Reichmann had to keep his eye on. In November came another blow: a challenge to Maggie Thatcher's leadership of the Tory party led to her replacement as prime minister by John Major. The Gulf War and the change of British leadership were but two more of the increasing uncertainties surrounding an unprecedented gamble.

Paul Reichmann was in the midst of spending at least Can$3.5 billion on the first phase of a project that would produce no net return for years. Part of the Reichmann myth had always been that the brothers had deep, even bottomless, pockets, but the pockets really belonged to the banks. It was the Reichmanns' hands that were in deep, and now Reichmann needed to dig even deeper.

20

Shadowy Figures

"BY SPENDING MORE, I RISK LESS," SAID PAUL REICHMANN OF
Canary Wharf. Like Reichmann's other homely aphorisms, such
as "Build on cost, borrow on value," this seemed to have a
comforting ring. If he had said, "By borrowing more, I risk less,"
bankers might have been a little less easy. But that, in effect, was
what he was saying.

Paul Reichmann once confided to one of his Toronto bankers:
"We have virtually unlimited access to money." It was a message
designed to both comfort and disturb the banker. Anybody with
unlimited access really did not need the money — the banker's
dream. But anybody with unlimited access might also choose not
to borrow from your particular bank — the banker's nightmare.
Paul Reichmann played banks off against each other in his quest
for ever-larger borrowings. The astonishing aspect of the relationship was that he managed to do it without ever showing the
vast majority of his lenders O&Y's books.

Secrecy had always been a key element of the Reichmanns'
operation. Initially this had much to do with the family background and the fact that it was, after all, a private company. But as
they grew more successful, this secrecy became a critical contrib-
utor to the Reichmann mystique. The mystique was enhanced
because Paul Reichmann was regarded as a brilliantly innovative
financier. From his days as a developer, he had gone beyond
bankers to insurance companies and other institutions to raise
money. He used mortgages and complex back-to-back arrangements; he had gone to both the bond and commercial paper
markets.

The Reichmanns seldom sold buildings because sales meant

taxes. It was considered more efficient to borrow against buildings as their rentals and value increased. But as the property
market boomed, driving building values up faster than rentals, and
thus drawing rental yields down, there was always the temptation
to overborrow. Prudently, the Reichmanns based their financings
on the projected rental incomes of the properties rather than their
market values. Nevertheless, even these borrowings held the risk
that projected incomes might turn out to be less than expected.

The heart of the Reichmanns' fortune was the Uris package,
the Manhattan buildings bought in 1977. They provided the collateral for the huge borrowings that financed both the World
Financial Center and the brothers' acquisition binge. Typically,
money was raised against these buildings innovatively, and with an
air of mystery. When Paul Reichmann had put together an unprecedentedly large mortgage with Salomon Brothers in the early
1980s worth almost U.S.$1 billion, an innovative financing backed
by three Manhattan properties, the restrictions on viewing O&Y's
financial information were reported to be almost bizarre. Documents were taped to a desk at the company's Park Avenue headquarters so they could not be removed, and no note-taking was
permitted. Four junior Salomon executives were each assigned the
task of memorizing a certain number of pages.

The Reichmanns were able to raise money on the Eurodollar
market in mid-1985 while revealing virtually no corporate details.
They pulled off this feat by having a subsidiary of insurance
company Aetna Life, with whom they had had a long relationship,
guarantee the loan. The offering circular for the U.S.$125 million
financing contained the astonishing statement: "Neither the delivery of this Offering Circular nor any sale made hereunder shall,
under any circumstances, create any implication that there has
been no material change in the affairs [of O&Y or Aetna] since the
date hereof or that information herein is correct as of any time
subsequent to the date hereof."

In other words: "Just give us the money."

And the investors did.

This desire for secrecy significantly determined the structure of the Reichmann corporate and financial pyramid. Projects were financed on a stand-alone basis. New borrowings were made with particular buildings as collateral. The mother company sometimes guaranteed these loans, but seldom if ever showed its own books. At any other time or place, the Reichmanns' secrecy might have been a turnoff, but in the late 1970s and 1980s, when the name of the banking game was "whacking up assets," the Reichmanns and the banks were made for each other.

The Reichmanns' main banking relationships in Canada were with the Canadian Imperial Bank of Commerce and the Bank of Montreal. The brothers had done business with the CIBC since they had been putting up warehouses and factories in the early 1960s. They still kept one of their two operating accounts at the bank's Yonge and Eglinton branch, where, so the story went, Samuel Reichmann had made that deposit "big enough to choke a horse" when he moved to Toronto. The brothers' relationship with the Bank of Montreal had developed with the building of First Canadian Place as the bank's headquarters. O&Y's other operating account was held in the main branch there, at King and Bay.

The CIBC and the Bank of Montreal received more information than other lenders, including figures for all the Reichmann companies, plus organization charts. However, these figures were usually eight months out of date, so there always existed the possibility that a problem could creep up without the bank knowing. Moreover, the company was *always* reorganizing for tax purposes. The annual review of Reichmann loans by the banks — a process carried out for all big lenders — was always a complex nightmare.

The Bank of Montreal's brilliant but autocratic chairman, Bill Mulholland, was unusual in the upper echelons of Canadian banking in that he had not risen within the bank. He was an American, born in Albany, New York, who had spent seventeen years with Morgan Stanley before becoming president and chief executive of the Churchill Falls (Labrador) Corporation Limited, builder of the second largest hydroelectric plant in North America. When the plant was completed, in 1974, Mulholland was brought in as president of the Bank of Montreal, with a mandate to shake it up. Mulholland was unusual in another way in the Canadian banking community: he was not keen on doing business with Paul Reichmann.

There had been some souring of the relationship with the Bank of Montreal due to the wrangles over First Canadian Place and the division of profits related to the bank's ownership of a quarter of the land under the development. The formula was complex and the Bank of Montreal felt that O&Y was always trying to take the deal beyond its reasonable limits. There was also the question of O&Y's allowing another bank into the project, which the Reichmanns had countered with what were considered hairsplitting arguments that the Exchange Tower was not really the same project.

The Reichmanns' importance as lenders meant they were invited to the intimate soirees on the sixty-eighth floor, when the bank would bring in big-name speakers like Henry Kissinger. Nevertheless, Mulholland was wary about a closer relationship. He had thought that Paul Reichmann would ruin himself with the World Financial Center. He hadn't, but Mulholland had a sneaking suspicion he might blow his brains out somewhere. Mulholland was also generally suspicious of financially complex structures like O&Y. Although he was speaking not about O&Y but about other businesses at the time, he once said: "I have spent thirty-three years in the financial industry one way or another, and one of the main reasons that people create complicated financial structures is to create veils."

And indeed, although it appeared an unseemly analogy for one of such somber aspect, Paul Reichmann had always produced a financial dance of the seven veils both for the bankers and for the press — a glimpse of asset ankle, a peek at cash-flow calf. But nobody got to see the big picture. Even to suggest such a thing would have been indecent. After all, the brothers were men of extraordinary honesty; their word was as good as their bond; a handshake was as good as a month of due diligence.

Paul Reichmann used to do most of the financing negotiations himself, backed up by Ken Leung, a Hong Kong accountant, and sometimes Gil Newman, the Reichmann bulldog. The CIBC and the Bank of Montreal knew about most loans from other banks, but they did not know the terms or the pricing, and it was considered unethical to try to find out. Paul Reichmann was very tough to deal with, but was always gentlemanly in his dealings. He never took the egotistical give-me-the-money-or-else tone that some big borrowers did. But then he knew he didn't have to.

If an impasse came in negotiations, a bank executive might return to head office to find out that Paul Reichmann had taken terrifying action: he had paid off a loan. For a banker, it was awful to have a man like Paul Reichmann repay loans, because it indicated displeasure, and that you might not get any more business. You'd know not to be quite so argumentative the next time.

Reichmann's lieutenants, too, were typically tough. Oskar Lustig, who played a key role in the empire's system of central cash management, would spend an hour on the phone arguing over $8,000. Lustig, Leung, and Newman would push every argument to the limit, take advantage of every loophole or gray area in any contract or arrangement. Far from obeying the standards of "my word is my bond" that were endlessly regurgitated in the press, O&Y had been known to quibble at, or renege on, verbal agreements. One example was a promise by Paul Reichmann to back a personal loan by the Bank of Montreal to Bob Campeau. The bank returned several times to Reichmann for the letter, but somehow the details could never be worked out. The letter was never forthcoming. The loan to Campeau went sour. The Bank of Montreal was left holding the baby.

O&Y would also sometimes make demands on its bankers that bordered on the ridiculous. On one occasion, the company had failed to deposit money with the CIBC and the Bank of Montreal on a Friday afternoon, thus potentially losing interest for the weekend. O&Y had requested that the CIBC pay the interest even though they had not had the money in the bank. The CIBC had done so. The Bank of Montreal had refused.

Banks also frequently helped the Reichmanns with a little

financial window dressing in the form of "daylight loans." The bank would lend the money for the course of a day when a balance sheet was being struck. The money would never leave the bank and would be "repaid" immediately after the balance sheet had been prepared, showing plenty of cash on hand. The bankers got an effortless fee but, as one says, "It was a crazy thing to do." The bank was only making O&Y look good in terms of its presentations to other banks. There was nothing particularly unusual in what O&Y did. Many corporate customers did it. But where this fit in with notions of truth, honor, and fair dealing was a little murky.

In 1985, the CIBC was envied within the world of banking when Paul Reichmann agreed to go on its board. Canadian bank boards are less instruments for monitoring and policy-setting than they are gatherings of the banks' largest customers. Other bankers considered it a coup. Not Bill Mulholland. He knew why Paul Reichmann had gone on the CIBC board: to get more money.

The Third World debt crisis and corporate debacles at Dome Petroleum and Chrysler, among others, led bankers to forsake the asset-building binge of the 1970s and early 1980s and to start looking at their loans not only in terms of size but in terms of profitability. To any even semisophisticated outside observer, it appears astonishing that they had not done so from the beginning. They started preparing "customer profitability models." These demonstrated that in some cases banks were losing money on Reichmann loans. The Reichmanns did not pay fees or allow decent spreads. This made some of the bigger banks fall out of love with them in Canada.

The Toronto-Dominion Bank stopped lending to them completely in 1987. The Bank of Montreal, too, cut back on its exposure which, at one time, had equalled the entire equity of the bank. The Bank of Montreal still talked as if it was the "relationship bank," but it was lending less and less money because Mulholland did not *want* the money lent. The bank told the Reichmanns that they would have to find more profitable deals for the bank to do. Otherwise, it wasn't worth dealing with them.

So the Reichmanns simply went to other Canadian banks: to the Royal Bank and the Bank of Nova Scotia and the National Bank of Canada, which had been burned by Campeau but was desperate to make it into the big time. The problem was that these banks just did not have the capacity to fill the Reichmanns' borrowing needs.

Most of the big Canadian banks had suffered from the Dome Petroleum fiasco. Although Dome was eventually sold to Amoco Canada, the crisis had threatened at one time to take one or more of the major banks down. As a result, regulatory authorities had placed a limit on any bank's loans to any one corporate customer of an amount equal to one quarter of the bank's equity. This would turn out to be a very wise provision. Nevertheless, it meant that although some Canadian banks would love to have lent more to the Reichmanns, they just couldn't. As a result, the Reichmanns turned to foreign bankers.

In Canada, the "schedule B" foreign banks were eager to do Reichmann business. In the latter half of the 1980s, the Reichmanns were *the* people to lend to. Bankers really got off on being able to casually drop the line: "I met with Paul Reichmann today." And indeed, any foreign bank with an office in Toronto was probably going to get flak from headquarters if it did not have a piece of some Reichmann syndicated loan on its books.

The brothers' social reclusiveness and business secrecy had fed the myth of them as magic men with virtually limitless resources, and the money had come begging to be borrowed. In banking relationships, secrecy tends to be directly proportional to the amount of money involved.

Another great part of the Reichmann myth was that the brothers were conservative financiers. They were not. They often used floating rates. Most real estate developers try to match their borrowings and rates with the projected returns on the project. But O&Y did not want to get locked into long-term financing because they were always refinancing, looking for better deals to shave off a point or two. Still the bankers came flocking.

Paul Reichmann had said from the beginning that he would finance Canary Wharf initially from North America, not only because it was the source of the Reichmanns' cash flow and collateral, but also because North American interest rates were lower. That meant borrowing against both buildings and the investment portfolio.

The Japanese, in particular, were eager to lend money backed by the Reichmanns' North American assets. Some of the Reichmanns' existing bankers, like Citibank, were pleased to make introductions. Citibank led a group of Japanese banks into a U.S.$500 million loan backed by the Reichmanns' holdings in Carena, the company that in turn controlled Trizec. Tokai Bank took a whopping U.S.$300 million of this loan. Fuji Bank, Daiwa Bank, the Industrial Bank of Japan, and Mitsubishi Bank also came in for a piece of the action. But it was the Sanwa Bank that wound up with the biggest exposure of any Japanese bank to O&Y. The Sanwa made loans of U.S.$752 million to O&Y's U.S. operations. These included a U.S.$480 million first mortgage on one of the towers of the World Financial Center and a U.S.$271.7 million first mortgage on One Liberty Plaza. Sanwa also took a piece of the Can$450 million loan backed by Scotia Plaza. The Sumitomo group, which includes a bank, trust, and life insurance company, loaned U.S.$726 million to O&Y's U.S. operations, including, like Sanwa, huge mortgages on New York buildings. Investment giant Nomura Securities masterminded an enormous U.S.$800 million financing on a building in the World Financial Center.

In January 1989, the Hong Kong and Shanghai Banking Corporation muscled its way in front of all the other banks clamoring for Reichmann business, lending U.S.$750 million as part of a larger loan, the mother of all loans, the "Jumbo Loan" for a stunning U.S.$2.5 billion. The loan, at LIBOR (the London Interbank offered rate) plus three-eighths, was with a consortium of banks from all over the globe. Apart from the Hong Kong and Shanghai, Germany's Commerzbank International kicked in U.S.$287.5 nillion; France's Crédit Lyonnais bellied up to the lenders' bar with US$262.5 million; Canada's Royal Bank contributed U.S.$250 million; Japan's Dai-Ichi Kangyo Bank put up U.S.$180 million; and the Cayman Islands branch of the Swiss

Bank Corporation contributed U.S.$150 million. Assorted other French, German, Finnish, Italian, and Japanese banks contributed the rest.

This huge loan was backed by the Reichmanns' common shareholdings in Gulf and Abitibi, which at the time barely covered the value of the loan. Moreover, dividends from Gulf and Abitibi would come nowhere near to covering the interest costs, so an essential part of the support for the loan was a "full recourse guarantee" by Olympia & York. Under this agreement, O&Y had to furnish annually a certificate prepared by chartered accountants that its net worth was at least US$2.5 billion. It also agreed that O&Y would "make available once annually a senior financial officer to discuss the affairs and finances of OYDL [Olympia & York Developments Limited] with officers and lenders."

The loan amounted to an extraordinary act of faith in O&Y. Once again, the central company was not required to open its books. It merely had to supply a certificate of net worth prepared by its accountants. Moreover, an awful lot could go wrong in the period between certificates. In effect, the bankers were making a leap of faith based on the myth of the deep Reichmann pockets. Nevertheless, even for the two banks that got to look at the Reichmanns' figures, the Bank of Montreal and the CIBC, when the Jumbo Loan was made, O&Y looked, in the word of one of their executives, "bulletproof."

The Citibank-led Carena loan for U.S.$500 million was also made on the basis of backing from O&Y and a certificate of U.S.$2.5 billion net worth. O&Y also entered into more than a dozen other loans backed by its "marketable securities." The biggest of these were Can$200 million from the Bank of Nova Scotia and Can$162 million from the Bank of Montreal. In total, O&Y would borrow more than Can$4.5 billion against its investment portfolio. The problem was that the dividends from these securities came nowhere near covering the interest costs. This meant that the shortfall had to be made up by rental incomes from O&Y properties. But the properties too were in the process of being mortgaged up to the hilt. For example, in 1988 the

Reichmanns had issued Can$475 million in bonds backed by First Canadian Place, by far the largest such financing in Canadian history.

By the fall of 1990, the Reichmann empire was already the greatest private borrower in the world, with estimated debts of around Can$17 billion. But it needed more. Some banks were beginning to ask questions. In fact, the company had already started a process of "rationalizing" its investment portfolio, although it stressed this had nothing to do with needing money.

In September 1990 came an announcement that sent ripples round financial markets: the Reichmanns were putting 20 percent of their U.S. real estate assets on the market. Inevitably, the word went out that the Reichmanns needed the money for Canary Wharf. O&Y stoutly resisted any such notion. Michael Dennis claimed that the sale "is not intended to finance Canary Wharf. What it does reflect is a desire by some individuals to redeploy their assets. I can tell you that one thing has nothing to do with the other."

But which individuals? The U.S. assets, like everything else in the Reichmann empire, were owned by the family. Redeploy where? For what? Did some family members want to get cash out in case Paul Reichmann had bet the farm on Canary Wharf? Unannounced internal transactions within O&Y over the next six months would tend to confirm that opinion. But the biggest question was: if the Reichmanns were selling, why would anyone be buying?

Paul Reichmann intimated to journalists in the summer of 1990 that Canary Wharf would be worth one-and-a-half times its cost by the time the first phase was completed, and that he would be able to finance two-thirds of its value. Even the less financially sophisticated members of the media, perhaps feeling incisive in their calculation, could work out that this arithmetic, rather neatly, projected that the first phase of the project's entire cost of around £1.5 billion could be safely financed on the back of the project itself. But it was not working out that way.

Financing depended on the projected success of Canary

Wharf, and projected success depended on leasings. But leasings were running behind schedule and rentals were flagging. Although Paul Reichmann stressed that rates were still up at £27 to £32 per square foot, it was the concessions given to lessors that determined the final present value of leases, and thus the financings that could be done against them. As the future dimmed, present values dropped, and so did financeability.

U.K. lenders were becoming a little jittery about the huge increase in their exposure to real estate. Back in 1987, when the Reichmanns had taken over Canary Wharf, the governor of the Bank of England, Robin Leigh-Pemberton, had warned banks about their exposure to property. He had repeated the warning in a speech in 1989. Now, at last, the banks were beginning to take him seriously at the worst possible time for the Reichmanns.

Nevertheless, in November 1990 Paul Reichmann succeeded in negotiating a £500 million construction loan with a consortium of eleven banks, known as the "Club of Eleven," led by Lloyds. He also negotiated a £100 million loan from the European Investment Bank. But that left at least £900 million still being financed in part by borrowings such as the U.S.$2.5 billion Jumbo Loan. Servicing that and other loans backed by Reichmann investments was already proving a drain on the brothers' North American real estate portfolio. Moreover, the brothers had to make sure their net worth stayed above U.S.$2.5 billion.

In October 1990, Donald Trump was bumped off *Forbes* magazine's list of the 400 richest Americans. The magazine declared his net worth was possibly within "hailing distance of zero." But the Reichmanns were still up there with the multi-billionaires. But then how could Donald Trump be in trouble and the Reichmanns *not* be in trouble? Of course, it was because the Reichmanns were not ego-driven media-hounds like Donald Trump. They were still magic men. They had the crystal ball. They were conservative.

Why the Reichmanns were different from Donald Trump was put to Lionel Dodd. Dodd said Trump was more interested in the size of his yacht. "The whole mind-set is different. There has been no motivation on the part of Paul and Albert in terms of the size of their empire. They don't put their names on their buildings. The whole motivation for being in business is different. I suspect the way Trump has applied debt and used debt is very, very different. O&Y has traditionally put lower loans against buildings than could have been carried, so it underfinances. There are also buildings with no loans against them. If you contrast with Campeau, some of his buildings have loans against them higher than what an independent appraiser might say the value of the building is. In the case of Trump too, the feeling is that the market value is less than the loans that are against them. The Reichmanns are more conservative in borrowing against buildings. Of course, the building loans are also nonrecourse. Trump apparently signed a loan where he personally guaranteed $500 million. I don't know any precedent for that here. It's a more conservatively financed operation. The amount of debt against the public company side, although I don't know exactly what it is, is certainly less than the public company side can support."

Dodd appeared to want to discourage pointless probing. "You can develop some values on the asset side. The part that you cannot get at is how much debt is against that. That is part of the private company's financial statements, which are not disclosed. There have been certain financings that have been disclosed, but you never know if you're seeing the total picture. In fact, you don't even know what the draw is against the loan facility on some of those financings."

Better, Dodd was suggesting, not to think about it.

But Dodd's revelations — or lack thereof — were fascinating. *Forbes, Fortune,* and other magazines were cheerfully printing figures for the family's net worth when even O&Y's own senior executives claimed they did not know what it was. Moreover, Dodd might claim the Reichmanns were relatively conservative, but in an industry populated with Trumps and Campeaus, even relative conservativeness could look pretty scary.

Certainly, Canary Wharf was proving to be not the least bit conservative. Moreover, when it came to motivations, was the desire to have a bigger yacht scarier than a seemingly relentless urge to make more and more money, even if it was described as "adding value"? Lionel Dodd knew all about the complexities that the added-value philosophy was causing in the Reichmanns' investment portfolio.

21

Complex Choreography

LIONEL DODD WAS TRYING TO MAKE IT A LITTLE SIMPLER FOR the visitor who came to his office in July 1990. The low-key former Gulf executive who was now chief operating officer of O&Y Enterprises Inc., the public company arm of O&Y Developments, pulled out the organization chart with its score or more of corporations descending from the mother company and acknowledged that although it had grown opportunistically and looked like a mish-mash, there *was* a rationale. "Most of what we've done on the public company side, you can see there was a real estate genesis to it. That's not apparent to a lot of outsiders. With the benefit of history rather than foresight, you can say that O&Y had a real estate emphasis, developed a public company emphasis, and is now developing a real estate emphasis again."

Dodd took a piece of paper and began to draw an alternative model of the Reichmann empire. This model was not pyramidal or wheel-and-spoke — the normal organizational forms. It was cosmological. Dodd started drawing orbits, but not the orderly orbits of a Newtonian, mechanical universe, moving in stately harmony. This was more of a Velikovsky-like system, where orbits crossed and worlds collided. And yet, as with Newton's view of the universe, there was still a Guiding Hand, a figure who also, as it happened, had a beard and sat upstairs.

Dodd finished sketching in the planetary paths and began to fill in the names of the companies whirling in this corporate space, explaining how they fit in with the Great Plan. "There are three groups of companies orbitting O&Y Enterprises. One is the real estate group: Trizec, Landmark, Stanhope, and then Campeau and Santa Fe. Santa Fe overlaps with the natural resource orbit: Gulf,

Abitibi, Interhome, Consumers' Gas. The natural resource orbit is the biggest one. The third orbit consists of Trilon and Allied-Lyons, overlapping with Campeau and Santa Fe. Campeau emerged on a real estate orbit, but went into department stores. We were deficient on that orbit. Santa Fe Pacific is on all three orbits. There was a real estate business and we were able to add value almost immediately in the way that business was run, but there's an oil and gas company and a pipeline, which puts it on the natural resource orbit too. Then there's the railroad, which goes on the third orbit, another area where we have no expertise. So there's real estate, then natural resources where the [Reichmann] mind-set can create value. And along the way we've picked up extraneous things which are not logical. We would not say department stores or railroads were a logical step, but the balance is logical."

The visitor was struggling to hang on, like a layman at a Stephen Hawking lecture.

Dodd turned from his graphic rendition of the system and began to expound on the laws of this corporate universe. "The way you create value in a resource business is the same as in a real estate business. I find that in the resource orbit, the Reichmanns can add value with relative ease. They have a value-creation mentality, a long-term focus, the financial strength to be able to endure the long term, and skills in innovation. In the resource sector — take Gulf with its frontiers — O&Y is able to deal with the very long-term focus that's required."

But a question occurred to the visitor: Why? Long-term focus for what? A well-known quotation from the British economist John Maynard Keynes came to mind: "In the long run, we're all dead." And although Paul Reichmann had said in the past that he was building something for his children, this was a ridiculous rationalization, like wanting to leave your children a hundred spinning plates to keep in the air, or a nuclear reactor to run. Unless you shared the obsession with "adding-value," the Reichmann empire, built to unprecedented size at breakneck speed and with alarmingly little underlying structure, would represent an enormous burden. Moreover, the corporations whizzing round in the Reichmanns' constantly changing orbits were finding that being under the constant threat of cosmic reorganization was a tiresome, and tiring, process.

The Reichmanns had once been reported, in hushed tones, to be "patient investors," the antithesis of the slice-off-the-top, get-rich-quick crowd. Yet in the wake of the Campeau debacle, their investment portfolio had been through — and was still undergoing — a series of restructurings and asset sales of bewildering complexity.

Like British playwright Tom Stoppard's Rosencrantz and Guildenstern, the parts of the portfolio felt like actors aware that they were part of something bigger, but not quite sure what it was. Like Stoppard's Hamlet, Paul Reichmann was a shadowy and pensive figure who would appear and disappear suddenly and unexpectedly. His intentions were never fully explained. This was only partly due to his penchant for secrecy; it was also because he was making it up as he went along. No part of the Reichmann portfolio was more aware of this than Gulf Canada.

In 1985, apart from being taken over and split up by the Reichmanns, Gulf had been persuaded to buy Abitibi-Price from the brothers to provide the bulk of the funds for its own acquisition. In 1986, the Reichmanns had used it to take over Hiram Walker Resources, and it had found itself a huge conglomerate. Then, in 1987, in an arrangement of Byzantine complexity, featuring shareholder communications as big as doorstops, the Reichmanns had "deconglomerated" their interests — splitting off Abitibi and the rump of Hiram Walker — and Gulf had found itself an oil company once more. Apart from Abitibi, the brothers' other main investment interests — primarily the remaining parts of the Hiram Walker conglomerate — were now held in another public company, GW Utilities Limited. Within GW, Interprovincial Pipeline had been merged with Home to form a new company, Interhome. GW also held the stake in Consumers' Gas. Finally, in the fall of 1987, at the suggestion of Allied-Lyons, O&Y's 49 percent stake in HW-GW had been exchanged for convertible preferred shares in Allied-Lyons. On conversion, those shares would give the Reichmanns just under 10 percent of the British company's equity.

Paul Reichmann, concerned by criticism that he had used Gulf as a financial cat's-paw, had in 1987 declared that Gulf would be revitalized. He had himself appointed head of a committee of Gulf directors set up "to guide the new initiatives for frontier and international exploration and development." He also took a contrarian stance in favor of Beaufort Sea exploration and development — although there were technical reasons for enthusiasm, primarily Gulf's huge, Can$674 million Arctic drilling fleet, which, despite a sale and leaseback arrangement that removed its debt burden from Gulf's balance sheet, forced Gulf to keep drilling.

Perhaps the most bizarre aspect of the Gulf takeover was that it was imagined that Paul Reichmann, a man with no direct experience of the oil and gas business, would somehow help the company's exploration prospects. The Reichmann mystique was certainly a key selling point for the record Can$519 million Gulf Canada equity issue in June 1987, an issue that was peddled not only in Canada but in the United States and Europe. But Paul Reichmann proved to be no oilman. Indeed, he could hardly have bought Gulf at a worse time. His skill was demonstrated simply in squeezing as much value as he could from the situation.

Despite the complexities of the Gulf shuffle and the Hiram Walker fandango, Paul Reichmann did not lose his acquisitive urge. Indeed, he seemed to have decided that hostile takeovers might not be such a bad idea after all. While the 1987 Gulf issue was still warm, and although he had just committed O&Y to Canary Wharf, Paul Reichmann drew a bead on Santa Fe Southern Pacific Corp., a Chicago-based railroad, real estate, and resources conglomerate.

When Mickey Cohen turned up at the Chicago office of Robert Krebs, Santa Fe's chief executive, on August 24 to announce O&Y's interest, Krebs told him that, in the legalese of Securities and Exchange Commission statements, Santa Fe "would not welcome" a stake above 5 percent. In other words: go to hell.

Nevertheless, there was a clear rationale — in terms of "adding value" — in O&Y's interest in Santa Fe. Like Gulf, which had just gone through the process, Santa Fe was a clear candidate for deconglomeration. O&Y was in a unique position to understand the company's real estate values. They had been looking closely at oil and gas. They could find out about railroads. But Paul Reichmann was not the only man interested in Santa Fe. Michael Dingman, chairman of Henley Group, according to the *Globe and Mail*, a "SWAT team of workaholic MBAs" based in La Jolla, California, ran an organization that specialized in corporate makeovers.

Despite Krebs's cold shoulder, O&Y kept buying shares. The stock market crash of October 1987 did not appear to dampen the Reichmanns' ardor. Krebs turned to Henley as a potential white knight, and Henley offered a cash-and-share package worth U.S.$9.9 billion for Santa Fe. The Reichmanns were then asked by Krebs to make an all-cash bid for the same amount, but, although they claimed they were considering such an offer, they decided against it and carried on buying shares.

Early in 1988, the Reichmanns reached an accommodation with Santa Fe. Paul Reichmann and Mickey Cohen wound up on the Santa Fe board; Santa Fe leveraged itself up to the hilt so it could pay a special dividend; and the Reichmanns bought more Santa Fe shares. Once he was on the Santa Fe board, Paul Reichmann was in a position to pass on the benefit of his real estate experience. His main piece of advice was to adopt the strategy he always used at O&Y: never sell property. Instead, he recommended that Santa Fe borrow against its real estate. That way, the company realized the same amount of money but held onto real estate's inflationary upside, which was still considered virtually limitless. In July 1988, Henley sold out to Itel Corporation.

As Dodd was expounding on the cosmic theories of the Reichmann corporate universe in July 1990, Santa Fe was in the process of splitting itself into its three constituent parts — energy, resources, and transportation. On December 4, 1990, the Reichmanns and Santa Fe's other shareholders were given shares in the three new companies: Catellus Development Corporation, Santa Fe Energy Resources, Inc., and Santa Fe Pacific Corporation.

By then, Paul Reichmann had concluded that his investment adventures were an enormously time-consuming, not to mention expensive, distraction. The investments had proved much less than a resounding success. And despite the inevitable brave corporate faces, they were showing signs of strain at being put through the Reichmann value-added wringer.

At the 1989 Gulf annual meeting, retiring chief executive Keith McWalter declared that the coming decade would be "a rewarding time for shareholders." McWalter claimed Gulf was at a turning point. The turning point was to be yet another corporate reorganization: a proposed merger with Home Oil, which had been announced a week before. The new company, said Mc-Walter, would be "truly poised to become the premier upstream oil and gas company in Canada."

Symbolically for such new beginnings, back in Calgary the atrium and public-access floors of Gulf's mist-enshrouded headquarters had just been given a typically tasteful Reichmann makeover — all marble floors, tinkling fountains, ceiling mirrors, and Art Deco torchieres — making it look like a setting for a Busby Berkeley musical. But Gulf was beginning to show corporate weariness at the convoluted choreographies through which the Reichmanns had been putting it for five years. In fact, the elegant polish of Gulf's ground floor was — despite the optimistic noises of the annual meeting — in marked contrast to the perennial uncertainty stalking the corporate offices above.

One year later, McWalter's successor, C.E (Chuck) Shultz, who had joined Gulf in October 1989 from Tenneco Oil Company, had to acknowledge a less-than-rewarding start to the decade. The company was losing money. The share price was languishing.

At the 1989 meeting, when he had been introduced to the

shareholders, Shultz had told them he had joined Gulf because he saw a well-managed company with an outstanding inventory of business opportunities. He was being diplomatic. He had been brought in by the Reichmanns to tighten, streamline, and generally smarten things up. He was described by a Toronto analyst as "a typical ass-kicking American, but then somebody had to sort Gulf management out."

Shultz had certainly made changes. He had moved Gulf's exploration thrust away from the frontiers toward Western Canada and overseas, where there would be a quicker payoff. He had also announced that a bundle of assets, including half Gulf's 25 percent stake in the Can$5 billion-plus Hibernia project, was on the block. But one thing he could not do was disguise the fact that the Reichmanns' investments in oil had proved both controversial and disappointing. The companies involved had all suffered from the Reichmann penchant for treating their corporate holdings as so many pawns in a gigantic game of "value-creation," played from Olympian heights with constantly changing rules.

Significantly, Mickey Cohen did not stick around very long at O&Y Enterprises. The former bureaucrat had rapidly become tired of being kept in the dark. His position had also at times been embarrassing. In 1988, he had arranged a meeting in London with the senior executive of another company on O&Y business. When he had turned up for the meeting, the executive had been a little surprised and confused. He said he was pleased to see Cohen, but Paul Reichmann had been by the day before and settled the matter. Again, in the wake of the Hiram Walker takeover, Cohen had made a slew of speeches preaching the joys of conglomerates and how important such organizations were if Canada was to play a part in the new global economy. Then Paul had decided to split the whole thing up!

When the top job became available at the Canadian brewing giant Molson, Cohen grabbed it with both hands. Paul Reichmann had reportedly disapproved of Cohen's high corporate profile, particularly after media suggestions that Cohen might be taking the organization in new directions. Cohen was replaced by Dodd, who was much more of a professional manager and much less of a schmoozer. Dodd also showed all the signs of having become a true believer in the Reichmann mystique. "Paul himself is far more impressive than even his image is from outside," he said. "The outside world has built him up, but he is higher. But if you sit down with him in an interview, you would say, 'This is Paul Reichmann? This can't be the guy at all.' You can't capture his thinking skills, his strategic skills, in an interview. His mind thinks extremely strategically . . . for example, I used to think the business was unstructured because Paul didn't understand organization. He understands structure. He's unstructured because that is the way he wants to run his business. He's perceptive in areas you wouldn't think he was perceptive. Albert also is easy to misjudge. He's a far more important member of the team than the outside world realizes. He plays the role of the older brother and chairman. He is a stabilizing influence. He's much more externally focused, as a chairman often is. He's much more involved with the community. In a way it seems very appropriate. He is also an extremely deft participant on the real estate side. Paul is much more involved on the company side. Albert is also far more likely, if he is on a board, to be at the meeting. He's more comfortable with structure, more patient with structure. The differences between the two make them very strong as a team."

Continued Dodd: "The number of challenges he deals with in a week is incredible. He and I will sit down and deal with issues in a half a dozen public companies. He will remember the last conversation we had on the issue. He will have thought about some of those issues since the last time we talked. He will have some creative input. The number of problems he solves in a week is phenomenal."

But Dodd was at great pains to note that the investment side of the business was firmly under control. Nor were they rationalizing and selling assets because they needed money. Rather, the myriad changes since 1985 had all been part of Paul's "learning process." Following the Gulf acquisition, "there was a lot of restructuring. There was a lot of effort to understand what we had acquired, a lot of examination of how to create value."

In 1988, O&Y had commissioned Morgan Stanley to analyze its holdings. Then the brothers had sat down with Dodd and other senior executives to examine the relative performances of their real estate interests and investment portfolio. They concluded, according to Dodd, that they had underestimated their international potential in real estate, which promised better returns than resources.

O&Y had spent much of 1989 developing a strategic plan to reorganize and sell off major parts of its public company holdings, and began implementing it early in 1990. As a result, O&Y had taken one company, GW Utilities, private, and sold GW's most valuable asset, Consumers' Gas, to British Gas PLC for Can$927 million. Gulf had bought Imperial's stake in Interhome for Can$492 million, and Interhome had been split. O&Y had also masterminded the split of Santa Fe into its constituent parts.

But the strategic change clearly acknowledged the puncturing of Paul Reichmann's supposed dream to create a Canadian resource conglomerate. The centerpiece of that plan was to have been Gulf, but Gulf had evolved from being the core of a dream to a corporation exhausted by the fancy financial footwork it had been asked to perform in the name of creating value. Also, the Reichmanns' carefully laid plans had begun to run into roadblocks.

A key part of the all-new, totally revised Reichmann strategy was that, following the Interhome split into its original oil and pipeline interests — Home and IPL — Home would be merged with Gulf so that, as Keith McWalter had said, it would be "truly poised to become the premier upstream oil and gas company in Canada." But the merger proposal met unexpected opposition.

For Gulf, Home's attraction was its position in Western Canada, which would theoretically fit with Gulf's frontier and overseas interests. But most analysts — and the market — thought a Gulf-Home merger made more sense for Gulf than for Home. Home's birds were in the hand, Gulf's in the bush. When the plan

was announced, Interhome's shares fell and Gulf's rose. Interhome's chief executive, Dick Haskayne, was disappointed at the
prospect of splitting up the company he had just spent three years
putting together. Although he was not the architect of Interhome's
creation, he believed there were synergies between the two companies at the managerial, financial, and tax levels.

The Reichmanns proposed that Home be acquired with Gulf
paper. This required evaluations by both sides. These evaluations
had become more important since the Ontario Securities Commission had tightened up on non-arm's-length transactions. An
independent committee of Interhome directors was set up, headed
by Donald Campbell, chairman of Toronto-based media conglomerate Maclean Hunter Limited. The committee balked at
Gulf's evaluations and its merger terms. The Reichmanns had
won no friends when they had caviled at a suggestion by Haskayne
that, due to the enormous amount of work the independent directors had to do on the valuation, they should be paid double fees.
The deal had fallen apart in the midst of the Gulf War.

Dodd admitted that some transactions were "immensely complex, but we never back away from a transaction because it's too
complicated." The priority, he emphasized, was the creation of
shareholder values. "A lot of my interface with the CEOs revolves
around the creation of values for the shareholder. There is certainly imperfect understanding on the part of CEOs about how
you should think about that. They're trained to look at organizations, maximize market shares, cut costs, or increase production.
But they're really never trained to run a company in the interests
of the shareholders."

But there seemed to be a dimension missing from the
Reichmann world view. Too narrow a view — a purely dollars and
cents view — of shareholder values could damage corporate morale, which in turn could damage earning ability. Insensitivity to
corporate culture and morale had been one of the main criticisms
of a decade of finance-driven leveraged buyouts based on satellite-
photo analysis that ignored people. Many of these takeovers had
demonstrated that dominant shareholders were not always wise

shareholders. Robert Campeau had provided abundant proof of that.

Gulf had changed immeasurably since its takeover, but it was difficult to claim it had changed for the better. Although Haskayne was reluctant to criticize the Reichmanns, whom he claimed were good shareholders, he admitted: "I can have a lot of empathy for the employees of Gulf. Six years ago, they were part of one of the Seven Sisters. They had a lot of autonomy here in Canada. They were a fully integrated company, active in Western Canada. They were involved in significant discoveries in the frontiers. They were an active refiner and marketer. They had chemicals. And then of course came the Chevron takeover. That was a hell of a shock. The Canadian thing was up in the air for a year or so. Then the Reichmanns acquired it and all this corporate trauma arrives. It's just a different world they're living in. Meanwhile, oil prices have gone to hell in a handbasket. Prices are half of what they were six years ago. This has hardly been a happy time for any of us."

But although the main source of Gulf's problems, like those of the whole industry, was low oil and gas prices, there was widespread employee concern that the company had been loaded with debt and drained of cash to fit the needs of its major shareholder rather than its own best long-term objectives. The Reichmanns inevitably wanted their public investments to maintain dividends because they had so much borrowed against them. This might not always have been in the companies' best interests. At the 1990 meeting, for example, Gulf announced that the Reichmanns would be cashing in their preferred shares in the company and taking out Can$265 million immediately and Can$265 million when Gulf sold further assets. Typically, this was O&Y's idea, not Gulf's.

Yet again, the controversies surrounding the investment portfolio seemed to clash sharply with the image of the Reichmanns as sensitive and fair-minded businessmen. Paul Reichmann's maneuvers outside real estate betrayed a relentless acquisitiveness and will to win, combined with a carefully calculated but disturbingly cold desire to rationalize and reorganize. They also revealed the inevitable limits of his business powers. As Ira Gluskin, the iconoclastic Toronto-based fund manager and former real estate analyst who had followed the Reichmanns for years, put it: "What we've learned after ten years is that when it comes to running Abitibi or Gulf, hiring professional managers, or giving valuable input at the board, Paul Reichmann has no particular magic touch."

By the beginning of 1992, there had been a change in bankers' attitudes. No longer did bankers' eyes go misty with warm admiration at the mention of the Reichmann name. They were daring to ask questions: about Canary Wharf, about values, about the rationale behind the Reichmanns' grab bag of public companies.

Bankers and other lenders were terrified at the prospect of a Reichmann default, both individually and collectively, because bankers, in particular U.S. bankers, had already seen their balance sheets damaged by Third World loans, and had also loaned heavily on real estate. In fact, by the beginning of 1992, O&Y *had* already defaulted on a number of agreements, but had been able to negotiate both their lenders' compliance and silence.

22

The Crunch

BY THE BEGINNING OF 1992, PAUL REICHMANN WAS ENGAGED
in an elaborate psychological game with his bankers, trying to
cajole additional loans, trying to soothe increasing concerns. One
of the most concerned lenders was Citibank, the Manhattan-based
giant that had found itself front and center in so many disastrous
loans in the 1970s and 1980s. It had headed the march into the
Third World; it had led a consortium into the Dome Petroleum
morass; it was a major lender to Campeau. According to a Citibank
insider: "Citibank thought they knew how to make big loans.
They were hungry for big loans and the big fees that went with
them." Nobody wanted big loans more than the Reichmanns, and
nobody was more prepared to provide them than Citibank.

One executive of Citibank Canada, on whose board Paul
Reichmann briefly sat, ventured in 1986 that "Paul is a real
gentleman. If he gave me his word, I'd back it with $100 million of
Citibank's money." There was another good reason for the
banker to take Paul Reichmann's word: he wasn't going to get to
see the O&Y books.

In 1987, when O&Y had bought its huge position in Santa Fe,
Citibank had bankrolled the whole deal, a whopping U.S.$750
million. Stunningly, the loan had been unsecured, not even backed
by the Santa Fe shares on which it had been spent. The rationale
was that the Reichmanns needed the shares to be unencumbered so
that O&Y could offset the borrowings for tax purposes. Citibank
had been none too happy when it discovered that O&Y had
subsequently pledged the Santa Fe shares to other lenders.

By the first quarter of 1991 — by which time Citibank had also
led a consortium of banks into a U.S.$500 million loan backed by

the Reichmanns' interests in Carena — the Santa Fe loan had been paid down to U.S.$250 million, but Citibank was becoming increasingly concerned about its lack of security. Paul Reichmann's word was suddenly no longer considered good enough. The bank demanded to see some figures. What they were shown failed to comfort them, indeed, it horrified them. An internal Citibank study completed in the first quarter of 1991 forecast a 20 percent chance of O&Y foundering by the first quarter of 1992, and an 80 percent chance of it going bankrupt by the final quarter of 1992. It all depended on Paul Reichmann's success in raising more money.

Throughout 1991, Citibank, with one eye on the day the music would stop, pressured Paul Reichmann to provide security for its outstanding U.S.$250 million. In the end, Reichmann agreed to provide some low-grade real estate backing for the loan. However, there would be a price: more money. Citibank lent another U.S.$75 million to a company it was projecting would go bankrupt.

However, the conditions of this desperately needed extra U.S.$75 million had adverse effects elsewhere. In the latter half of 1991, Paul Reichmann had also been working on an additional U.S.$250 million line of credit with four Canadian banks: Canadian Imperial Bank of Commerce, the Royal Bank, the Bank of Nova Scotia, and the National Bank of Canada. An agreement was reached late in 1991, but then, when the four banks discovered the additional security that had been given to Citibank, they became annoyed, demanding additional security for themselves. This additional security would in turn later infuriate other lenders.

Those bankers most closely involved with Paul Reichmann saw increasing signs that he was short of money. He would call from overseas with requests for amounts that would previously have been regarded as mere petty cash. They became increasingly concerned about the vulnerability of O&Y's commercial paper. Paul Reichmann had attempted to calm them, saying there would be no problem, everything was under control. But he could say nothing else; he had run out of alternative sources of finance. He had to handle the banks with the delicacy of a bomb-disposal expert.

From the beginning of 1992, there were growing indications that the empire was on the point of foundering. The most obvious was the dispute between O&Y and Morgan Stanley over the Morgan Stanley building at Canary Wharf.

In 1990, Morgan Stanley had changed its original agreement with O&Y, under which the merchant bank would build its own office block on land at Canary Wharf leased from O&Y. Under the new agreement, once Morgan Stanley had built the property and moved in, it had the right to sell to O&Y for U.S.$240 million between December 12, 1991, and June 30, 1992. On December 12, Morgan Stanley had decided to exercise its option. For Paul Reichmann, the timing could not have been worse.

Reichmann went to Morgan Stanley's president, Robert Greenhill, and persuaded him to postpone payment until the end of January. Reichmann had presumably hoped that he could gain the funds elsewhere. When the money was still not forthcoming, Morgan Stanley treated the reversal as bad faith and sued O&Y.

Deeply concerned about a flood of stories questioning its condition, in January 1992, O&Y released a flood of financial information. But the move backfired. It missed out on the details people needed to know. It looked like smoke and mirrors. O&Y declared its net worth was Can$8.5 billion. It claimed its debt-to-equity ratios were a modest 65 percent. But whose estimates of equity were the brothers using? And what was the total debt? Meanwhile, the company pointedly refused to release more critical financial figures, in particular cash flow, the key element of liquidity and thus immediate viability. Neither would they say how much had been borrowed against the non-real-estate portfolio. Far from assuaging fears, these sketchy details tended to unnerve the market further.

In an interview with *Business Week* that appeared on February 3, 1992, Paul Reichmann acknowledged that the recession was "the worst I've seen." He admitted that O&Y was "suffering in this downturn." He confessed that "cash flow is much worse than it was two years ago." Nevertheless, the interview clearly was not intended to undermine faith in O&Y. But then Paul Reichmann ran out of credit as he ran out of credibility. The commercial paper collapsed; the Morgan Stanley decision went against him; the bankers got cold feet.

On March 6, the day O&Y was "dragging its feet" on the commercial paper, the company was also forced to grant a second mortgage on Scotia Plaza and a third mortgage on First Canadian Place to the Canadian bank consortium, as backing for the U.S.$131 million forwarded under the U.S.$250 million line of credit. But the banks would forward no more. O&Y then announced its intention to restructure. But Paul Reichmann certainly did not consider the game over.

On March 24, 1992, two days after acknowledging to a stunned global financial community that it was being forced to "rework" its debt, O&Y named Thomas S. Johnson, the former president of Manufacturers Hanover Trust Company, to the position of president.

Johnson, 51, was a long-time banker who had been president of Manufacturers Hanover for three years, but had wound up in second spot after a merger with Chemical Bank, for which, ironically, he had worked for two decades before moving to Manny Hanny. He had been president at Chemical from 1983 until 1989. "Reichmann," according to one lender, "had retained a banker to deal with bankers. We couldn't have been more satisfied." But for anybody who understood the way the Reichmann empire was run, and who understood Paul Reichmann, the notion that he would cede any real power to an outsider was a delusion.

A New York analyst said: "Johnson has been a stickler for detail — very much a numbers-oriented type of manager — and I think from that standpoint he would fit in." The analyst clearly didn't know that Paul Reichmann had once said: "You can go broke if you depend too much on numbers." Some who knew Johnson reckoned he was the wrong man for the job *because* he was a numbers-oriented, black-and-white kind of guy. Paul

Reichmann certainly was not going to be in a two-plus-two-equals-four mode, much less a two-minus-two-equals-nothing frame of mind. For his part, Paul Reichmann may have underestimated Johnson's sense of independence. Johnson would find the Reichmanns' attitude toward their bankers little short of bizarre, especially in view of the fact that O&Y's position was nothing less than desperate.

The day Johnson's appointment was announced, O&Y also revealed that it had selected J.P. Morgan & Co., Incorporated, James D. Wolfensohn, Inc., and Burns Fry Limited to serve as financial advisers to the company on its debt restructuring. Wolfensohn partner Robert S. (Steve) Miller would, it was declared, "devote substantially all of his time to this effort."

Miller was a former vice-chairman of Chrysler who had been instrumental in the U.S. car giant's bail-out in the early 1980s. Tall and bespectacled, with a bald, shiny dome, Miller, unlike Johnson, was renowned for a somewhat quirky sense of humor. In the spring of 1980, he had walked into a roomful of Chrysler bankers and declared the company had just filed for bankruptcy. Lenders' hearts went into fibrillation. Then a grinning Miller pointed out that it was April Fool's Day. On another occasion, he brought a water pistol to a negotiating session and held it to his own head, threatening to shoot himself if they couldn't make a deal. Miller also distinguished himself by rescuing the bail-out contracts from an office fire hours before Chrysler would have run out of cash. At the champagne victory party, Miller tore off his suit and shirt to reveal a Superman outfit.

And yet the Reichmanns had never exhibited a penchant for either practical jokes or fancy dress.

O&Y announced the formation of a "Planning and Finance" committee, of which Johnson would be chairman, and Miller, vice-chairman. Other members included John Zucotti, the distinguished lawyer, former academic, and ex-deputy mayor of New York who had been appointed head of O&Y's U.S. operation, Michael Dennis, and Gil Newman. Neither Paul nor Albert, it was announced, would be directly involved in the day-to-day talks on the debt. The appointment of the negotiating group, it was said, would allow Paul more time to devote to Canary Wharf. The restructuring could be worked out while Paul was dealing with more important things.

It was announced — presumably as reassurance — that the head of the Royal Bank, Allan Taylor, was to become directly involved in negotiations. The CIBC's head, Donald Fullerton, was also reported to be heading a "crisis team" within the bank. Cedric Ritchie, chairman of the Bank of Nova Scotia, declared: "I read in the papers that everybody seems to think it's a controllable situation. I would tend to agree with that. It's absolutely a proper observation." Everything was OK, declared the bankers who had been asleep at the Reichmann lending switch. They were all now awake. Everything was under control.

The first meeting between the new O&Y Planning and Finance committee and the bankers took place in Toronto on March 27. There, Reichmann and Johnson met with about twenty bankers and announced that they were working on an "interim plan" that they intended to present on April 6 to all of O&Y's lenders. Johnson told his fellow bankers they would receive all the financial information they needed. Paul Reichmann thought they didn't need too much.

On March 31 and April 1, the day Miller had made his big joke to Chrysler's bankers eleven years earlier, O&Y became involved in a slew of defaults. The planned meeting with the bankers was postponed until April 13 and extended to all of its ninety-one international lenders. Thomas Johnson was reported to be working "night and day" to comprehend O&Y's complex financial position and to cobble together a restructuring proposal. But his main problem was comprehending Paul Reichmann.

On April 9, O&Y narrowly missed defaulting on the more than U.S.$900 million of Eurobonds secured by three Manhattan buildings. The good news on that day, however, was that John Major's Tory government had been returned to power in Britain. There had been fears that a Labour government would have been hostile to Canary Wharf and thus less inclined to be helpful.

The delay in the meeting with O&Y's bankers was caused only partly because of the complexities of the situation. Equally significant was the growing tension between Reichmann and Johnson. Johnson wanted to open the books. Reichmann said absolutely not. They would play this the way they had always played it: tough and tight-lipped.

The final showdown came over Johnson's pay. Johnson had been promised U.S.$1 million a year and a U.S.$2 million bonus upon a successful restructuring. However, when guarantees were not forthcoming, he resigned, demanding a substantial severance. Paul Reichmann offered a token sum. Johnson threatened to go public. In the end, Albert, who had been more inclined to play it Johnson's way, insisted that Paul pay Johnson's $2 million severance out of his personal bank account.

On April 13, the day of the big bankers' meeting, O&Y issued a terse announcement, including a joint statement on behalf of O&Y and Johnson: "There were certain conditions to the proposed agreement between Olympia & York Developments Limited and Mr. Johnson which could not be met. Accordingly, the parties have mutually determined not to proceed."

In the Old Testament, during the ritual of Yom Kippur a "scapegoat" was a creature "symbolically laden with the sins of the Israelites and sent into the wilderness to be destroyed." The sin Johnson was widely accused of in the press was asking for too much money. With unconscious irony, "sources" within O&Y — that is, Paul Reichmann — accused the man installed to deal with the company's financial problems of one of Reichmann's own chief failings: corporate greed. Johnson collected his payoff, participated in a bland joint statement, and kept his mouth shut. The Reichmanns partially buried the real reason for Johnson's departure, which was Paul Reichmann's unwillingness to cede the driver's seat in negotiations with the banks over the family empire's survival.

Johnson was replaced by Gerald Greenwald, another former Chrysler executive. Nicknamed "the Hoover" because of his ability to suck up large amounts of information, Greenwald had first worked with Miller at Ford's Venezuelan operation in the 1970s. Both had been recruited by Lee Iacocca as part of the "Gang of Ford" brought in to help rescue Chrysler.

On April 13, Paul, Albert, Greenwald, and Miller met with nearly 400 representatives of ninety-one banks from around the world in the ballroom of Toronto's Sheraton Hotel. The first ninety minutes of the three-and-a-half-hour meeting were taken up with a verbal presentation about the company's financial status, a presentation that bordered on fantasy. Miller, while acknowledging that O&Y had direct debt of Can$14.3 billion, with another Can$4 billion or so in subsidiaries, whistled a happy tune about the empire having a net value of Can$5.5 billion, and stated that O&Y was not asking the banks to "take a haircut." It was merely offering them scissors and a mirror.

When a banker asked Paul Reichmann about O&Y's willingness to issue equity, Reichmann refused even to address the question. The figures the company delivered in a 270-page document were more than a year out of date. Astonishingly, the Reichmanns' plan seemed to be to seize the initiative from the banks via a strategy of "divide and conquer," seeking to separate the discussions into different lending consortiums, and dealing with assets in different countries. They also wanted the banks to kick in a fresh Can$300 million. The bankers were stunned by the arrogance of this approach. According to one Bay Street investment adviser who had been close to the family: "They didn't realize that they looked different than they did six months ago. Their mystique was gone. People knew they had nothing."

What Miller and Greenwald really thought of the Reichmann tactics they weren't saying. Nevertheless, the evening of the bankers' meeting, when he was having supper with Michael Dennis in the exclusive Camberley Club Hotel in Scotia Plaza, Miller had a taste of O&Y's arrogant style himself. Dennis claimed to make "100 decisions a day," and expressed disdain for consultants. "Consultants are people who advise, not people who do," he said. But then, realizing that Miller was a consultant, he added: "Except for consultants with a big C like you. They're different."

Dennis and other senior O&Y executives now began a desperate search worldwide for new investors. Previously, the Reichmanns had come close to the Saudi royal family and the sultan of Brunei and the sheik of Dubai only in those lists of the megarich in *Forbes* and *Fortune*. Now O&Y representatives waited for audiences in their royal antechambers. Others flew to Singapore, Hong Kong, and Japan.

Meanwhile, once the full import of the April 13 meeting had sunk in, the bankers were outraged. Who did the Reichmanns think they were? What were they trying to pull? They determined to put O&Y on minimal life support, a "drip-feed" of cash just sufficient to keep the business going.

In the following month, the situation inevitably continued to deteriorate. There were defaults on a U.S.$800 million Eurobond issue backed by one of the towers of the World Financial Center. O&Y failed to make a principal payment on a mortgage held by Sanwa Bank on One Liberty Plaza in New York. Appeals to the Canadian and Ontario governments for loan guarantees to help the sale of Exchange Tower were turned down. Moreover, the Canadian Superintendent of Financial Institutions, Michael Mackenzie, told the House of Commons finance committee that the banks could survive an O&Y "meltdown." To cap off a trying month, on April 30, Robert Campeau made a most unwelcome reappearance.

Through the first half of 1990, following the Chapter 11 filing, Campeau had begun a skillful, if futile, game of playing the Reichmanns, Edward DeBartolo, and the National Bank of Canada against each other. Ultimately, this maneuvering only caused further tensions among the major players.

Bob Campeau was nothing if not resourceful. He came up with a new scheme. He made a deal with the National under which he could take back control of the Campeau shares he had pledged against the Can$150 million loan the bank had made him in return for two payments of Can$40 million, the first when the shares were handed over and the second when a restructuring of Allied and Federated had been worked out. But who in their right mind would lend Bob Campeau Can$40 million? The answer, it seemed, was a "mystery investor." And who was the mystery investor? None other than Bob Campeau's old friend and nemesis, Paul Desmarais.

The extent of Desmarais's commitment was never revealed. Bob Campeau's master tactic was to keep all those involved separate in order to give himself maximum leverage. But although Desmarais may have held discussions regarding the Campeau situation, Campeau likely implied a little more concrete commitment from his "mystery" man, without identifying him, than Desmarais ever indicated. Nevertheless, the National Bank considered him real enough to strike their tentative deal with Campeau on the Campeau Corporation shares.

The deal with the National Bank was just part of an elaborate scheme worked out by Bob Campeau to "save" his company. The mystery investor would not only lend money to Bob Campeau, he would also come up with funds that would "flow through" to the United States to help salvage the situation down there. The other parts of Bob Campeau's scheme were first, that debenture holders, the most important of whom were the Reichmanns, would settle for perhaps 17 cents on the dollar, a little above where the public debentures were trading, and second, that Campeau would settle with DeBartolo by giving him a package of Canadian real estate.

By linking the National Bank's recovery of at least half its loan with a plan for the Reichmanns to take a haircut, Campeau cleverly placed the National Bank on the side of the shareholders and himself, and against the Reichmanns. If the Reichmanns could be shamed into settling for 17 cents on the dollar, then the mystery investor would not be needed. It was a brilliant bluff.

Rumors of this sketchy plan — which was never formally put to the Reichmanns — induced incredulity at O&Y. Not only did Bob Campeau expect them to suffer a huge loss on their debentures so that funds could flow through to the common shareholders, principally Bob Campeau himself, but the real estate he wanted to give to DeBartolo was already pledged against loans to the Reichmanns! In the Reichmanns' view, Bob Campeau had lost touch with reality. He was still trying to pull rabbits out of the hat when the show was over. O&Y thought his scheme "harebrained."

Paul Reichmann increasingly found dealing with Campeau not only taxing but bizarre. Campeau would say to him in one breath: "Paul, you have to trust me," and in the next threaten to sue. Soon after the Chapter 11 filings in January 1990, Reichmann had refused to speak with Campeau further. That task was deputed to Lionel Dodd, who had to listen to Campeau's constant litany of complaints.

The Reichmanns wanted Bob Campeau to step away from the whole process. He naturally felt that if he was not there, then there would be nobody to protect the shareholders, principally himself. He claimed, with some justification, that the Reichmanns had a conflict of interest on the Campeau board, because they were not there primarily as representatives of shareholders, but as secured and unsecured creditors.

Shortly after the initial Chapter 11 proceedings in the United States, it was put to Campeau that he should give up the position of chief executive while retaining the title of chairman. He responded with threats to sue for wrongful dismissal. The Reichmanns backed away, unwilling to be seen as Campeau's corporate assassins, and horrified at the thought of further negative publicity.

By mid-year, the mystery investor had disappeared. With Campeau management struggling to deal with secured and unsecured creditors and Bob Campeau running off hatching increasingly wild schemes, the time had come to clip the former high-flier's wings.

Campeau, following the annual meeting, finally agreed that he would step down as chief executive but would remain as chairman. When that appointment came up at a meeting on August 10, Campeau, who participated by phone from Europe where he was attending his son's wedding, declared that, of course, he would still like to carry on dealing with Edward DeBartolo! This was the last straw, and the National Bank directors were finally persuaded to join the board representatives of Olympia & York in ousting Robert Campeau from the positions of both chairman and chief executive.

On November 9, 1990, Stanley Hartt, a lawyer who had served both as deputy minister of finance and chief of staff to Prime Minister Brian Mulroney, was appointed to the Campeau hot seat. Hartt's close relationship with senior bankers from his stint at Finance, and his experience at the heart of Ottawa's political intrigue, were reckoned to be crucial qualifications for his new job as chairman, president, and CEO.

Hartt's most important function was to preside over an elaborate game of financial musical chairs, in which all the stakeholders were circling and whistling and pretending there were enough chairs to go round when they knew there were not. He would be helped by the fact that everybody wanted to keep up appearances, minimizing the accusations that they had lent unwisely and had not exercised due diligence.

In September 1991, an agreement was signed with O&Y under which the Reichmanns would wind up with two-thirds of the shares in the "new" Campeau, named Camdev. O&Y also purchased the remainder of Scotia Plaza by assuming the debt backed by the building. Paul Reichmann had obtained his "trophy" at last, but he had paid a hefty price. His involvement with the mercurial French Canadian had cost him more than Can$600 million. Bob Campeau, meanwhile, wound up with less than 2 percent of the corporation that had all too eagerly shed his name. The shares of Camdev Corporation started trading in mid-February at $18.75, and immediately slid. By mid-year they would be below $4.

On April 30, 1992, Bob Campeau at last did what he had been threatening to do for two years: he sued the Reichmanns — now fighting for their own lives — for Can$1.25 million. O&Y treated the suit as frivolous. But like Robert Campeau, when faced with the loss of his own equity, Paul Reichmann would also appear to stuggle with reality, or at least with reality as perceived by his lenders.

23

Seeking Protection

FOLLOWING THE FIRST MAJOR MEETING WITH ITS BANKERS ON April 13, O&Y had been told in no uncertain terms to come up with both more comprehensive and up-to-date figures and a more realistic restructuring proposal. The new proposal was announced at a meeting with fifty representatives of the company's fifteen largest lenders at Canary Wharf on May 7. Paul Reichmann, who had said little at the April 13 meeting, now reportedly looked "relaxed and composed." He went round the table, shaking hands and smiling.

The new proposal was put by Miller and Greenwald. Greenwald declared that "after decades of total private family ownership, the company is inviting lenders to join hands as partners." Miller looked much less chipper than he had at a meeting with London reporters the previous week. Michael Dennis looked like death. Following the meeting, Dennis, Miller, and Greenwald had to undergo the indignities of a "photo opportunity." They forced incongruous smiles and thumbs up. Michael Dennis gave what appeared to be a "time out" signal. Paul - Reichmann posed for no pictures. Neither did any of the bankers.

Once again, the "terms" offered by O&Y were considered no reflection of the reality of the situation. O&Y was demanding enormous concessions. It wanted principal payments deferred for five years. Shortfalls of interest would be made up with shares in O&Y, up to a maximum of 20 percent of the company and 30 percent in Canary Wharf. But the O&Y shares would be nonvoting. Also, the company sought another £300 million for Canary Wharf and the remainder of the Can$250 million under its recent agreement with the four Canadian banks.

Said a disgruntled Canadian lender: "They offered an inch when they should have offered three feet." Following meetings that dragged into the night, the banks agreed to extend another £21 million to keep Canary Wharf alive for a few more weeks. One of the toughest stands during the meetings in Canary Wharf's main tower was taken by the CIBC, which was demanding a more realistic attitude from its previous star borrower. Meanwhile, in a demand that seemed to display a distinct lack of faith, lenders under the 1989 "Jumbo" U.S.$2.5 billion loan insisted that O&Y deposit the Gulf and Abitibi shares that backed the loan with the Toronto-Dominion Bank, the one big Canadian bank that was not on the hook to the Reichmanns.

In a report that somehow summed up the press's monstrous misreading of the Reichmanns' position in the past, the London *Sunday Times* on May 10, at the end of the week of tough negotiations between O&Y and its lenders at Canary Wharf, declared in an annual review of Britain's wealthiest people that the - Reichmanns were up there at number four, worth U.S.$15.6 billion. In fact, the Reichmanns were worth less than nothing. They appeared to believe their only hope of retrieving the situation lay in fighting a guerrilla legal war, and this attitude was infuriating their lenders.

While the talks had been going on in London, on May 5 bondholders of First Canadian Place had decided to push O&Y into default. That meant they could — after a statutory delay — seize the Reichmanns' flagship building unless O&Y came up with their interest payment. The bondholders were applying pressure on the banks as much as on the Reichmanns, because the banks held security on First Canadian Place that ranked beneath both the bonds and other mortgages. Also, a seizure of the building might lead to cross-default proceedings that could bring the whole corporate edifice tumbling into bankruptcy, and hence the horrors of liquidation in the worst real estate market since the Second World War.

The week of Monday, May 11, saw two further dramatic developments. On Tuesday, May 12, J.P. Morgan, one of O&Y's own advisers, declared O&Y in default on a New York loan. Two days later, in London, a British court upheld the previous order for O&Y to pay Morgan Stanley the U.S.$240 million under their Canary Wharf agreement.

On Thursday, May 14, faced with the loss of its best-known Canadian building, O&Y decided to file for protection against its creditors. A few days later, the wood-paneled courtroom of the Ontario General Justice Division on Toronto's University Avenue was packed to the rafters with black-gowned lawyers representing the Reichmanns' creditors. They spilled over into the dock; they sat on the floor alongside their crates of documents; they clamored outside the door trying to get in. As the gray-bearded and crimson-sashed Justice Robert Blair moved up to the bench, he joked, "I'm just sorry we weren't able to get Roy Thomson Hall [home of the Toronto Symphony] for this event." There was an almost carnival atmosphere. But this was not joyful business.

At 8 P.M. on May 14, David Brown, a distinguished lawyer and banking specialist from Davies, Ward & Beck, began to lay out O&Y's situation and why it needed protection from its creditors. He was applying under the Companies' Creditors Arrangement Act (CCAA), an obscure piece of legislation dating from the Depression era.

As Brown made his presentation, several hundred miles to the southeast, in a tranquil New York suburb, two lawyers surprised a bankruptcy clerk in her small home and produced a stack of petitions seeking Chapter 11 protection for a number of O&Y companies with U.S. assets. O&Y's main U.S. operation did not file for protection, even though its condition was as desperate as that of its Canadian and British counterparts.

CCAA, unlike Chapter 11, a much-used U.S. legal provision with rigid rules, left a great deal of discretion in the hands of the judge. After a three-and-a-half-hour hearing, Blair declared: "I grant the order, but do so with caution." Blair gave O&Y five months to come up with a workable restructuring proposal. By October 21, 1992, they had to have a plan accepted by 75 percent of the creditors on the U.S.$8.6 billion of debt involved in the proceedings.

Court documents showed that far from having a net worth of

Can$5.5 billion, as Miller had claimed the week before, O&Y's net worth was zero. Nevertheless, Miller put on a brave face. Asked at a press conference the next morning whether this was the end of O&Y, Miller said: "Absolutely not. Olympia & York is continuing in business. If I can make an analogy for you, it's as though you're walking down the street; you notice it's raining; you open your umbrella and keep going. The Companies' Creditors Arrangement Act filing in Canada is the equivalent of opening the umbrella. We are still moving forward."

Singin' in the rain.

Although Chapter 11 had still been avoided for the main U.S. operation, Texas Democratic Senator Henry Gonzales, chairman of the U.S. House of Representatives banking committee, declared in Washington: "I look on this as sort of a high-level Donald Trump operation. These old boys are just more sophisticated and worked on a much broader international scale, but essentially the same."

"Old boys!" Oh the indignities of no longer being the bottomless-pocketed ones.

Besides the fate of the main U.S. operation, the filings for protection in Toronto and New York still left one enormous question mark: the fate of Canary Wharf. One of the concerns of the creditors was that the Reichmanns would use cash flow from assets the creditors held as security in order to continue to fund Canary Wharf. Their fears were confirmed five days after the filing when a group of bondholders of 55 Water Street were told there was no money to pay their interest. It had been taken out by the Reichmanns and shipped to London. The bondholders' only recourse was to seize a building badly in need of renovation, the majority of whose leases were coming up for renewal. Nevertheless, the Reichmanns' action on 55 Water Street and other New York buildings from which they had taken rents to keep Canary Wharf going led to a flurry of applications in Toronto to segregate the Reichmanns' various assets and cash flows so they might not be transferred.

Meanwhile, in London, O&Y was asking the Club of Eleven

lenders to extend more money to Canary Wharf for its completion. For two weeks, the groups met late into the night. O&Y's last-ditch effort was an offer — thrashed out during a fifteen-hour meeting at Canary Wharf on Wednesday, May 27 — of 80 percent of the equity in the first two phases of Canary Wharf and 35 percent in the remainder of the project in return for an additional £595 million revolving term loan. But just one of the problems was that the loan was contingent on the British government moving into 350,000 square feet of space. John Major's government, for its part, was sensitive to any accusation of bailing out people whom the *Sunday Times* had declared only weeks before to be the fourth richest in the world. If the government did a deal, it had to be on an arm's-length, commercial basis. O&Y was reported to have offered space to the Department of the Environment at £12 a square foot, but although the figure was less than half what Paul Reichmann had been projecting four years previously, still there were other Docklands projects prepared to offer cheaper space.

The Reichmanns' initial tough negotiating stance was now coming back to haunt them. In the words of one banker quoted by the *Wall Street Journal*: "O&Y wasted too much time, and they needed too much money."

In addition, there was a split among the eleven Club lenders. Citibank, Crédit Lyonnais, Credit Suisse, and a Finnish bank wanted to extend more money. But the other seven, including the big Canadian lenders and the British giants Lloyds and Barclays, said no.

For Paul Reichmann, who did not attend the London meeting but was kept informed by phone in Toronto, this was a devastating blow. It meant that Canary Wharf would have to be put into "administration," a form of bankruptcy protection far less amenable to debtors than either the U.S. Chapter 11 or Canada's CCAA. Under administration, debtors lost management control, which was placed in the hands of court-appointed insolvency accountants.

At 9:30 A.M. on the morning of Thursday, May 28, Ernst &

Young insolvency partner Stephen James Lister Adamson walked
into the High Court in London, knowing he was about to take
over a task that had eluded the world's most ambitious property
developer: to salvage Canary Wharf. Only Adamson's job was not
to save Canary Wharf for the Reichmanns, it was to rescue as
much as possible for the lenders.

From the High Court, Adamson drove to Canary Wharf for a
meeting with O&Y's 400 shell-shocked London staff members.
They learned that all debts had been frozen and construction work
had stopped. Adamson and his colleague, Nigel Hamilton, had
been given just £10 million to keep Canary Wharf on the most
basic life support for three months while they solicited proposals
for the project's survival. That meant that virtually all O&Y's
London staff would have to go. For people who had shared the
Reichmann dream, it was a terrible blow. A press conference was
called for noon in the tower's Cabot Hall. There, Michael Dennis
and Steve Miller, both looking drained, admitted defeat, although
a strain of defiance remained. Miller declared: "This family in
Toronto has invested more money in the U.K. than all the Japanese automakers put together." Given the Japanese banks' exposure of over U.S.$3 billion to O&Y, that may have been an
infelicitous comparison.

Moving the Reichmann team out of the driver's seat meant a
further critical blow to an already doomed cause. Ironically, it
seemed to make much more sense to leave the Reichmanns managing Canary Wharf than either the Toronto or New York real
estate because Toronto and New York were going concerns.
Canary Wharf had been the world's greatest juggling act. Far from
maintaining the project's momentum, slim as it was, the administrators — with their tight budget — were bound to lead to a sharp
reversal of whatever confidence was left. How could they take
over the running of a dream?

Tenants due to occupy space at Canary Wharf, such as American Express, now began to pore over their leases, looking for
possible escape clauses. Part of American Express's deal had been
that the Reichmanns would take over their old space in the City.

With administration, there might be no money to carry out that agreement. That might leave Amex with two sets of rent. Before administration, Canary Wharf had held on to the vestiges of being an address in the making; now it threatened to become at best a back office location, at worst a ghost town. The government was still sticking to its condition that the Reichmanns, or whoever took over the project, put up £400 million of the cost of the underground extension.

Meanwhile, tenants who had moved in were nervous about upkeep and maintenance on their space, and annoyed about commitments O&Y had made to them that the Reichmanns were now in no position to keep. A spokesman for advertising company Ogilvy & Mather said: "If they fall back on their commitments that they have made to us, then we will have to relook at the commitments we made to them."

Back in Toronto, Justice Robert Blair had moved the wranglings over O&Y to the largest courtroom in the University Avenue courthouse, Courtroom 6-1, which was usually reserved for murder trials.

There, the debate centered upon two issues: how the creditors would be grouped, and who would pay the costs of restructuring. Those with senior debt on the trophy buildings objected to having lesser-secured creditors lumped in with them, as O&Y had proposed. Blair found in the secured creditors' favor. As a result, on June 5, six creditors' groups were announced, ranging from those whose loans were backed by prime real estate to those whose loans were backed by nothing but the hope that something would turn up.

As for who would pay for the restructuring costs, bondholders who felt they were well secured objected strongly to having rents from "their" buildings used to fund the legal and financial advisers who were fighting them. There was particular annoyance every time Steve Miller turned up at a meeting with a large entourage — which the creditors dubbed "The Steve Miller band" — because the creditors knew they were paying the band's salaries. A battle quickly developed in court over why the Reichmanns were not prepared to put more of their own money into the restructuring, since they would be the principal beneficiaries of the business's survival. Lawyers for the bondholders accused the Reichmanns of the intent "to deliver as little information as possible as to all of these financial matters so as to shield O&Y Group and Reichmann family assets for their obligation to fund GAR [general, administrative, and restructuring] expenses."

In the course of a search for unencumbered assets within O&Y that might be used to pay for their own legal and financial costs, it was discovered that the tile business, the brothers' first venture in Canada, which had grown to become highly successful and continent-wide in its scope, had been bought by "certain of the Reichmanns" — in fact, Ralph — from O&Y in January 1991. It was also discovered that the company had accounts receivable from entities controlled by the Reichmanns for close to Can$150 million.

Representatives of the Canadian buildings' bondholders put up a powerful challenge to the notion that their security had any place in the CCAA proceedings. Indeed, they attacked the validity of the proceedings themselves, noting that the refusal of governments to become involved in the affair indicated that no "public interest" was involved. They argued that Miller's original claim on April 13 that there was a "franchise value" that had to be protected in order to maintain values was also untenable. O&Y's business as a property developer was over; its active and passive management of equity interests in other companies was due to end with the orderly liquidation of these assets to pay down debts; only its real estate ownership and management business would be left. That business could easily be taken over by other companies. Indeed, due to the company's cash-strapped position, it could not manage its buildings well, particularly in a tight market, because it could not offer inducements to new tenants. There was also a potential conflict in that O&Y might favor one building over another. The bondholders' lawyers pointed out that many of the tenants who had moved from First Canadian Place to BCE Place had had their leases in the Reichmann building taken over by the landlords of BCE Place, the old "used car" technique. These landlords, in turn, were in a stronger financial position to sublease the space in First Canadian Place than the empty space controlled by the Reichmanns. They also noted that O&Y's failure would not involve the loss of large numbers of jobs, since the building managements would still be needed whoever owned the buildings. The only beneficiaries of the plan, said the bondholders' representatives, were the Reichmanns. The initial restructuring proposals by the Reichmanns offered no advantages to secured real estate lenders and "quite probably, potential serious disadvantage."

Perhaps the biggest issue the bondholders raised was that the Reichmanns' actions would have enormous potential impact on capital markets in Canada. In particular, the Reichmanns' actions threatened to kill the whole market for nonrecourse project finance. Put simply, the Reichmanns were claiming that lenders to a project could not come after O&Y if the project ran into trouble, but if O&Y got in trouble, then O&Y could come after the project! Henceforth, lenders could not afford to lend without looking at the financial strength of the ultimate controller of any project. Single-project financing would be killed. The Reichmanns had to go down, said the bondholders' lawyers, so that the system and the law could be seen to work.

The matter of cost sharing was not settled until the beginning of July, following a week of round-the-clock negotiations. Even then, the cost-sharing plan was only settled for the period until the end of August. Under the plan, O&Y had to sell, and be allowed to borrow against, a package of unencumbered assets, including Paul Reichmann's corporate jet. The undersecured creditors, such as the lenders of the Jumbo and Carena loans, were forced to kick in. But O&Y had to ditch two of its advisers, Burns Fry and J.P. Morgan.

Despite the anger of the bankers, Paul Reichmann was still receiving a largely sympathetic treatment from the press. A *Wall Street Journal* story on June 1 opened with a reported *cri de coeur* from

Reichmann about his crumbling relationship with his former main Canadian bank, the CIBC: "Why are they doing this to me? These people are my friends."

The answer of course was that they were doing it to him because they were fed up with him doing it to them. The story claimed that "Mr. Reichmann's slow, trusting, Old World style of sealing deals has been ill-suited to the task of putting together a strategy quickly to overcome a cash crisis." In fact, Paul - Reichmann was still trying to negotiate as if he were on top. He was also giving off-the-record briefings blaming everyone but himself for O&Y's problems: the commercial paper had collapsed because of DBRS's downgradings and because a "junior treasury official" in the Ontario government had panicked; it was all Morgan Stanley's fault that the Canary Wharf financings had fallen apart; Thomas Johnson had been too greedy; it was Miller and Greenwald who had hatched the get-tough-with-the-banks strategy that had so disastrously misfired; the British government was at fault for not taking space in Canary Wharf.

But then, at the end of June and the beginning of July, a New York court case and the revelation of O&Y's financial status challenged both Paul Reichmann's reputation and the empire's solvency.

In 1981, as he had plotted the financing of the World Financial Center, Paul Reichmann had entered negotiations with Teachers Insurance and Annuity Association of America that led to an agreement in 1983 to borrow U.S.$250 million of permanent finance backed by one of the towers. The agreement was subject to subsequent negotiations that proved long and complex. At the end of 1983, Paul Reichmann had notified Teachers that he would terminate the loan agreement imminently unless the association finalized the negotiations and agreed to forward the money, even though the previously scheduled closing of the agreement was more than a year away. O&Y had borrowed elsewhere. Teachers had sued. The case had been going for several years. In June 1992, a New York judge ruled that O&Y was liable for breaking off the loan agreement. The judge refuted Reichmann's claim that the parties were at an impasse and maintained that Paul Reichmann had no right to make his demands for an immediate closing. The issue of damages awaited a later trial.

A further blow to Paul Reichmann's credibility came with the publication, at last, of O&Y's financial statements for the year ending January 31, 1992. Far from having the "equity cushion" that Paul Reichmann had quietly intimated to his journalistic conduits, the figures showed that O&Y was truly bankrupt. After asset write-downs of Can$1.4 billion, the company had a net loss for the year of Can$2.1 billion. Consolidated cash flow had slumped from Can$583 million to just Can$77 million.

In fact, these figures told only half the story. After a behind-the-scenes battle with its accountants, Price Waterhouse, O&Y had refused to write down its Can$3.6 billion investment in Canary Wharf, even though most analysts put its value at little more than Can$1 billion. In its auditors' report, Price Waterhouse declared: "In our opinion, the value of the development has been materially impaired. Generally accepted accounting principles require that the amount of the impairment in value should have been estimated and provided for in these financial statements."

Ironically, Price Waterhouse's report was addressed to the very shareholders who had stopped it from making any adjustment. If Canary Wharf's reduced value had been included in the figures for the year to January 31, 1992, O&Y's loss would have been over Can$4 billion, one of the largest in global corporate history.

In the July 20 issue of *Forbes*, the magazine issued a qualified *mea culpa* for its inclusion of the Reichmanns in its 1991 list of billionaires. *Forbes* acknowledged that in assessing the brothers' net worth at U.S.$7 billion, "We seem to have been off by a nice, round $9 billion." But then, just to prove it hadn't grown too much wiser over the interceding year, the magazine announced, "Are the Reichmanns really underwater? We doubt it. . . . We think that when the smoke clears, the Reichmanns will still be very rich. But for now they are off our list of the superrich."

The myth of deep pockets, it seems, dies hard.

The September 1992 issue of *Fortune* would be less apologetic about its gaffe in pegging the Reichmanns' wealth at U.S.$12.8 billion the year before. "Canada's Reichmann family, No. 4 on last year's list, have traceable wealth outside the beleaguered Olympia & York of less than $1 billion. But who knows?"

Deadlines continued to be missed. Claiming insufficient time and too many demands for information, O&Y asked for, and was granted, an extension of the July 13 time limit for filing a restructuring agreement. The court set a new deadline of August 21. Paul Reichmann meanwhile quietly traveled the globe looking for investors who would back him in a bid to buy Canary Wharf, an action that seemed somehow inappropriate.

The wrangling and posturing continued on three fronts. In Toronto, O&Y engaged in round after round of meetings with creditors as it attempted to come up with an acceptable debt restructuring plan by its court-imposed deadline. In New York, the U.S. operation struggled to stay out of Chapter 11 and to persuade its creditors to come to a voluntary arrangement. In London, although Canary Wharf was under administration, Paul Reichmann had still not given up hope of regaining control.

Chief Reichmann negotiator Steve Miller apparently kept his sense of humor. Following yet another long confrontation with lenders in a law firm's office in Scotia Plaza in August, Miller rose to go with the words: "Well, if someone will open the window, I'll leave now."

An increasing frustration for the bankers was Paul - Reichmann's apparent unwillingness to recognize his true condition. O&Y insiders claimed that he still saw the situation as "a challenge." And there was nothing that Paul Reichmann liked more than a challenge. He also remained apparently convinced that hard bargaining was still the best strategy.

On August 20, the day before O&Y was due under the revised court order to reveal its restructuring plan, the plan was ballyhooed via a press conference in Toronto. O&Y clearly still hoped to gain leverage through use of the media. Under this proposal, O&Y wanted a five-year moratorium in return for less secured lenders swapping $5.3 billion of debt for a 49 percent stake in O&Y. If they could not put things straight within that period, then the banks would wind up with 80 percent of the company via the conversion of O&Y-issued bonds. The - Reichmann family, it was claimed, was prepared to kick in the 20 percent of its U.S. real estate assets owned directly rather than through O&Y, but it was reckoned those assets were as debt-burdened as the rest of the empire. A suggestion that the different lending groups should vote at different times was seen as another attempt at the "divide and conquer" strategy. Once again, the proposal was regarded as smoke and mirrors, designed to leave the Reichmanns in control. Moreover, there were huge gaps in the 105-page plan. It did not even deal with the best-secured real estate lenders, who, it was assumed, would wind up with equity in the buildings against which they had loans. "There's nothing there," one banker said. Another claimed: "We want flesh on the bones. It's not good enough to have the skeleton. We want the flesh." In the end, the sketchy proposal was rapidly rejected.

A few days after the plan was revealed in Toronto, the London administrators of Canary Wharf announced they were opening up the top floor of the building to sightseers, who would pay £3 to take the 55-second ride to the top. The decision was made, according to the administrators, to "generate and maintain interest in the Docklands." They denied suggestions that this was a way to raise cash. Indeed, it was calculated that 187 million visitors would be needed to cover the project's direct debt.

When the three-month deadline under the original administration order came up in August, the administrators asked for more time, declaring that there were talks going on with ten potential buyers. By far the highest profile, and most controversial, was a consortium containing Paul Reichmann.

In August, a trio of Manhattan financial mavens announced an offer to inject money into Canary Wharf: Laurence Tisch, the president of CBS, Sanford "Sandy" Weill, chairman of Primerica, and Lewis Ranieri, former vice-chairman of Salomon, who now ran a Manhattan-based company called Hyperion. All were long-time associates of Paul Reichmann. Reichmann had discussed a bail-out of Campeau with Tisch. He had negotiated American Express's tenancy at the World Financial Center with Weill when Weill had been at Amex. He had known Ranieri through O&Y's huge New York real estate financings and had backed Ranieri when he had been ousted from Salomon.

In fact, Reichmann's role was reportedly greatly exaggerated. This did not help the consortium's status with the banks. Neither did the size or nature of the consortium's offer of £350 million. The loan had stringent conditions, including a requirement that it rank in front of existing loans, and that the investors have no responsibility for the subway extension. In return for the loan, which would receive commercial rates of interest, the consortium would also take a 50 percent equity interest in the project. The proposal bore all the trademarks of the ultra-tough Reichmann negotiating stance. At the end of August, the size of the cash injection offer was reduced to £235 million.

In September, an advertising campaign was launched by the London Docklands Development Corporation to boost the Docklands. In full-page ads in major British newspapers, it pitched "The Docker" against "The Knocker." The Docker was an enlightened risk taker who, among other attributes, "happily got wet to hear Pavarotti. . . . Sees a secretary as a colleague not a slave. . . . Says the Channel Tunnel's a good idea, even if it only means you get a decent croissant." The Knocker, by contrast, "finds, in the spring, his fancy turns to thoughts of a new lawn-mower. . . . Would not have built Concorde. . . . Buys Christmas cards in January sales for the coming year."

Interspersed with such contrasting adventurous versus stick-in-the-mud characteristics were similar attitudes toward the Docklands. The Docker "knows that cities, like businesses, must develop or they'll decay. . . . Has a healthy suspicion of experts. . . . Believes the 30-year-old trees in the Docklands are well worth £1,000 each. . . . Knows beyond doubt that London Docklands will be a success." The Knocker "has never visited London Docklands, even as a tourist. . . . Would rather 'lose' a few people than cut overheads by moving. . . . Can't believe that Heathrow is twice as far from St. Paul's as London City Airport."

The *Financial Times* noted, "The campaign has been greeted with as much derision as acclaim." And indeed, it seemed to be marked by the same self-righteous paranoia that had characterized O&Y's attitude to those who had earlier dared to question the wisdom of Canary Wharf.

At the end of September, American Express and Chemical Banking Corp. joined the list of "the knockers" by announcing they were pulling out of their leases. A few days later, the bid for Canary Wharf by the U.S. consortium containing Paul Reichmann was rejected by a majority of the project's eleven leading bankers. At the beginning of October, the leading O&Y executives in London, including Michael Dennis, were laid off.

Meanwhile, back in Toronto, on September 11, after O&Y had asked for more time to fit together the "pieces of a complex puzzle," the Toronto court order protecting O&Y was extended to December 30. The Reichmanns were given until October 27 to submit their restructuring plan. Said Justice Blair: "There must be a finality to this process, both because real deadlines are what bring negotiations in a process like this to fruition and because there are limits on how long creditors may fairly be asked to stay their hand."

In New York, which had been perhaps the quietest, or at least best-contained, area of dispute, things began to heat up as lenders grew tired of Reichmann tactics. Both Hong Kong billionaire Li Ka-shing and a consortium led by J.P. Morgan began to play hardball, threatening to put the Reichmanns into Chapter 11. John Zucotti, the well-regarded head of O&Y's U.S. operations, was reportedly threatening to leave.

Early in August, Zucotti and Meyer (Sandy) Frucher, O&Y's executive vice president of development in the United States, flew to Hong Kong to meet Li Ka-shing in an effort to "defuse the situation." Li felt he had been led down the garden path when he had taken the mortgage on 60 Broadstreet toward the end of 1991. He had "lost face." He was clearly angry with Paul Reichmann.

A deal was sketched out over 55 Water Street, under which a

state pension fund would acquire the building. The deal valued the property, which backed U.S.$548 million of secured debentures, at around U.S.$150 million. The building at 320 Park Avenue, part of the original Uris package, was sold in September to Mutual of America, a New York–based life insurance company, reportedly for around U.S.$20 million less than its U.S.$147 million mortgage. The building had been lying empty for a year because O&Y had not been able to afford to have the thirty-four-story building's asbestos removed.

Among the Reichmann U.S. assets, the real trophy was the World Financial Center. Apart from the building owned by American Express and interests by certain tenants, lenders believed the remainder of the equity belonged to Olympia & York, and that the Reichmann family had no direct interest. But in September it was revealed that the Reichmanns' old associates, the Edper Bronfmans, held a stake through a company called Battery Park Holdings Inc. Even more surprising was the revelation that the Reichmanns held a half share in Battery Park Holdings themselves. The company had been set up in 1989, but this was the first time the vast majority of lenders had ever heard about it. Observers wondered why the Reichmanns would want to buy a stake in a development they already owned via O&Y. The knowledge of the separate Reichmann stake reportedly came as a surprise even to the executives of O&Y's U.S. operation, although they had suspected it several months earlier. As a result, O&Y's Manhattan-based U.S. operation had stopped making payments to Battery Park Holdings since this apparently violated bank agreements that stipulated that the Reichmanns would not take money out of the U.S. operations during the negotiations with their bankers.

This revelation was of concern not merely because it had been concealed but because it indicated that the Reichmanns may have been strapped for cash as far back as the end of 1989. Part of the organization still controlled by Jack Cockwell had evolved into a merchant bank that specialized in "last resort" finance. One obvious reason for keeping the deal secret was that if it had been known, the Reichmanns' credibility would have been further damaged. As for the Edper organization, itself subject to declining profits, obviously the last thing it wanted was to be linked further with the floundering ship of the Reichmanns.

At the end of October, O&Y submitted another restructuring proposal. It envisaged splitting the company into three parts: a U.S. real estate and investment arm, a Canadian real estate arm, and a Canadian investment company, which would also have responsibility for Canary Wharf. The Reichmanns' major concession to their Canadian bankers was that the CIBC, Scotia, Royal and National Bank would now wind up with 80 percent of the equity in the three Toronto "trophy" buildings: First Canadian Place, Scotia Plaza, and Exchange Tower. Once again, the proposal called for a five-year moratorium. Once again, it left the Reichmanns in control.

The deal met immediate opposition from increasingly angry lenders and bondholders. "We're not happy with them even keeping a small ownership position," one banker was quoted as saying. "But this, this is ridiculous." Another unidentified senior banker declared, "I just don't see it as being a double deal. It comes down to how much confidence you have in the people running this. Once you lose credibility with the banker, it's gone. And he [Paul Reichmann] has lost credibility." Bondholders asked to take an interest cut were even more angry. Bill Maclean, chairman of the committee representing the First Canadian Place bondholders, declared: "Olympia & York's proposal is garbage."

Hostility to the plan forced the Reichmanns almost immediately to revise it. Under a hastily devised new scheme, it was declared that O&Y would turn itself into a property management company with perhaps 20 percent of the U.S. properties and 10 percent of those in Canada. The secured creditors would be able to seize all their collateral. It was declared that the changes were so extensive that a new information circular would have to be issued and that voting on the plan would have to be delayed yet again. Under the existing proposal, voting was meant to take place at the end of November. Now, however, it was claimed that it might not be possible before mid-January.

Ironically, O&Y's one hope appeared to be not that the market was improving but that it was deteriorating. But of course the whole exercise was a charade. The Reichmanns may still have seen themselves in the ringmaster role, but their corporate creation was now more like a wounded animal being circled by rival packs of predators, each of which was sizing up its opponents before moving in for the kill. The one indisputable fact was that there wouldn't be enough to go round.

24

Credit Where Credit Is Due

IS PAUL REICHMANN IN THE END A TRAGIC FIGURE, AN extraordinary man laid low by a fatal flaw? Certainly, he and Albert will always be known as great real estate developers. First Canadian Place, the World Financial Center, and Canary Wharf are all monuments to quality, embellishments to Toronto, New York, and London. Paul Reichmann's fatal flaws were excessive belief in his own powers, corporate acquisitiveness, and a penchant for larger and larger gambles. What ultimately killed the Reichmann empire was Canary Wharf. The seeds of destruction lay in Paul Reichmann's unquenchable ambition. However, he could never have taken his empire to the size it ultimately achieved — and the disaster it ultimately threatened — without the willing cooperation of a mesmerized banking community. Canary Wharf was conceived as a monument to the world's greatest family business; it wound up becoming a symbol of an unprecedented real estate bust encouraged by a spate of feckless lending.

On July 30, 1992, James Grant, editor of *Grant's Interest Rate Observer* and author of a brilliant book on credit, *Money of the Mind*, gave testimony in Washington before the House Banking Committee on the Olympia & York affair. Two years previously, Paul Reichmann had been annoyed at Grant's assertions that not even O&Y could flout the laws of financial gravity. Now Grant's simple assertion had been abundantly borne out.

Grant told the committee that real estate busts were both recurrent and global: "Overbuilding brought on by overlending is a recurring phenomenon, and the first bad real estate loan no doubt occurred along about the time the first bank opened." Moreover, "Whatever colossal delusions American lenders might have entertained about real estate. . . . were as common in Stockholm and London as they were in Dallas and New York."

Grant stressed that human psychology was at the root of the problems: "I do not mean to sound a note of pure fatalism, but the truth is that people with money, acting in crowds, periodically go off the deep end." He admitted, however, that the sheer persistence of real estate overlending in the 1980s was difficult to explain. He saw the roots of the phenomenon in federal deposit insurance and the notion that major banks were "too big to fail." This "socialization of risk" tended to make bankers less prudent. Nowhere were they less prudent than in real estate lending.

Grant's projections for real estate, and thus for any hope of a Reichmann restructuring, were not optimistic. "The trouble with real estate depressions is that they go on and on," he said, "because a new crop of expiring leases comes up for renewal and downward adjustment every year." Grant believed that the Manhattan office market was more overbuilt and vulnerable in the 1990s than it had been even in the 1930s.

One question only briefly alluded to by Grant, however, was why bankers should have lent so much, on the basis of little or no information, to one man. "Every banker is taught to secure adequate collateral and obtain current financial information about a borrower before lending," said Grant. "Bedazzled by the - Reichmanns' stature and reputation, however, many lenders forgot to ask. This absentmindedness was a hallmark of the boom."

What magic did Paul Reichmann have that made bankers want to lend him so much money? J.P. Morgan once said that the main thing he looked for in making a loan was "character." The growth of Paul Reichmann's character to that of "philosopher king" was in the end a self-feeding process promoted by his bankers. Paul Reichmann *had* to have an exceptional character and supernormal standards of integrity. Otherwise, why were the banks lending so much money to a man who wouldn't open his books?

Paul Reichmann was never a symbol of the regard expressed by bankers for honor or fair play or piety. Paul Reichmann was an example of how much deference bankers pay to naked wealth.

The banks lent Paul Reichmann so much money because he convinced them he didn't need it.

Not that the myth was without foundation. The Reichmanns' early achievements in real estate gave them a more-than-mere-human image. As one contrite banker acknowledged: "We go on track record. The problem is that we extrapolated success into infinity. Banking is ultimately a matter of trust and Paul - Reichmann had an aura. We look at balance sheets and profit and loss accounts and interest coverage and all the other ratios, but then there's the fuzzy part, the intangibles, the magic touch." Far from the brothers' secrecy being a turn-off for bankers, it somehow enhanced Paul Reichmann's image of invincibility.

When the going got tough, some of the bankers got defensive. Allan Taylor, head of the Royal Bank, Canada's largest financial institution, gave an interview to Peter Newman for *Maclean's* in which he told Newman: "The newspapers have been constantly wrong on the information they've put out on O&Y. They've been engaged in incremental fact-finding, publishing their guesses on loan exposures and expecting bankers to put them right. It's the responsibility of the media to get things right, while my responsibility is to my shareholders and the customers who have deposits with us."

Actually, one responsible member of the media had asked the Royal on what basis its loans were made, only to be told that this was "competitive" and thus "confidential."

Taylor told Newman: "You have to accept the fact that we're not completely irresponsible ... that we weren't making loans against nothing. The media have painted a picture of bankers as practically being idiots. There has been a great injustice done in portraying us as loaning against the Reichmann name, the implication that we did it just because it seemed to be an account everyone had confidence in. That gives no credit to the people who run banks."

Credit where credit is due. Among its loans, the Royal took a £100 million chunk of a loan to Canary Wharf, backed primarily by shares in Canary Wharf, at a time when the project was widely regarded as an enormous gamble. It took U.S.$250 million of the U.S.$2.5 billion Jumbo Loan in 1989. That loan was ultimately backed by a piece of paper, signed by O&Y's accountants, that declared that O&Y had a net worth of U.S.$2.5 billion.

Both loans turned out to be imprudent. They were not well secured. The Royal Bank had in fact acted irresponsibly. Its customers and shareholders should be mad. Heads should roll. In any other business, Allan Taylor would be forced to resign. The only justification for his not doing so seems to be that he has so much company.

For bankers, the Reichmanns' early successes provided the excuse to display their age-old tendency to lend in a pack. As the great economist John Maynard Keynes once noted: "A 'sound' banker, alas! is not one who foresees danger and avoids it, but one who, when he is ruined, is ruined in a conventional and orthodox way along with his fellows, so that no one can really blame him." Hence, almost one hundred financial institutions are up to their necks in the Reichmann debacle.

If the media bought the Reichmann myth, they took their lead from the banks. Also, the *Toronto Life* lawsuit was largely misunderstood. Many thought the Reichmanns were saying: "Don't dare to write about our business affairs." In fact, Paul Reichmann had always attempted to use the press, and the press had often allowed itself willingly to be used.

There had long been reasonable cause for concern about the strategic direction of the Reichmann empire. Paul Reichmann's diversifications were neither wise nor well-timed. When he took control of Abitibi, he persuaded himself that the newsprint cycle was a thing of the past; demand and profits were headed onwards and upwards for ever. When his advisers told him this could not be so, he became annoyed with them. The timing of the Gulf Canada takeover was terrible; its convoluted form left Gulf debt-burdened and sapped of morale. Gulf was then used to acquire Hiram Walker in an acrimonious and litigious battle, even though Paul Reichmann had previously claimed that he would never become involved in a hostile takeover, and that he did not believe in using lawyers. In the end, the Reichmanns lost the asset they most sought — Hiram Walker's liquor business. Santa Fe was also costly and time-consuming.

According to those closest to him, one of the features that set Paul Reichmann apart from rivals was his relentless willingness to look at new ways of doing things, never to accept the precedent as the rule. He always believed that there was a better way and was prepared to go to unusual lengths to find it.

Lionel Dodd claimed, before the crash: "I've often said with Paul that the way to be sure that you are going to do something is to say it can't be done. There may not be any CEO, certainly not one I've ever been exposed to, who will take the time, as Paul does, to try and be creative, to go down blind alley after blind alley after blind alley, trying to come up with that one idea that really works. There is extreme desire and pressure to innovate and be creative." Michael Dennis described it as "an unwillingness to do anything the same way a second time; a constant probing of the frontiers." David Brown, the retired investment banker who worked briefly for the Reichmanns, noted, "Paul always liked to move onto bigger and bigger deals. He never wanted to be perceived as standing still." But in the end, Paul Reichmann's great analytical strengths led him into a complex labyrinth of his own making, a labyrinth from which he could not escape.

His maneuvers indicated a degree of acquisitiveness that should have exploded the myth that Paul Reichmann was a "philosopher king," unmotivated by greed or ambition. Put most kindly, Paul Reichmann was like a corporate master chess player who relished playing more and more games simultaneously. Put less kindly, he had turned into a man who found it impossible to stop doing deals. Put least kindly, one could argue that he was the world's most egregious example of corporate greed in action, grabbing as much as he could as fast as he could, with little underlying rationale except the principle of "adding value."

Why couldn't Paul stop? Struggling to explain himself for a 1988 article, he said: "We have no particular interest in growing bigger. What drives us is usually the challenge, to be creative, to do something interesting. No successful businessman really has money in mind after a certain point. When we do something, we want to do it right. It's not monument building; it's more than that. The fact is, anybody who is able to do something well will want to do it until he is stopped by the force of time."

But claiming that he had "no particular interest in growing bigger" seems nonsense in hindsight. How could anybody have bought such a statement? Paul Reichmann was *obsessed* with doing larger and larger deals.

There is a tendency in writing about corporate moguls to emphasize style and appearance at the expense of common underlying psychological drives and the universal constraints of the market — the surest break on whimsical or unwise decisions. The fact that Paul Reichmann appeared without personal foibles — no huge yachts, no messy divorces — was at first a source of mystery, but ultimately it made him seem a less human figure, an obsessive dealmaker. It may turn out that Paul Reichmann, Bill Zeckendorf, Robert Campeau, and Donald Trump had far more in common than people imagined.

One common psychological trait in entrepreneurs — as understandable as it is potentially dangerous — is unwillingness to give up equity. The Reichmanns never wanted to share their achievements and reduce their risks by issuing shares. They were always reluctant to sell buildings, because then they would have to pay taxes. They preferred to borrow against their rising equity instead. When they did at last try to peddle 20 percent of their U.S. interests in the latter half of 1990, the market was already on the way down, but the Reichmanns refused to accept prices below their own inflated estimates.

Canary Wharf will rank as one of the greatest business disasters of all time, not to mention a severe political embarrassment to the British Tories. The project was a self-contradictory hybrid: a piece of boldly ambitious free enterprise that depended on government concessions. Although it was a de facto partnership, a devoutly noninterventionist government mistook providing infrastructure — a necessary role for any government — with government interference. Nevertheless, it should also be noted that Paul Reichmann's vision for Canary Wharf far outstripped anything originally conceived by the Thatcher government for the Docklands.

The Reichmanns' relationship with the Canadian government, too, ran into difficulties, particularly after Gulf Canada pulled out of the Hibernia megaproject early in February 1992, just before the Reichmanns' problems hit the headlines. The Tory government, which had trumpeted the heavily subsidized scheme as a critical piece of regional development for Newfoundland, was clearly annoyed with the Reichmanns. Some analysts felt that the federal government's unwillingness to help bail out O&Y may have been partly rooted in the belief that the Reichmanns had used up all their political credits. Government support and subsidy for the Reichmanns' acquisition of Gulf wound up doing as little good for Canada as Gulf did for the Reichmanns.

Canary Wharf had marked a return from non-real-estate acquisition to what the brothers were best at — development — but it was an extraordinary gamble. Paul Reichmann had to finance the enormously expensive early stages of the development out of North America, which placed an insurmountable burden on New York and Toronto just as the real estate market was experiencing its worst slump since the Second World War. In the end, Paul Reichmann simply could not keep all the plates in the air. This was exacerbated by his chronic inability to delegate. The danger was always that Paul Reichmann would simply experience system overload.

In the two years before the crunch, problems may have increased because Albert became less and less involved with the main business and devoted more time to helping Soviet Jews and to other philanthropic activities. He may be the only man who could have restrained Paul. And yet those who had witnessed the brothers together acknowledged that although Paul always gave Albert a respectful hearing, he also always wound up getting his own way.

Early in May 1992, O&Y had hired a man named William

Kennedy to help with the restructuring. In July, Kennedy gave a deposition in court. He acknowledged that O&Y had been slow in coming to grips with the ramifications of its insolvency, but that this amounted to a kind of corporate shock, a sort of institutional denial.

"I think that in fairness to Olympia & York, it is quite a transition to go from a healthy company to a company that is in trouble, where the tables are turned and different considerations come into play, and that took some time to sink in." Kennedy knew all about corporate denial. His previous employer had been Robert Campeau. The ultimate tragedy for Paul Reichmann was his perhaps inevitable failure to realize, like Bob Campeau, that the game really was over.

Chronology

1955-60   The Reichmann family arrives in stages in Toronto from Tangier. They start a tile importing business. This leads to commercial property development.

1965   The family buys Flemingdon Park, some 500 acres of mixed-use land in the northeast corner of Toronto, for around Can$25 million, and moves into high-rise development.

1965-74   Olympia & York Developments, the family holding company, builds a significant real estate portfolio, as well as building and managing for others. The buildings it owns include:
Place Bell Canada, Ottawa (1.5 million square feet)
Toronto Star Building, Toronto (900,000 square feet)
York Centre, Toronto (900,000 square feet)
Bell Canada Data Centre, Toronto (400,000 square feet)
Global House, Toronto (380,000 square feet)
Texaco Canada Limited Head Office, Toronto (240,000 square feet)
Mony Life Insurance Company of Canada Building, Toronto (220,000 square feet)
Shell Canada Limited, Data Centre, Toronto (165,000 square feet)
Province of Ontario, Ministry of Consumer and Commercial Relations, Toronto (120,000 square feet)

1974   O&Y starts building First Canadian Place. At seventy-two stories, its main tower is the largest building in the Commonwealth and the tallest bank building in the world.

1977   They buy the "Uris package," eight Manhattan skyscrapers, for U.S.$320 million. The transaction is subsequently dubbed "the deal of the century."

1978   They purchase 80 percent of Block Brothers, a Vancouver-based company specializing in residential real estate development and real estate brokerage. (They subsequently buy out the minority.)

1979   March. They take control of English Property, one of Britain's largest publicly owned real estate companies for Can$157.3 million. This gives them a majority interest (although not control) in Trizec, a Canadian real estate company with assets of Can$1 billion. Trizec is controlled by Edward and Peter Bronfman. They buy, for an unspecified price, just under 10 percent of Canada Northwest Land Ltd., a Calgary-based oil company.

1980   September. They buy 50.1 percent of petroleum and mining company Brinco for Can$95 million. The same month, they buy, for around Can$33 million, 9 percent of Royal Trustco, the parent holding company of Canada's largest trust company, with more than $26 billion under its administration, and the country's largest brokers of residential real estate. They subsequently take their stake up to 23.9 percent. They win the contract to develop the 8-million-square- foot Battery Park City in Lower Manhattan, the largest private commercial real estate development in the world.

1981   March. Following a bidding war, they acquire 16.8 million shares of Abitibi-Price, the world's largest newsprint manufacturer, at a cost of Can$537 million. (They subsequently increase their holdings, giving a final cost — for 94 percent of Abitibi's stock — of Can$560 million.) April. They buy 20 percent of MacMillan Bloedel for Can$214 million, and then tender it into Noranda's partial offer for MacMillan Bloedel. They are left with just under 10 percent of MacMillan Bloedel and a stake in Noranda.

They accumulate an initial stake in Bow Valley Industries of 5.3 percent for approximately Can$31 million. (They will later take this stake to 10 percent.)

They buy 5.9 percent of Hiram Walker Resources for around Can$130 million (again, they will later take this stake to 10 percent).

1983   They swap their 23.9 percent stake in Royal Trust for cash and shares in Brascan-controlled financial conglomerate Trilon. They receive approximately Can$40 million in cash, an immediate 12.5 percent share in Trilon's common stock, and warrants and convertible shares that can ultimately bring O&Y's voting interest in Trilon to more than 20 percent.

1984   June. They buy 16.2 million shares of Cadillac Fairview (22 percent) for Can$232 million.

1985   They buy 60.2 percent of Gulf Canada, Canada's second-largest integrated oil company, from Chevron for Can$2.8 billion.

As part of the deal, they sell 90 percent of Abitibi-Price to Gulf Canada for Can$1.2 billion, leaving the newsprint producer still effectively under their control.

1986   April. Gulf Canada, now under Reichmann control, pays Can$3 billion for 69 percent of liquor, petroleum, and gas distribution conglomerate Hiram Walker Resources.

July. Interprovincial Pipe Line swaps its Hiram Walker stake plus a package of cash and debentures reportedly worth Can$1.1 billion for Home Oil. There is also a legal battle over the sale, for Can$2.6 billion, of Hiram Walker's liquor subsidiary, Hiram Walker–Gooderham and Worts (HW-GW) to Allied-Lyons PLC of England for Can$2.6 billion.

September. Agreement is reached under which Allied will control 51 percent of HW-GW, and the Reichmanns 49 percent. All litigation between the two sides is ended, with each party bearing its own costs.

1987   June. Gulf Canada is split up. Abitibi becomes a separate company once more. GW Utilities is set up to hold the stakes in HW-GW, Interhome Energy, and Consumers' Gas.

Gulf Canada raises over Can$500 million in one of Canada's largest ever equity issues. Shares are sold in both the United States and Europe.

July. Paul Reichmann takes over the Canary Wharf project in London from a consortium led by G. Ware Travelstead. He commits to build more than 12 million feet by 1996, at a cost of between £3 billion and £4 billion, in a formerly derelict part of London, 2 1/2 miles east of the City.

O&Y accumulates shares in Santa Fe Southern Pacific Corp., a Chicago-based railroad, real estate, and resources conglomerate, and considers a bid for the company, which would cost close to U.S.$10 billion.

O&Y swaps its 49 percent stake in HW-GW for convertible preferred shares in Allied-Lyons. On conversion, those shares will give the Reichmanns just under 10 percent of the British company's equity.

November. *Toronto Life* publishes "The Mysterious Reichmanns" by Elaine Dewar.

1988   February. The Reichmanns and O&Y sue *Toronto Life* for libel.

The Reichmanns buy half of Scotia Plaza from Robert Campeau, who gained control of Allied Stores in 1986 for U.S.$3.6 billion.

Campeau buys Federated Stores for U.S.$6.6 billion.

The Reichmanns buy Can$260 million of debentures in Campeau Corporation.

1989   January. The Reichmanns arrange their U.S.$2.5 billion "Jumbo Loan" from a global consortium of banks led by the Hong Kong & Shanghai Bank.

December. O&Y becomes involved in a restructuring of Campeau Corporation and its U.S. retailing subsidiaries.

1990   January. Federated and Allied file for Chapter 11 protection.

April. Gulf Canada announces it will buy Imperial's 23 percent stake in Interhome for Can$492 million, then split Interhome into Home Oil and Interprovincial Pipe Line, and merge Home with Gulf Canada.

July. Gulf Canada reveals that it is planning a major investment in the Soviet Union.

August. Sadam Hussein invades Kuwait, leading to the Gulf War.

September. It is reported that O&Y has put 20 percent of its U.S. real estate portfolio on the block.

November. O&Y announces that the Gulf Canada/Home Oil merger has fallen apart due to disagreements over price. Nevertheless, it is announced that Consumers' Gas will be sold.

£500 million of long-term project finance is raised on Canary Wharf.

1991   February. GW Utilities sells its stake in Allied-Lyons for net proceeds of Can$487 million.

Consumers' Gas is sold to British Gas for Can$1.1 billion.

September. A restructuring of Campeau Corp. is announced under which the Reichmanns will control two-thirds of the company's equity and Robert Campeau less than 2 percent. The Reichmann losses on their Campeau involvement will total more than Can$600 million.

October. O&Y gains control of the half of Scotia Plaza it does not own in return for taking over its debt.

Hong Kong billionaire Li Ka-shing invests U.S.$57.5 million to bail out O&Y's 60 Broad Street in Manhattan.

1992   January. Morgan Stanley sues O&Y for U.S.$240 million over O&Y's commitment to buy the building Morgan Stanley has built at Canary Wharf.

February. Gulf Canada pulls out of the Hibernia project.

February/March. There is a run on O&Y's commercial paper, forcing the company to withdraw from the market.

March 22. O&Y admits liquidity problems and that it has to restructure its debt.

March 24. Thomas Johnson is appointed president of O&Y. Steve Miller, a former Chrysler executive now with New York–based Wolfensohn is appointed chief bank negotiator. J.P. Morgan and Burns Fry are also hired to help O&Y with restructuring.

April 13. At its first major meeting with ninety-one banks, O&Y releases figures fifteen months out of date and asks for more money. The bankers are not amused. Thomas Johnson resigns and is replaced by Gerald Greenwald, another former Chrysler executive.

May 4. O&Y misses a payment on the bonds backing First Canadian Place, setting in motion an action by bondholders to seize the tower.

   The Canadian federal government and the Ontario government announce they will not provide backing for an O&Y bail-out.

May 7–8. At a meeting with its leading bankers in London, O&Y requests a five-year moratorium on debt and a large cash injection in return for nonvoting shares worth up to 20 percent of the company.

The bankers are again not amused. Canary Wharf is "drip-fed" £21 million to keep it alive for three weeks.

May 14. A London court finds in favor of Morgan Stanley in the suit over its Canary Wharf building.

O&Y files for protection in Canada under the Companies' Creditors Arrangement Act (CCAA), and for certain of its companies with U.S. interests under Chapter 11 in the United States.

May 27. Canary Wharf is forced into administration by its lenders.

July. Canary Wharf's administrators announce they are negotiating with "more than half a dozen parties" interested in investing in Canary Wharf. O&Y defaults on the mortgage taken over by Li Ka-shing on 60 Broad Street. Li is said to feel he has "lost face" in the transaction.

July 10. O&Y announces a net loss for the year to January 31, 1992, of Can$2.1 billion. Price Waterhouse declares that the company should have written down the value of Canary Wharf, which is still on the books at Can$3.6 billion. If the depreciation in the value of Canary Wharf had been taken into account, the company's loss would likely have been over $4 billion, the largest in corporate history.

August 20. O&Y unveils a sketchy new restructuring plan seeking a five-year moratorium and offering a 49 percent stake in O&Y to less secured lenders. The plan is almost immediately rejected by O&Y's bankers.

The London administrators of Canary Wharf open the tower to sightseers to "generate and maintain interest in the Docklands." They also seek, and are granted, an extension on the three-month deadline to find a solution to the development's problems.

A U.S. consortium consisting of Laurence Tisch, president of CBS, Sandy Weill, chairman of Primerica, and Lewis Ranieri, former vice-chairman of Salomon, makes an offer to lend £350 million to Canary Wharf in return for 50 percent of its equity. The offer, which is backed by Paul Reichmann, is subsequently reduced to £235 million.

September 11. The Toronto court order protecting O&Y is extended to December 30. The Reichmanns are given until October 27 to submit their restructuring plan.

American Express and Chemical Bank pull out of Canary Wharf leases.

October. The U.S. consortium's bid for Canary Wharf is rejected. Michael Dennis and other top O&Y executives in London are laid off.

O&Y submits another restructuring proposal under which the company would be split into three but the Reichmanns would retain control of the bulk of their empire. The deal was rapidly rejected and a revised, with a projection that a new information circular, and hence and vote on the plan, might not now take place until January, 1993.

INDEX

Abitibi-Price Inc., 84-86, 108, 115-17, 248, 255, 298
Adamson, Stephen James Lister, 282
Aetna Life, 241
Allied-Lyons, 139-41, 143, 148, 153, 157, 165-78, 183-89, 191, 255-56
Allied Stores Corporation, 213-17, 223-24
Alster, Henri, 67
American Express, 66-67, 90, 209, 282-83, 291, 292
Art of the Deal, The, 229
As It Happens, 184

Baker, Neil, 108
Bank of Montreal, 30, 37-39, 85, 242-46, 248
Bank of Nova Scotia, 246, 248, 266, 270, 293
Bankers, The, 44
bankers: relationship with O&Y, 242-50, 264-66, 296-97; restructuring O&Y's debt, 270, 272
Bannon, Brian, 156, 158-59, 170, 175
Barclays, 281
Battery Park City, 51-53, 55-68. *See also* World Financial Center
Battery Park Holdings Inc., 292
BCE Place, 4, 284-85
Beattie, Peter, 136
Beaufort Sea, 103-04, 256
Bell Canada, 138, 142
Bell, Tom, 85, 86
Bennett, Avie, 232
Best, Patricia, 82
Black, Conrad, 17, 230
Blair, Justice Robert, 279, 283, 291
Blau, Otto, 36
Blauvelt, Howard, 107, 108
Bloomingdale's, 223
Boesky, Ivan, 139, 214
Bradman, Godfrey, 207
Brascan, 80, 82
Bregmann & Hamann, 31
British American Oil Company Limited, 101
British government, 192-93, 237, 238, 270, 281
Bronfman, Charles, 128
Bronfman, Edgar, 128, 149, 158, 171
Bronfman, Edward, 76-80
Bronfman, Peter, 76-80, 85
Brown, David, 85, 107, 133, 279, 299
Buchanan, Peter, 196, 214

Burns Fry Limited, 269, 285
Burr, David, 175
Burrough, Bryan, 219
Business Week, 93, 166, 193, 267

Camdev Corporation, 276
Campeau Corporation, 217-18, 221, 225, 274
Campeau, Robert, 80-81, 211-13; Allied Stores Corp., 213-17; deals with Reichmanns, 215-19, 221-25, 244, 273-76; Federated Department Stores, 217-18
Campbell, Donald, 262
Canadian Establishment, The, 75
Canadian government, 111-15, 301
Canadian Imperial Bank of Commerce, 39, 85, 242-46, 248, 266, 270, 278, 286, 293
Canary Wharf, 3-4, 194-97; business disaster, 295, 300; construction, 200-06; financing, 246-50, 277-79, 289-90, 295-98; media reports, 235-38, 249; Morgan Stanley, 267-68; plans for project, 197-99, 206-08; problems, 206-07; salvaging, 280-83; tenants, 209; value of, 287
Carena Properties Inc., 77, 247-8, 266
Carney, Pat, 110-11
Catellus Development Corporation, 258
Chapter 11 (U.S. legal provision), 273, 279, 280, 291
Chemical Banking Corporation, 291
Chevron, 105-08, 111, 115, 17
Chevron Canada, 105-06
Chrétien, Jean, 113
CIBC. *See* Canadian Imperial Bank of Commerce
Citibank, 5, 214, 247-48, 265-66, 281
City Investing, 64-65
Clemes, John, 140, 143, 172
Club of Eleven, 250, 280-81
Cockwell, Jack, 79-80, 292
Cohen, Mickey, 112, 113, 133, 150, 166, 170, 174-75, 179, 256-58
commercial paper market, 5-10, 266, 268
Commerzbank International, 247
Companies' Creditors Arrangement Act, 279
Connacher, Jimmy, 80, 106, 108, 130
Conoco, 106, 107
Consumers' Gas Company, 129, 255, 261
Coombes, Tony, 55, 58
Crédit Lyonnais, 247, 281
Credit Suisse, 281

Credit Suisse First Boston, 195, 209
Crombie, David, 31-32, 54
Cuomo, Mario, 73
Cushman, John C., III, 64

Dai-Ichi Kangyo Bank, 247
Daily Telegraph, 209
Davis, Bill, 196
Davis Oil and Gas, 129
DeBartolo, Edward, 214, 217, 222, 273-75
Dennis, Michael, 54, 63, 195-97, 200,
    208-09, 236-37, 249, 269, 272-73, 277,
    282, 291, 299
Desmarais, Paul, 218-19, 274
Dewar, Elaine, 230-31
Diamond, Eph, 33
Dickson, Ron, 167-69, 171-75, 177, 179-83
Dingman, Michael, 257
Dodd, Lionel, 222, 234, 250-54, 260-62,
    275, 299
Dome Petroleum, 102-06, 137, 190-91, 246
Dominion Bond Rating Service, 6-10
Downing, Bud, 123-24, 129-31, 136-38, 144,
    145, 147, 154, 166, 170, 176-77
Drapeau, Jean, 24
Drexel Burnham Lambert, 4

Edper Investments, 77-82, 292-93
Elders IXL Limited, 140, 165
Elliott, John, 140-41, 164
Ellis-Don, 202, 204
Ellsworth, Albert Leroy, 101
Emerson, Garfield, 107
English Property Corporation, 76-79, 192
Essential Talmud, The, 42
Exchange Tower, 7, 38-39, 243, 273
Executive, 75
Eyton, Trevor, 77, 79-81

Federated Department Stores, 217-21,
    223-24
Fennebresque, Kim, 215
Financial Post, 138, 147, 160, 235
Financial Times, 140-41, 291
Financial Times of Canada, 87, 90
Fingas, 142-44, 148-52, 181-82
First Boston Corporation, 213-14
First Canadian Place, 4, 30-39, 242-43, 249,
    268, 278-79, 284-85
Fitzhenry, Robert, 232
Flemingdon Park, 25-27
Forbes, 250, 287
Forbes, Bob, 136

Fortune, 2, 13, 91-92, 225, 228, 288
Francis, Diane, 183-84, 231
Freeman, Ron, 108
Frucher, Meyer (Sandy), 291
Fullerton, Donald, 270
Fung, Bob, 108

Gallagher, "Smilin' Jack", 103-04, 190
Gimlin, Bob, 86
Girvan, Gary, 136, 144
Globe and Mail, 9, 87-89, 93, 114, 119, 148,
    154, 155, 200, 227, 231-32, 257
Gluskin, Ira, 264
Going for Broke, 215
Goldberger, Paul, 47, 49, 60
Goldenberg, Susan, 87
Gonzales, Henry, 280
Gordon Capital, 80, 106, 116, 117
Gordon, Donald, 24
Grabino, Harold, 46, 47
Grant, James, 227, 295-96
Grant's Interest Rate Observer, 227, 295
Greenhill, Robert, 267
Greenwald, Gerald, 271-72, 277
Griffiths, Richard, 201-04
Guinness Book of Records, 39
Gulf Canada, 100-04, 248, 298, 301; assess-
    ment of takeover, 120-21, 189; bid for
    Hiram Walker, 123-24, 130-35; deal for
    minority shareholders, 118-20; Govern-
    ment concessions, 111-15; plans to re-
    vitalize, 256, 261-63; purchase
    negotiations, 105-09, 115-17; under
    Reichmann management, 132-33, 255-56
Gulf Oil Corporation, 100-01, 105-06
GW Utilities Limited, 255, 261

Hamilton, Nigel, 282
Harper's, 57
Hart-Scott-Rodino Antitrust Improvements
    Act, 178, 179, 188
Hartt, Stanley, 276
Haskayne, Dick, 123-24, 262-63
Hatch, Clifford, Jr., 126, 129, 139, 142, 171,
    175-76, 182, 183
Hatch, Clifford, Sr., 125, 127-29, 176
Hatch, Harry, 126-27
Hay, Bill, 26, 53
Heaps, Leo, 231-32
Henderson, Gerry, 121
Henley Group, 257
Heule, Bob, 131, 134, 145, 152
Hibernia project, 102, 259, 301

Hiram-Walker Gooderham & Worts, 125-30, 165-74, 182, 187, 189
Hiram-Walker Resources, 106-07, 255, 298-99; arrangement for shareholders, 160; assessment of takeover, 189-90; Fingas, 142-44, 148-52, 181-82; hostile takeover, 123-25, 130-35; Interprovincial Pipe Line, 129-31, 134-35, 144-48, 152-53; liquor busines, 125-30, 148, 155-60, 162-84; Reichmanns' objectives, 138
History of the Jews, A, 16
Hitler, Adolf, 11
Holden-Brown, Sir Derrick, 139-42, 144, 164-66, 168, 170, 178, 187-89, 191
Home Oil, 123-24, 132, 135, 142-43, 145-46, 187, 255, 258, 261-62
Hong Kong and Shanghai Banking Corporation, 247
Hopper, Bill, 110-12
Hudson's Bay Oil & Gas, 106
Huxtable, Ada Louise, 59

Iacobescu, George, 201, 202, 204-06
Iacocca, Lee, 272
Imperial Oil, 129, 134
Independent, 236
Interhome, 255, 261-62
Interprovincial Pipe Line Limited, 129-31, 134-35, 144-48, 152, 187, 255
Investment Canada, 166, 184

Jackaman, Michael, 144, 180
Johnson, Paul, 16
Johnson, Thomas S., 268-71
Judaism: relationship to Reichmanns' business success, 16-17, 41, 89

Kahan, Richard, 51-52, 62
Kennedy, William, 302
Keynes, John Maynard, 254, 298
Koch, Ed, 73
Krebs, Robert, 256-57

Ladner, Tommy, 165
Lambert, Allen, 123, 146-47, 154
Lehrer-McGovern International, 201
Leigh-Pemberton, Robin, 250
Leung, Ken, 244
Li Ka-shing, 291
"Little Egypt Bump", 111-17
Lloyds, 250, 281
London: financial deregulation, 193, 198

London Docklands Development Corporation, 193, 290
Lustig, Oskar, 244

McAfee, Jerry, 101
McAlpine, Robert, 202, 204
McCallum, Archibald, 136
McClelland & Stewart, 231-32
McCurdy, Howard, 167
Macdonald, Howard, 137
Macioce, Thomas, 214
Mackenzie, Michael, 273
Maclean, Bill, 293
Maclean's, 86, 88, 90, 297
McNish, Jacquie, 219-20
McQueen, Rod, 82
McWalter, Keith, 115, 132, 161-62, 168, 258, 261
Macy's, 219
Maier, Gerry, 146, 147
Major, John, 238, 270
Manufacturers Hanover, 209, 268
Marks and Spencer, 209
Matter of Trust, A, 2
media: Canary Wharf project, 235-38; Reichmanns' coverage in, 1-2, 190, 229-30, 233-35, 285-88
Medland, Ted, 108
Men of Property, 87
Mendoza, Roberto, 136-38, 143, 152-53
Mernit, Dan, 70-71, 90
Merrill Lynch & Co. Inc., 72-73
Milavsky, Harold, 78, 79
Milken, Michael, 4
Miller, Robert S. (Steve), 269, 272, 277, 280, 282, 283, 288
Milne, Al, 174-75
Minskoff, Edward, 45, 53, 63-64
Money of the Mind, 295
Moneyspinners, The, 82
Montgomery, Justice Robert, 151
Morgan, J. P., 296
Morgan, J. P. & Co., Incorporated, 268, 278, 285, 291
Morgan Stanley, 195, 209, 261, 267-68, 279
Muir, Jimmy, 24-25
Mulholland, Bill, 39, 242-43, 245
Mulroney, Brian, 112-13
Mutual of America, 292

Nathanson, Paul, 85
National Bank of Canada, 246, 266, 273-75, 293

National Energy Program, 102-05, 110, 113
National Kinney Corporation, 45-46
Ness, Elliot, 126
Newman, Gil, 107, 133, 188, 244, 269
Newman, Peter, 20, 75, 297
New York City: Battery Park City, 51-53, 55-68; lenders threaten Chapter 11, 291-92; real estate purchases in late 1970s, 44-49; vacancy rates, 4
New York Times, 13, 47, 59
Nicholson, Ronald, 48
Nomura Securities, 247
Noranda, 116
Norris, John, 68-70, 192

Ogilvy & Mather, 209, 238, 283
Olympia & York Developments Limited: Abitibi-Price, 84-86; assessment of Gulf takeover, 120-21; assessment of Hiram Walker takeover, 189-90; bankers, 242-46, 296-97; Battery Park City, 51-53, 55-68, 72-74; commercial paper, 5-10, 266, 268; company started 19-29; construction of Canary Wharf project, 201-06; deals with Campeau, 215-19, 221-25, 273-76; diversification, 86-87; Dodd's organization chart, 253-54; English Property, 76-79; financial information, 240-42, 267, 287; financial troubles in early 1980s, 90-94; financing Canary Wharf, 246-50, 277-79, 289-90, 295-98; First Canadian Place, 31-39; forced to rework debt, 267-73; Government concessions in Gulf Canada purchase, 111-15; Gulf's minority shareholders, 118-20; interest in Santa Fe Southern Pacific Corp., 257-58; Interprovincial Pipe Line acquired, 145-48; investment portfolio, 5; legal and political battle with Allied, 156-60, 169-89; Morgan Stanley building at Canary Wharf, 267; nature and structure of Reichmanns' empire, 94-97; New York lenders threaten Chapter 11, 291-92; plans to revitalize Gulf, 256, 261-63; protection from creditors, 277-80, 283-85; reaction to sale of Hiram Walker's liquor business and Fingas, 148-53; real estate holdings, 2-4; real estate purchases in New York City, 44-49; restructuring plan, 288-89, 291, 293, 302; salvaging Canary Wharf, 280-83; sold parts of public companies,

261; takeover of Gulf Canada, 106-09, 115-18, 189; value of Canary Wharf, 287. *See also* Reichmann family
Olympia Floor & Wall Tile, 16, 29
Ontario Securities Commission, 118, 262
OPEC crisis, 99

Paroian, Leon, 168, 180-83
Pelli, Cesar, 55-59, 199
Petro-Canada, 108, 110-12, 117
Petroleum Incentive Payments, 103-05
Peterson, David, 158
Phillips, Lazarus, 24, 26
Pickens, Boone, 105
Pitblado, Jimmy, 136-38
Place Ville Marie, 22, 24-25
Powis, Alf, 116-17, 119, 120, 134
Price Waterhouse, 287
Prince Charles, 199

Ranieri, Lewis, 289-90
Reichmann, Albert, 5, 15, 20, 27, 39, 81, 87, 95-96, 123-24, 219, 271, 301
Reichmann, Edward, 15
Reichmann family: banking relationship, 242-50, 264-66, 296-97; business skills, 88, 152, 188, 190, 262-64; compared to Dome executives, 190-91; integrity, 228-29; Jewishness, 16-17, 41, 89; management style, 43-44, 96-97; media coverage, 1-2, 190, 229-30, 233-35, 285-88; myth of being conservative financiers, 246; nature and structure of empire, 94-97; oil investments, 259; relationship with Establishment, 75, 83; secrecy, 190, 240-42, 246; *Toronto Life* article, 230-33; unwillingness to give up equity, 300. *See also* Olympic & York Developments Limited
Reichmann, Paul: Abitibi-Price, 84-86, 115-17; ambition, 297; assessment of, 299-300; Battery Park City, 61-62; Canary Wharf project, 195-97; childhood in Tangier, 11-15; compared to Campeau, 211-12; compared to Trump, 228-29, 250-51; described by Dodd, 260; diversification, 86-87; financial genius, 5-6, 17-18, 87, 97; First Canadian Place, 30-39; forced to rework debt, 267-73; Government concessions for Gulf purchase, 111-15; hostile takeover of Hiram Walker, 124-26, 148-84; Interprovincial Pipe Line takeover, 145-48; interviews

after Allied's purchase, 183-87; Orthodox Jewish beliefs, 41-43; portrayal in media, 229-33, 235; press conference, 170, 174-75; relationship with Albert, 95-96; relationship with Johnson, 270-71; Royal Trust, 81-82; started Olympia & York, 19-29; use of media, 1-2, 147, 154-60, 190, 233-35
Reichmann, Philip, 203, 229
Reichmann, Ralph, 5, 15-16, 284
Reichmann, Renee, 11, 14-15, 230-31
Reichmann, Samuel, 11-15, 20, 230, 233, 242
Reid, George (Chip), 136
Richards, Bill, 190
Ritchie, Cedric, 270
Roberts, Keith, 34, 58, 192
Robinson, James, III, 66-67
Rosehaugh, 207
Rosewell, Peter, 143-44
Rothchild, John, 215
Royal Bank, 246, 247, 266, 270, 293, 297
Royal Trust, 80-82

Salomon Brothers, 93, 108, 241
Sante Fe Energy Resources, Inc., 258
Santa Fe Southern Pacific Corporation, 256-58, 261, 265, 299
Sarlos, Andy, 84-85
Sanwa Bank, 247, 273
Schacter, Harry, 185
Scharffenberger, George T., 65
Schore, Benjamin, 229
Schreyer, William, 73
Schroeder, Walter, 6
Scotia Plaza, 212, 216, 221, 268
Seagram's, 127, 128, 149, 171
Shields, Bill, 156
Shortell, Anne, 82
Shultz, C.E. (Chuck), 258-59
Skyscraper, The, 60
Soden, James, 77
Soskolne, Ron, 32-33, 53-55, 58-59, 88
Spankey, Malcolm, 53
Standard Oil of California (Chevron), 105-08, 111
Steinsaltz, Adin, 42-43
Stevens, Sinclair, 114, 166
Stoakes, Dennis, 156-57
Strong, Maurice, 84-85
Sumitomo group, 247

Sun Life Assurance of Canada, 38
Sunday Telegraph, 235
Sunday Times, 278

Taylor, Allan, 270, 297-98
Taylor, Austin, 81
Teachers Insurance and Annuity Association of America, 286
Thatcher, Margaret, 192-93, 198, 207, 237
Thomson, Ken, 85-86
Thomson, Newspapers, 85-86
Time, 14, 233
Tisch, Laurence, 289-90
Tokai Bank, 247
Toronto-Dominion Bank, 245, 278
Toronto Life, 230-33, 298
Toronto Star, 183
TransCanada PipeLines, 142, 146, 153, 155
Travelstead, G. Ware, 194-97, 199, 201
Trilon Financial Corporation, 82
Trizec, 76-79
Trudeau, Dennis, 185
Trump, Donald, 214, 228-29, 250
Turner, John, 114

Ultramar, 118
Uris, Harold and Percy, 45
Uris package, 45-49, 90-91, 241, 292

Von Clemm, Michael, 193-95

Wade, Peter, 200
Wall Street Journal, 219-21, 225, 281, 285
Walsh, Michael, 238
Washington Post, 49
Wasserstein, Bruce, 213
Watchorn, Derek, 196
Webb & Knapp, 22-23, 25
Weill, Sandford, 66, 289-90
White, Ken, 81-82
Whiteford, William K., 101
Wilder, Bill, 106-07, 123-25, 146-47
Wilson-Smith, Ian, 175
Windsor Star, 156, 167-68, 175, 180
Wolfe, Tom, 57
Wolfensohn, James D., Inc., 269
Wood Gundy, 108
World Financial Center, 23, 67, 72-74, 90-91, 243, 273, 292

Young, Chuck, 195, 199

Zeckendorf, William, 21-25, 98
Zucotti, John, 269, 291